TOM WOLFE GOES TO THE DOGS:

Carving Dogs

Douglas Congdon-Martin

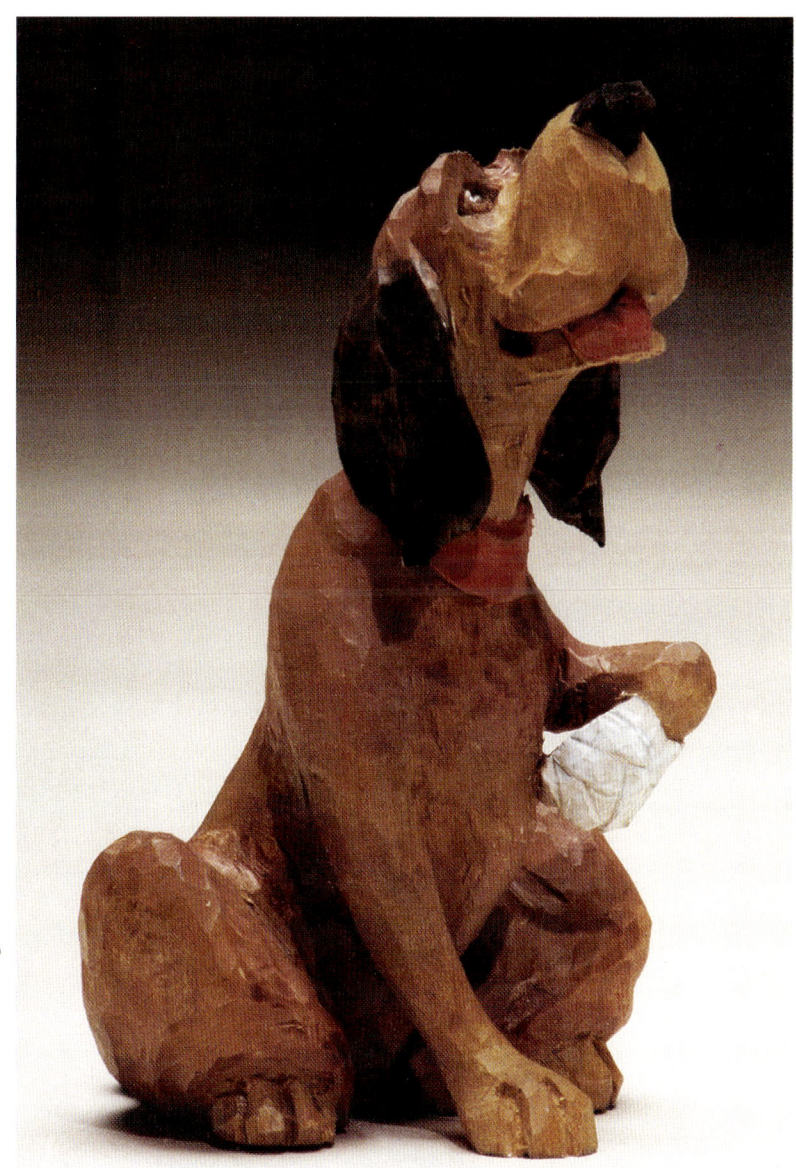

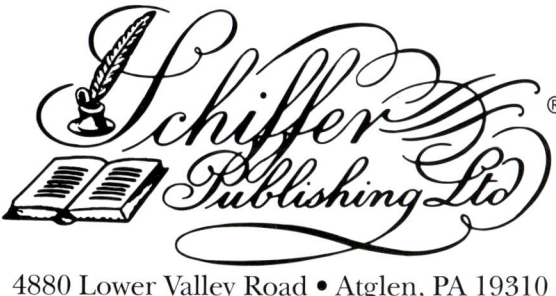

Schiffer Publishing Ltd®

4880 Lower Valley Road • Atglen, PA 19310

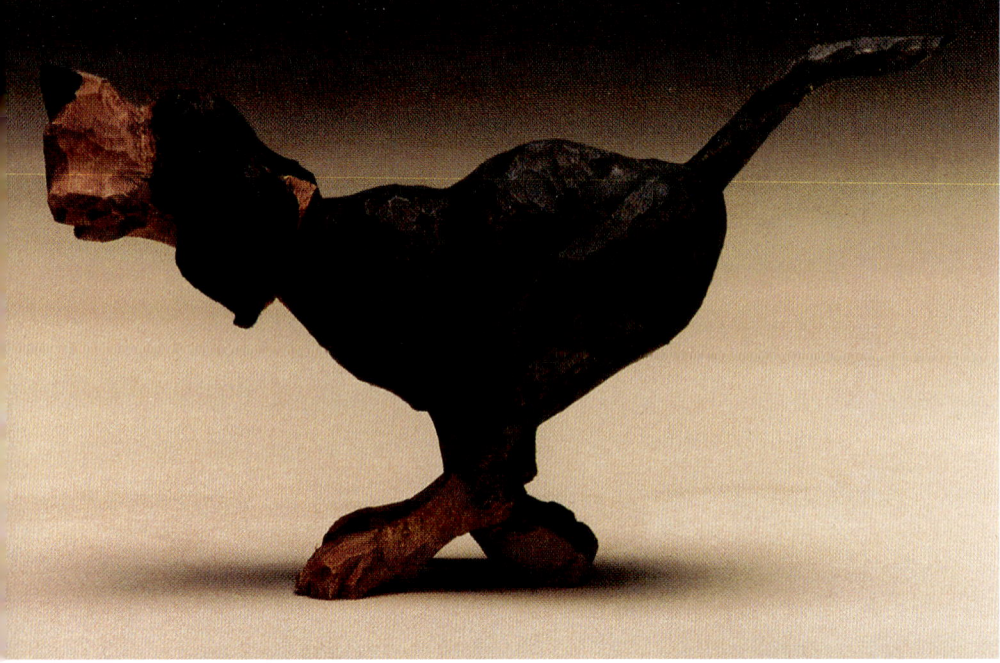

ISBN: 978-0-88740-367-5
Printed in China

Schiffer Books are available at special discounts for bulk purchases for sales promotions or premiums. Special editions, including personalized covers, corporate imprints, and excerpts can be created in large quantities for special needs. For more information contact the publisher:

Published by Schiffer Publishing Ltd.
4880 Lower Valley Road
Atglen, PA 19310
Phone: (610) 593-1777; Fax: (610) 593-2002
E-mail: Info@schifferbooks.com

For the largest selection of fine reference books on this and related subjects, please visit our website at **www.schifferbooks.com**
We are always looking for people to write books on new and related subjects. If you have an idea for a book, please contact us at proposals@schifferbooks.com

This book may be purchased from the publisher.
Please try your bookstore first.
You may write for a free catalog.

In Europe, Schiffer books are distributed by
Bushwood Books
6 Marksbury Ave.
Kew Gardens
Surrey TW9 4JF England
Phone: 44 (0) 20 8392 8585; Fax: 44 (0) 20 8392 9876
E-mail: info@bushwoodbooks.co.uk
Website: www.bushwoodbooks.co.uk

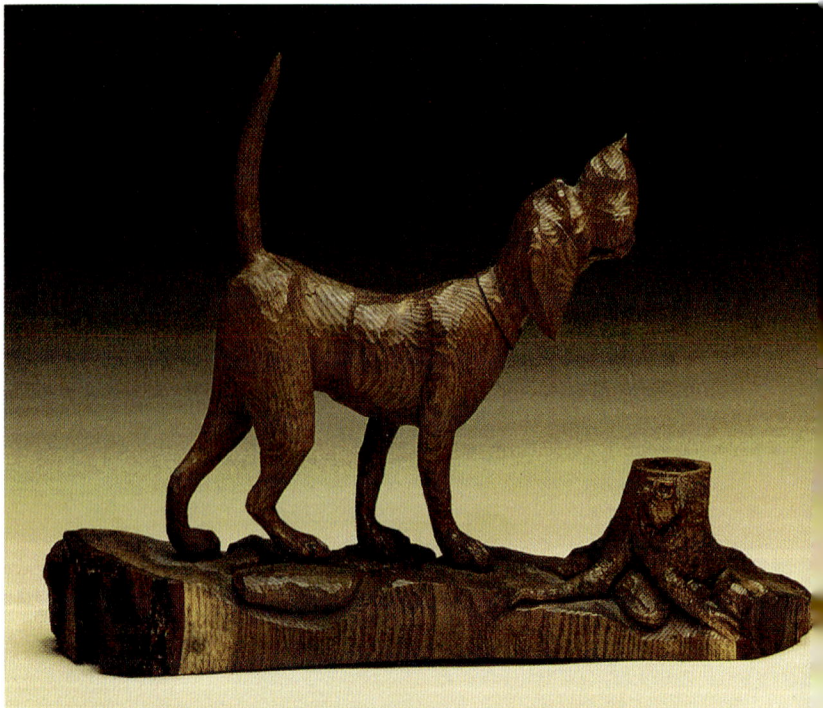

Contents

Introduction

Dogs have always been among the most popular carvings I do. I suppose it is because they are such an important part of our everyday life, man's best friends. It could also be because these dog carvings take on such great personalities. These can carry just about any human emotion, from love to loneliness, and from joy to anger. Dogs have been around people for so long that they begin to look like us.

Dogs, especially hound dogs, are especially important to hunters and other country folk. One time many years ago, one of my uncles saw an advertisement for a guaranteed coon hound. For $35 he would get a trained hunting dog, and if he wasn't completely satisfied he could get his money back. Well, back then $35 was a lot of money, but it was cheap for a good dog. Besides it was guaranteed, so my uncle sent off for it.

It was a nice looking dog, and friendly to boot. But the ol' dog wouldn't hunt. He would go into the field and be happy as a lark, but he would not hunt. All he would do is follow my uncle around, sniffing the ground he had already covered. Not much help in finding coons.

After a few days my uncle wrote for his money back. The check came in the next week's mail, and Uncle was pleased to get it. There was not any word about how to return the dog. My uncle waited a couple days for instructions, and when they didn't come he finally called the company on the telephone.

"What do you want me to do with this worthless dog," he asked.

"Well," said the voice at the other end, "if he's worthless, just take him out and shoot him."

The same idea has evolved through the years until now. Some dog dealers will advertise coon dogs at different stages of development: beginner, partially trained, trained, etc. They offer a money back guarantee with a 10 day trial period. For $100 they send out a beginner to the buyer. For the next ten days the dog gets trained in the field by an expert dog handler. At the end of the time he either keeps him or sends him back. Either way the dog dealer wins. Either he makes a quick $100 or the next time the dog is sent out he'll be able to charge more for a partially-trained dog. The more times the dog goes out the better he is trained and the more money he'll bring.

Of course, dogs also play a part in our humor. They easily become comic figures even in carving. One story I remember is about the drunk who brings his dog to the bar.

"Bartender," he announces, "my dog can talk. Give me a drink and I'll make him say something."

The bartender has seen all kinds of scams in his life and is naturally cynical. "This better be no joke. I don't believe it for a minute."

"Then I'll show you," says the man, who then turns to address the dog. "What is on a tree?"

"Bark, bark."

"Do you take me for a fool?" asks the bartender, "I won't give you a drink for that."

"Well then listen to this. What does sand paper feel like?" he asks the dog.

"Rough, rough."

The bartender goes into a rage. "Get outta my bar! And don't you or your dog ever come back."

"Just a minute." the man pleads. "Tell you what. You ask the dog a question and see if he doesn't answer."

The bartender thinks about it for a minute and then asks the dog "Who was the best baseball player that ever lived?"

"Ruth, Ruth," says the dog.

It is too much for the bartender and he kicks them out on the street.

Pulling himself up from the pavement the dog turns to the drunk and asks, "Who the hell was it, DiMaggio?"

If you find the dogs in this book talking to you, don't be surprised. They take on a personality of their own and will engage you in conversation as you go. I often find myself talking to my carvings, and in a way they talk back. Maybe I have gone to the dogs.

The projects in this book require only a few simple tools, and are perfect for the beginner and intermediate carver. They should also be challenging for the advanced carver.

I have carved a sitting hound dog, so you can see how it is done step-by-step. The other dogs are carved in a similar way. Good luck and good fun!

The Patterns

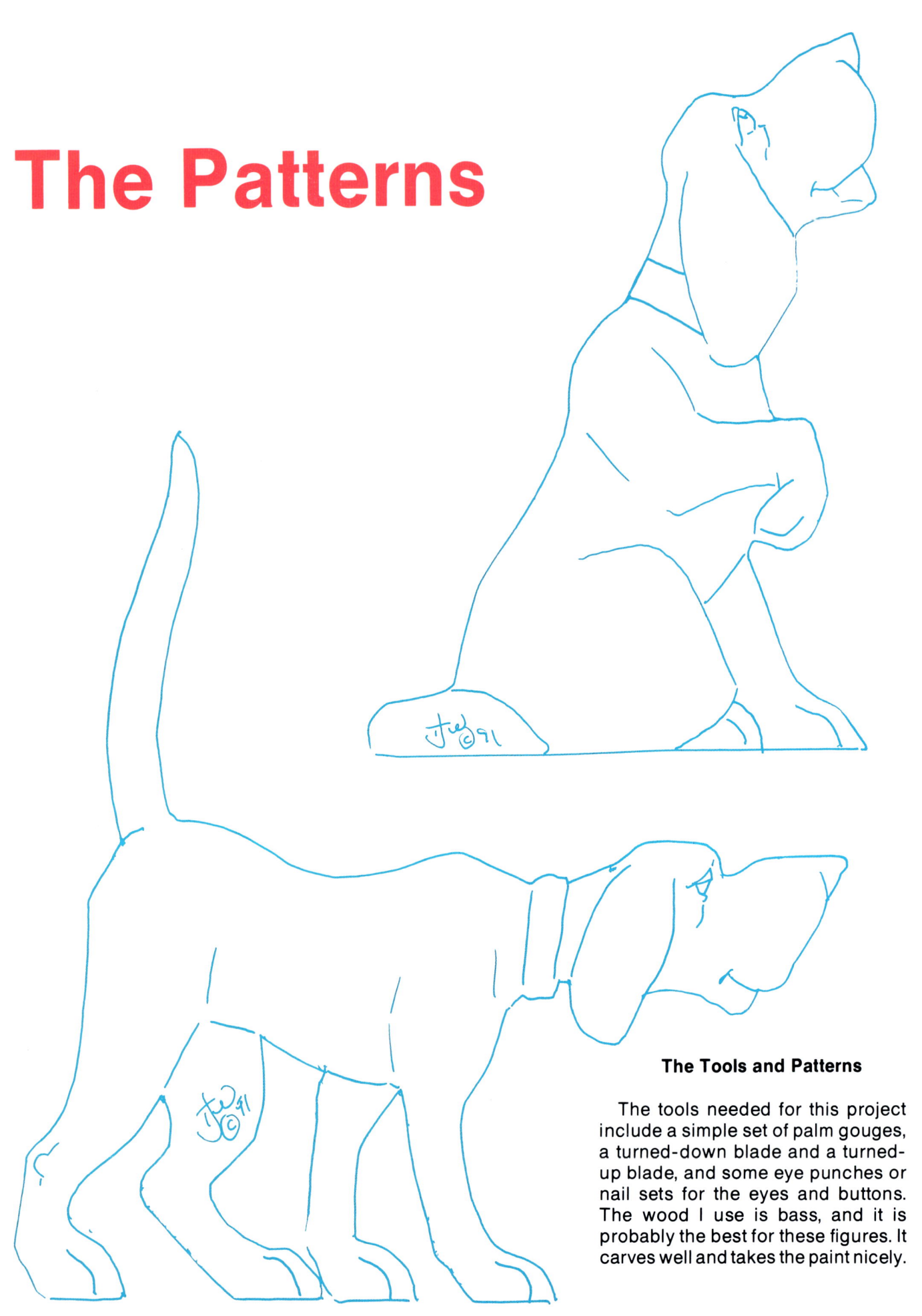

The Tools and Patterns

The tools needed for this project include a simple set of palm gouges, a turned-down blade and a turned-up blade, and some eye punches or nail sets for the eyes and buttons. The wood I use is bass, and it is probably the best for these figures. It carves well and takes the paint nicely.

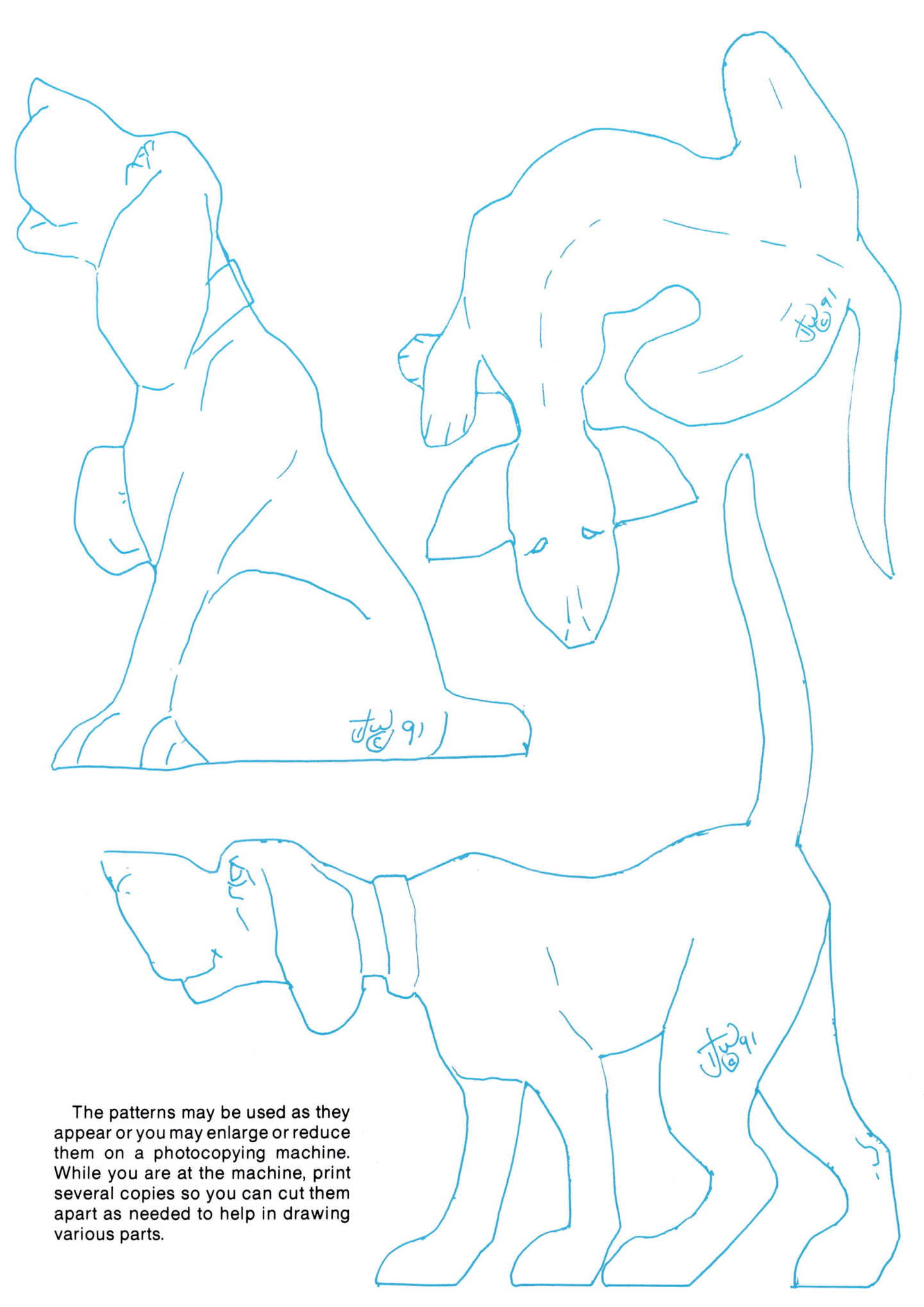

The patterns may be used as they appear or you may enlarge or reduce them on a photocopying machine. While you are at the machine, print several copies so you can cut them apart as needed to help in drawing various parts.

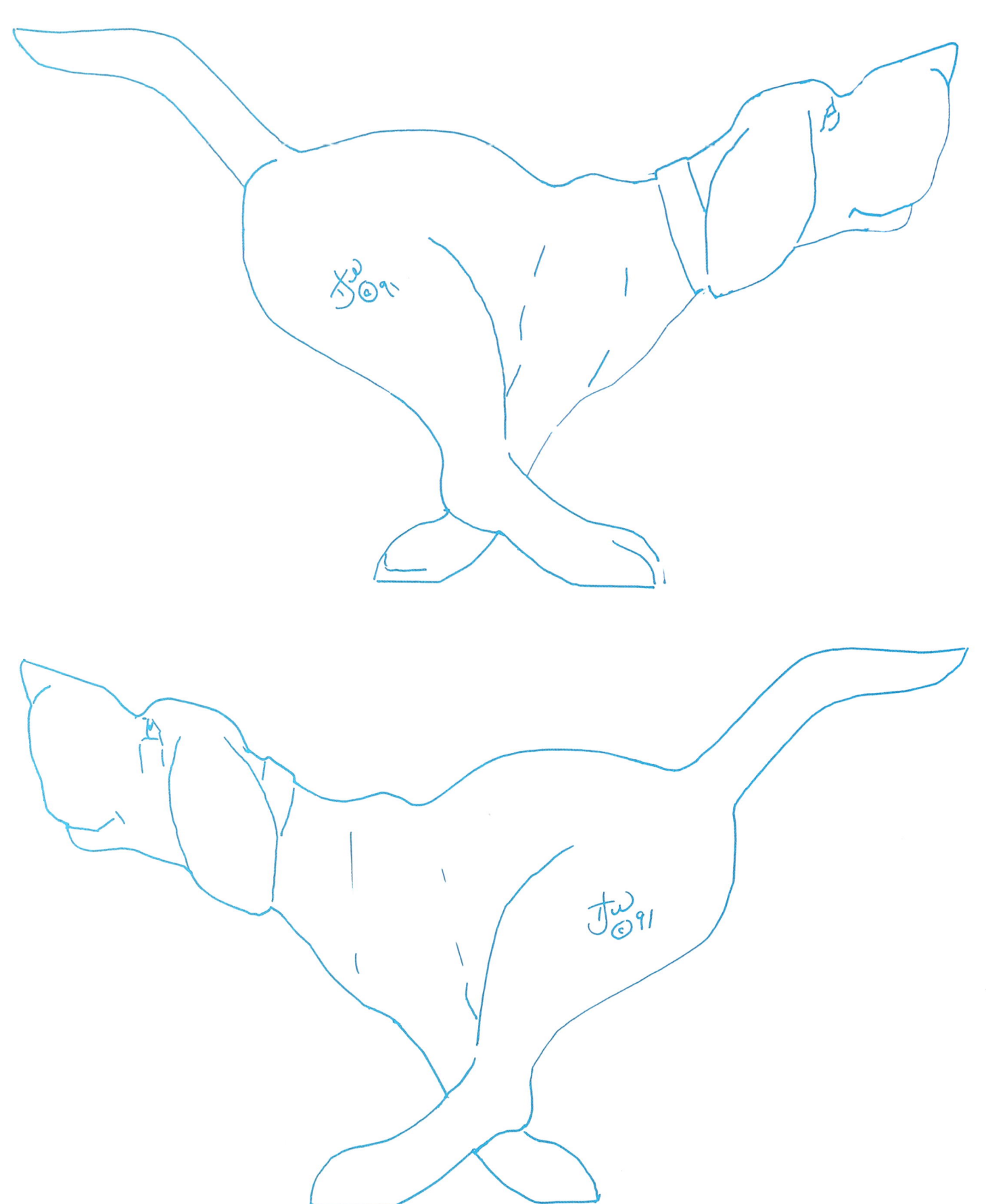

Carving the Dog

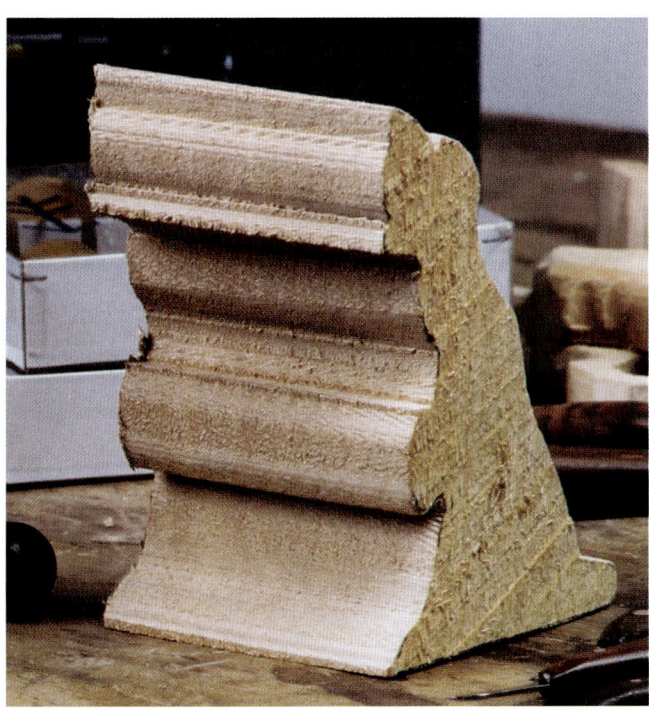

The blank is cut with a bandsaw. I prefer bass wood for this type of carving, although other woods can be used, sometimes with beautiful results.

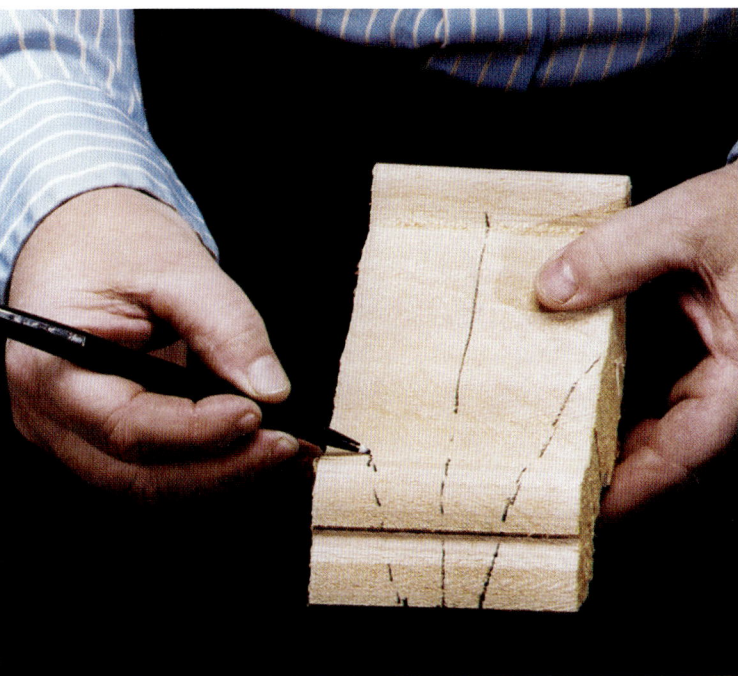

Mark the basic head-on shape of the dog, noting what is to be cut off.

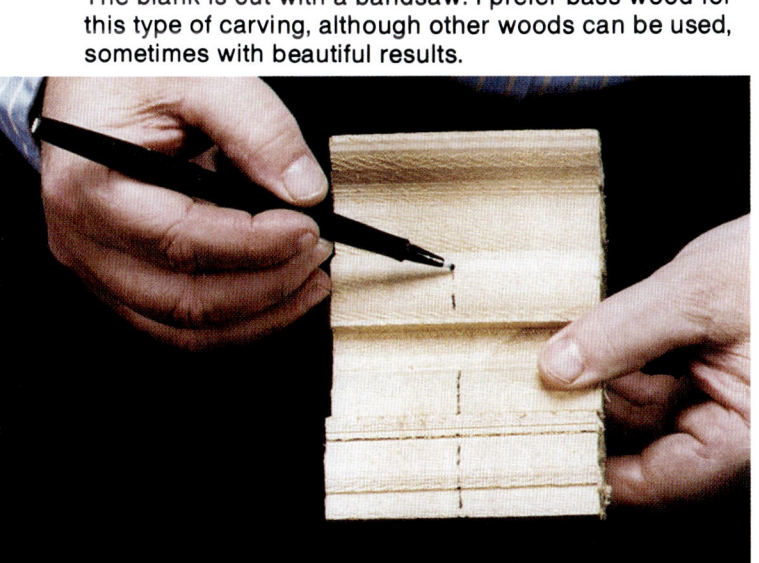

Mark a center line all around the blank.

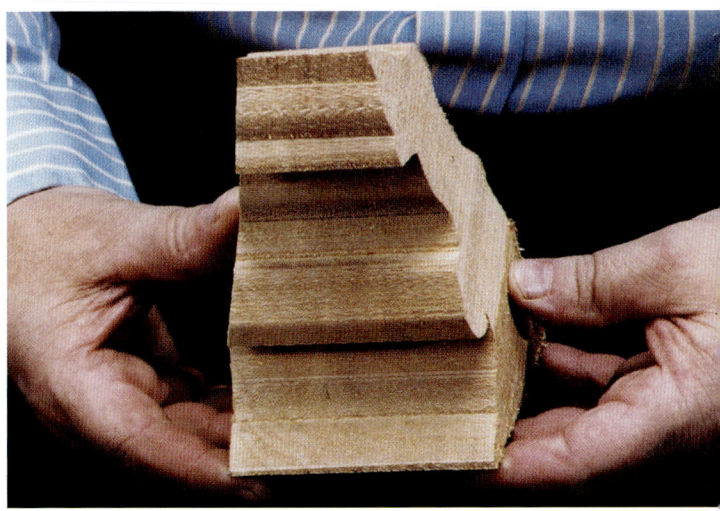

Remove the area marked with a bandsaw, to get this result.

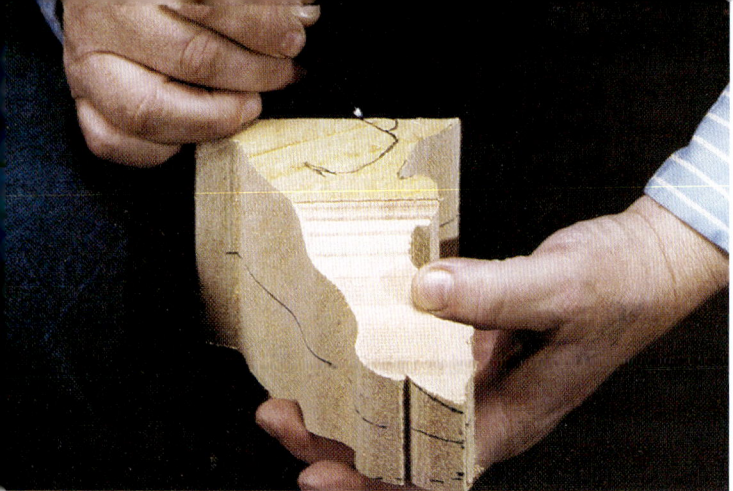

Draw the legs on both sides.

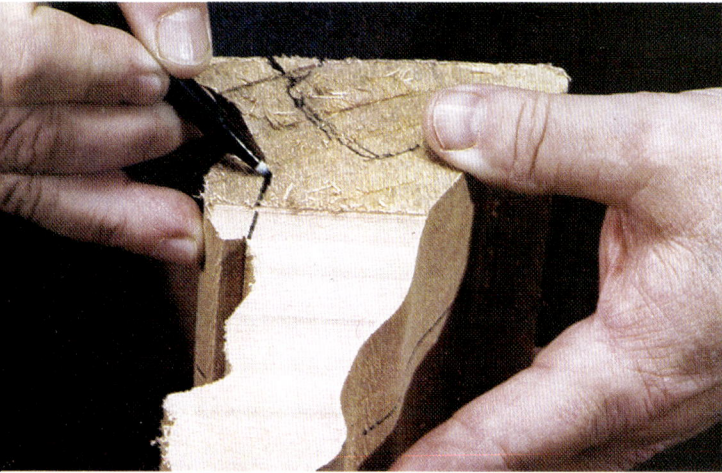

Decide which of the front legs will be held up and which will extend down to the floor. Look for flaws in the wood before you decide. Sometimes this is an opportunity to cut away a problem before it becomes one. I've chosen the front right to go to the ground, so I mark the top part of it to be removed.

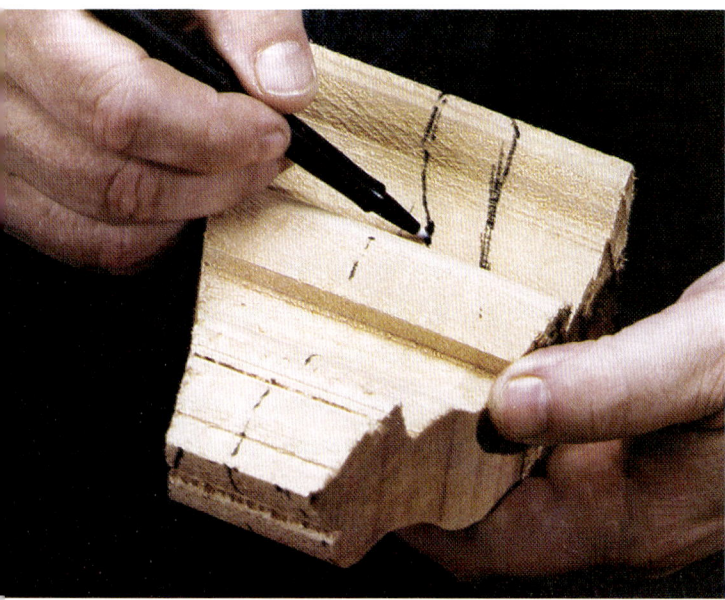

Mark the front leg that will go to the ground so it comes to the middle of the rear legs.

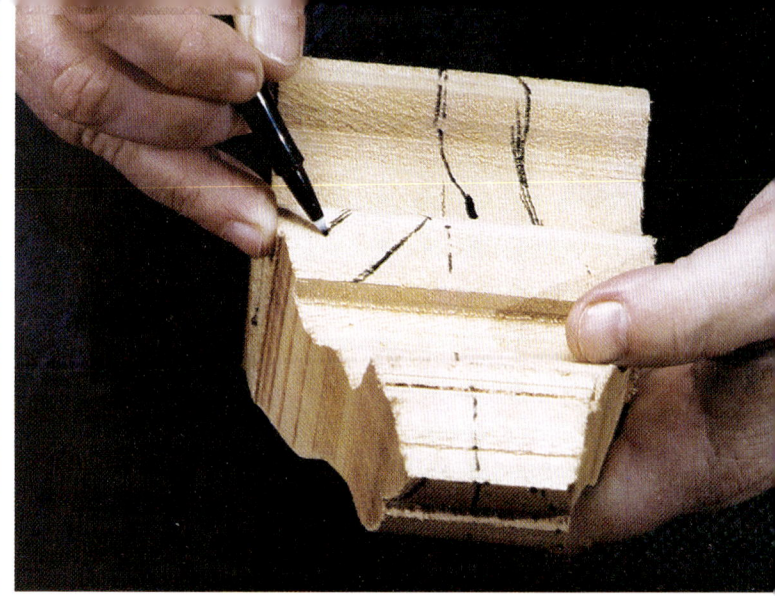

Mark the raised front paw at an angle.

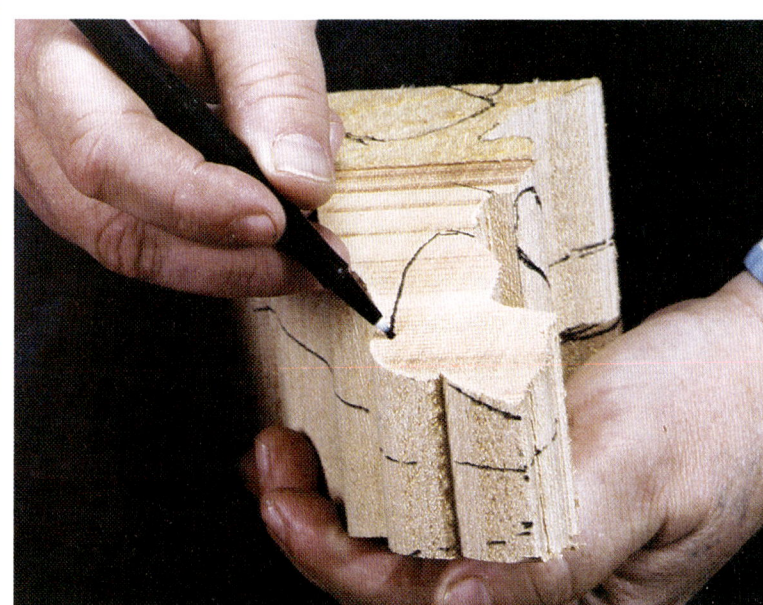

Draw the ears on both sides so we won't cut into them by mistake.

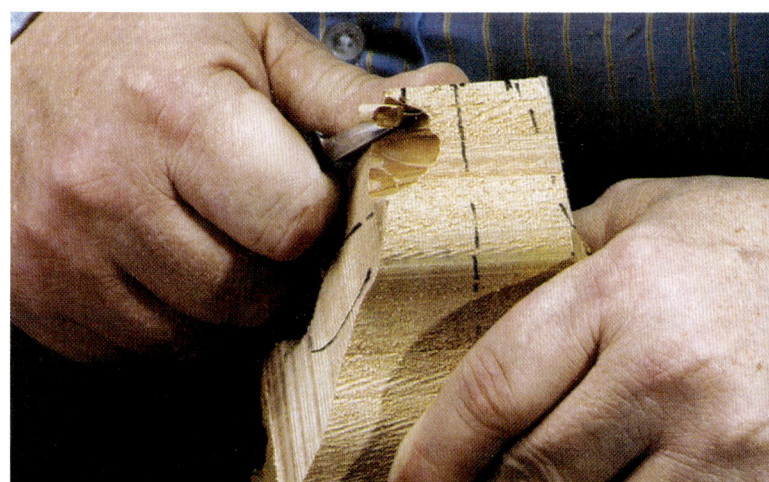

Start carving at the end of the nose. Use a narrow turned up knife, or any other sharp knife to remove the unwanted wood.

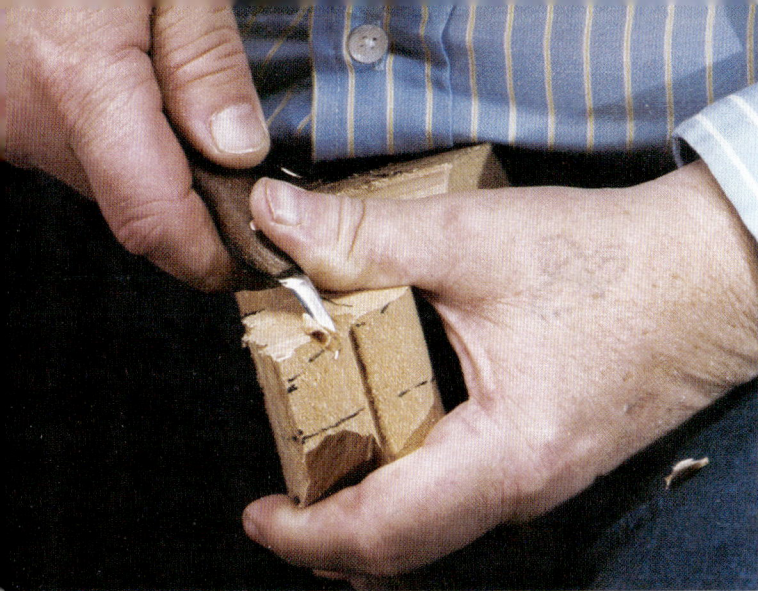

Lock your left thumb against the knife to give it good pressure.

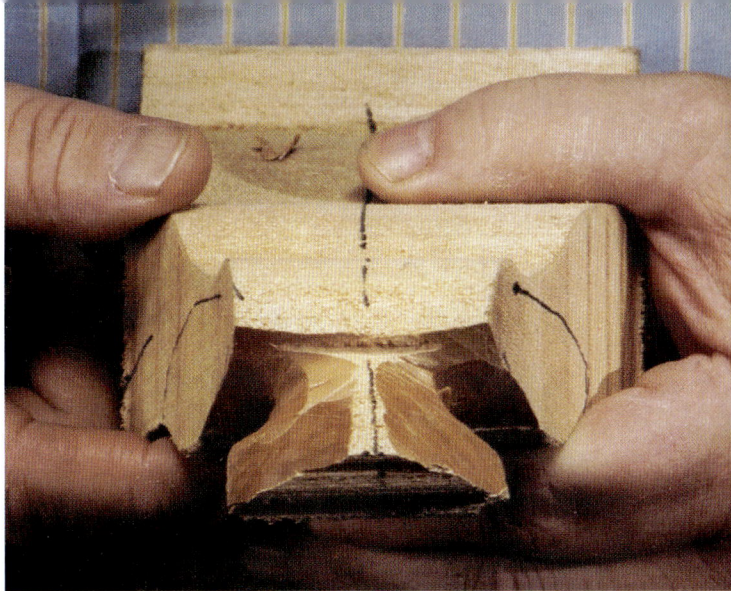

Leave the front portion full while you are shaping the muzzle. A large front portion gives the muzzle a more comical look.

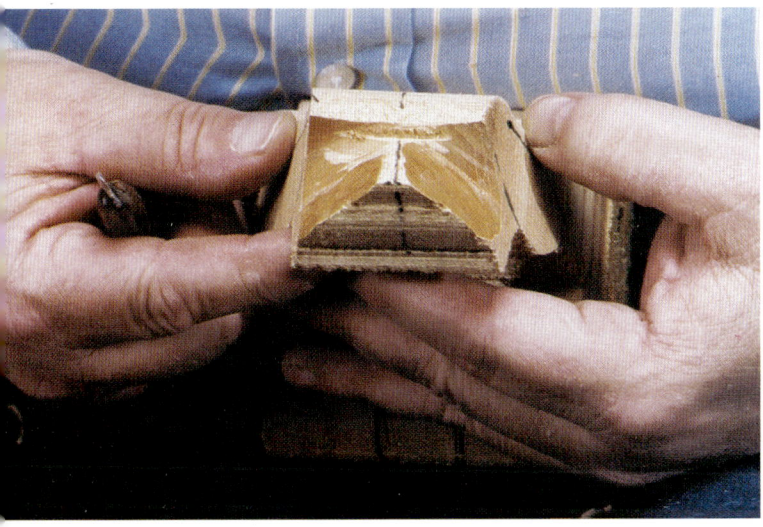

You want to create a ridge for the nose with the sides of the muzzle sloping down to the jowels.

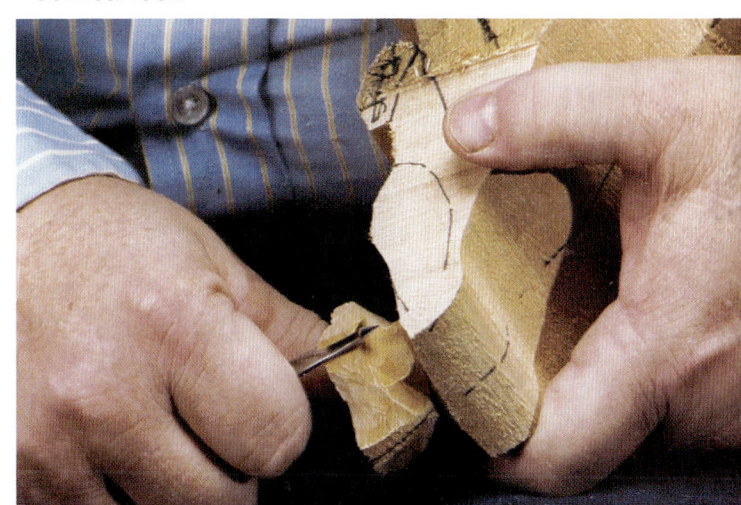

Shape the front of the muzzle. Use the grain when possible and pop off excess wood.

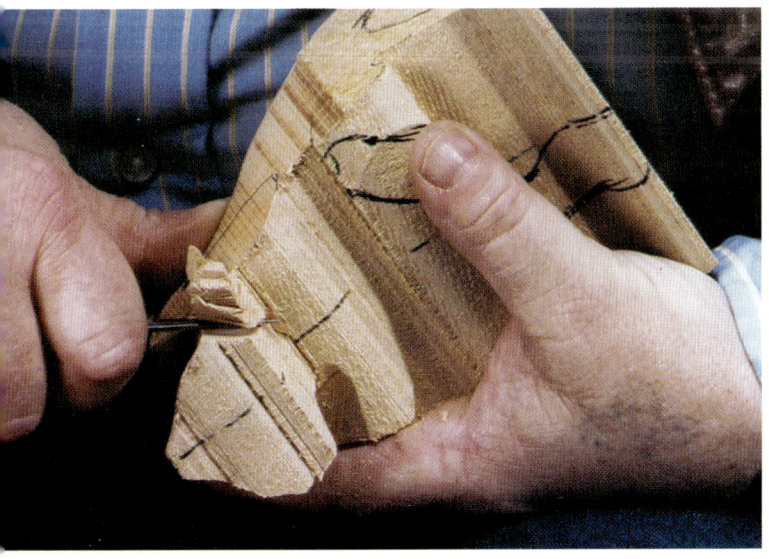

Carve the underside of the muzzle in the same way, until you arrive at the shape you seek.

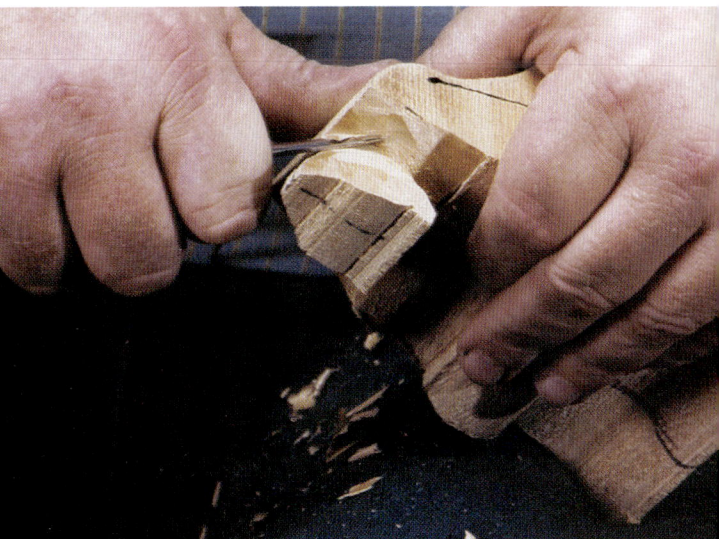

After the muzzle has the shape you want, go back and smooth it up.

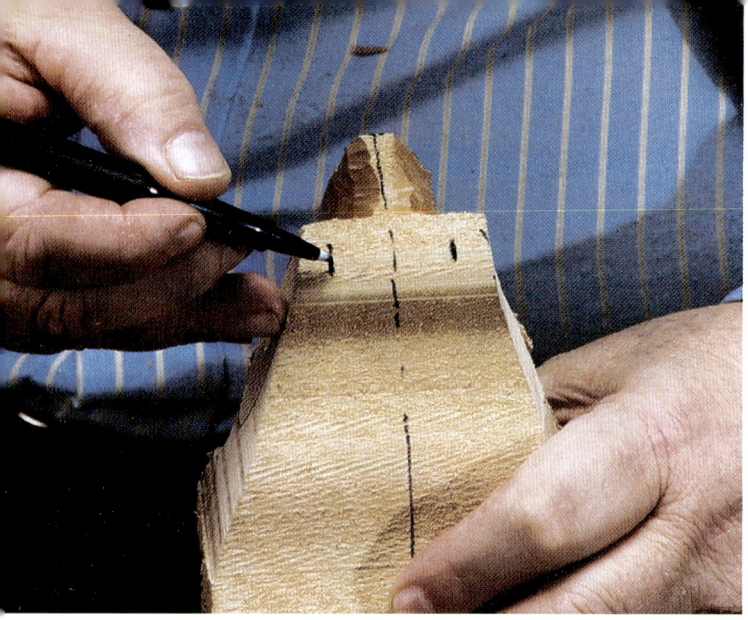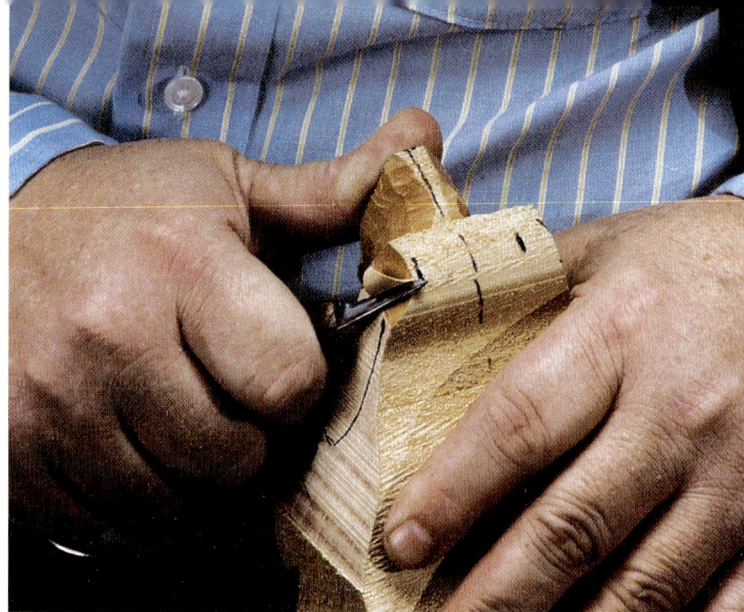

You want the head to be at least as wide as the muzzle. Mark it...

and trim the sides of the head to the marks...

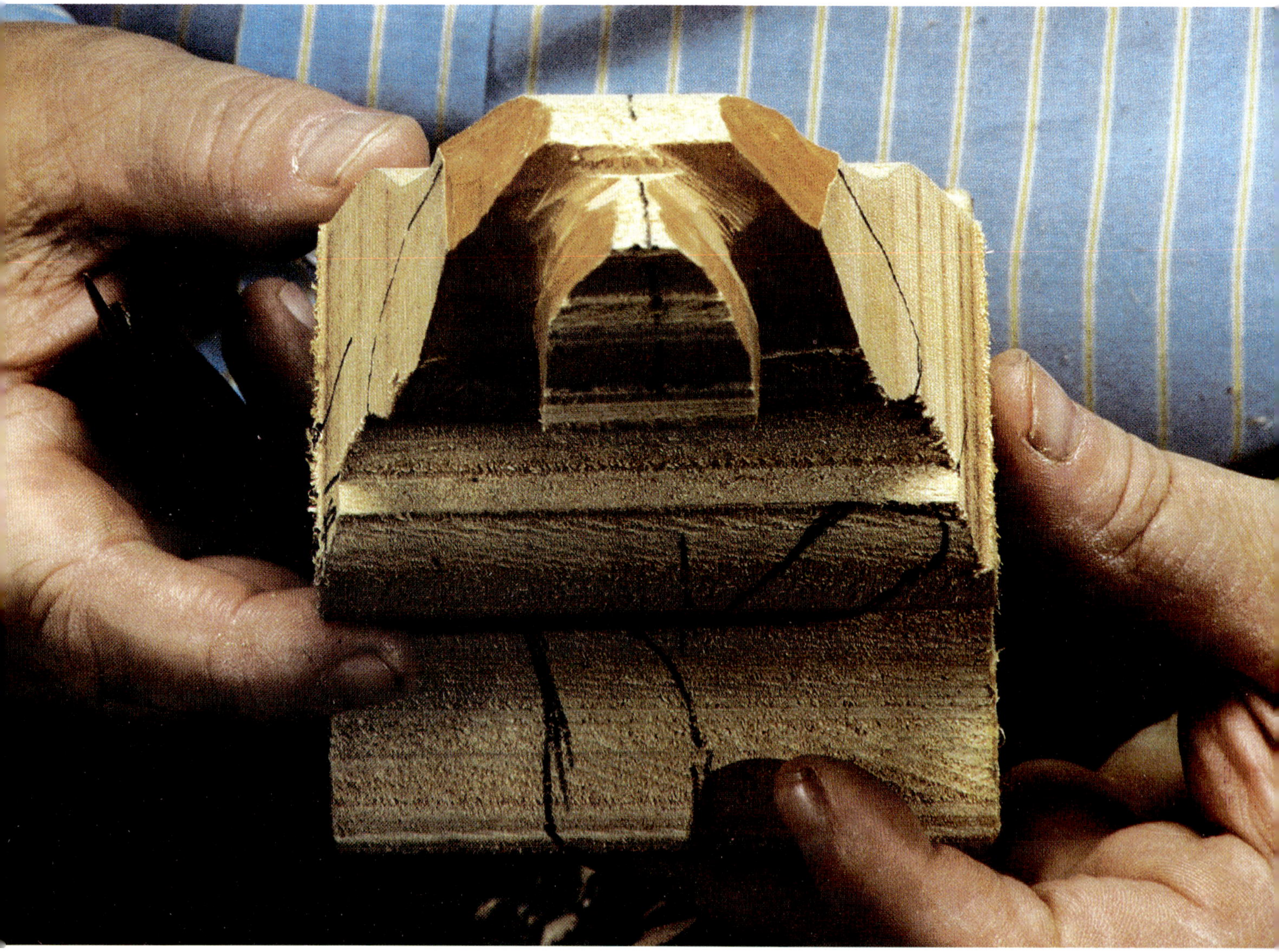

at a 45 degree angle.

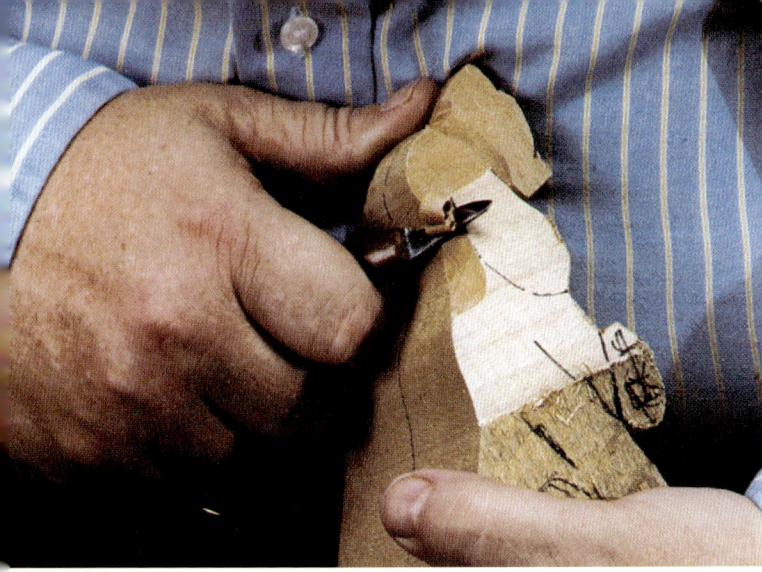

Trim around the ears, but don't make the mistake of carving the ears themselves too soon.

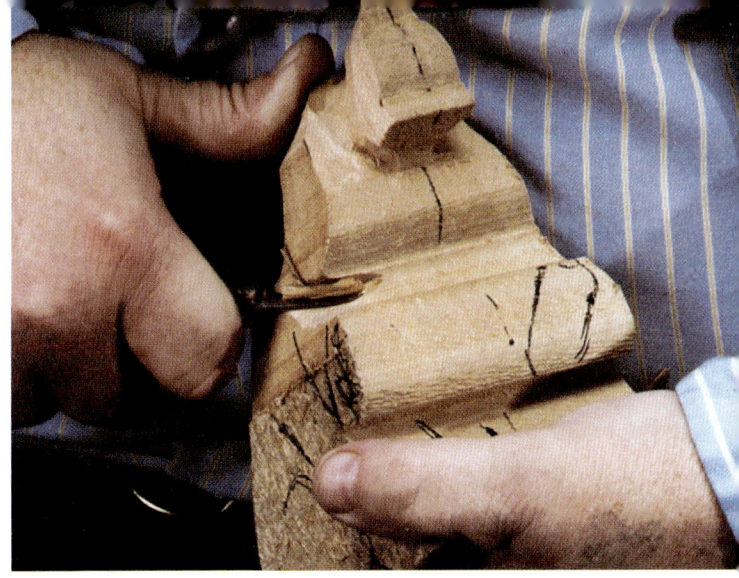

Continue the process of cutting stops and trimming back to them to thin the neck. Nothing looks weirder than a hound dog with a fat neck.

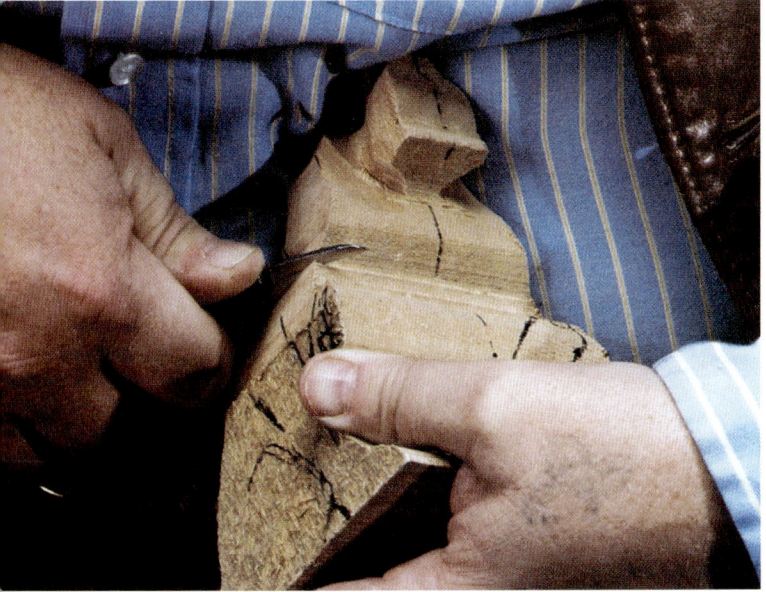

Cut a straight stop at the bottom of the ear by pushing and rocking.

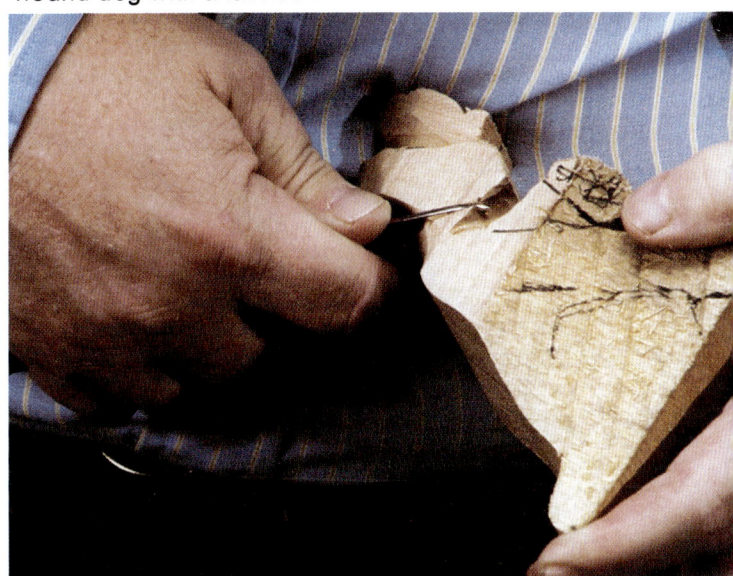

Continue around the ear with the stop cut...

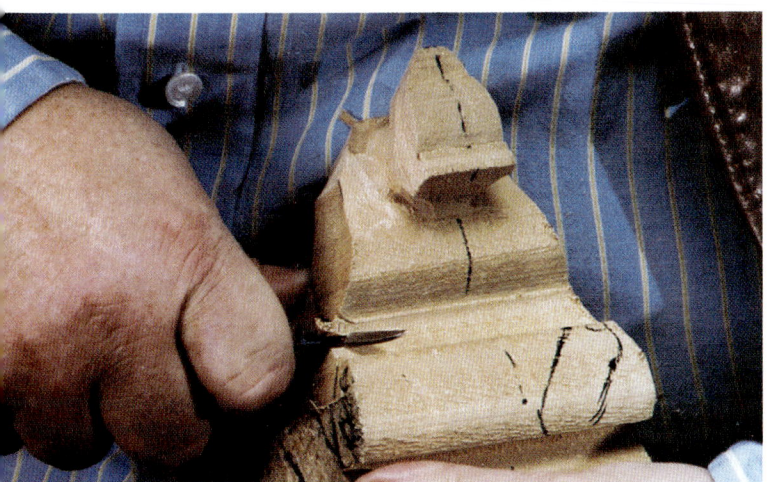

Cut into the stop from the shoulder. The stop is the most basic of cuts, used to define shapes while safely removing unwanted wood.

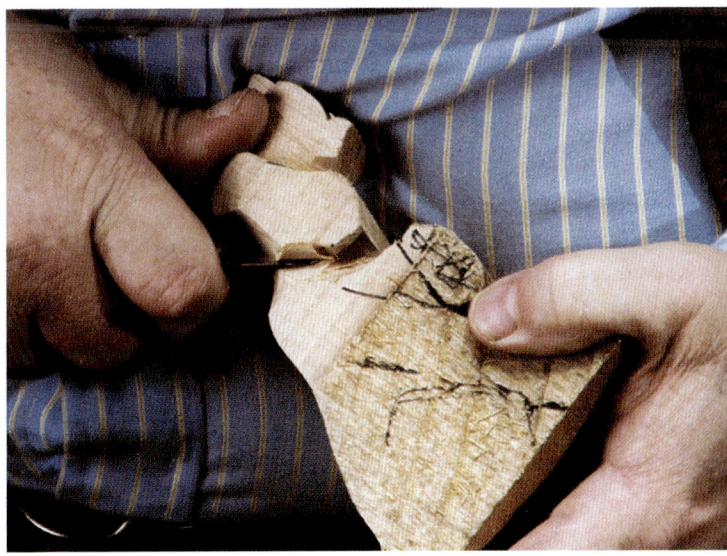

and the trim.

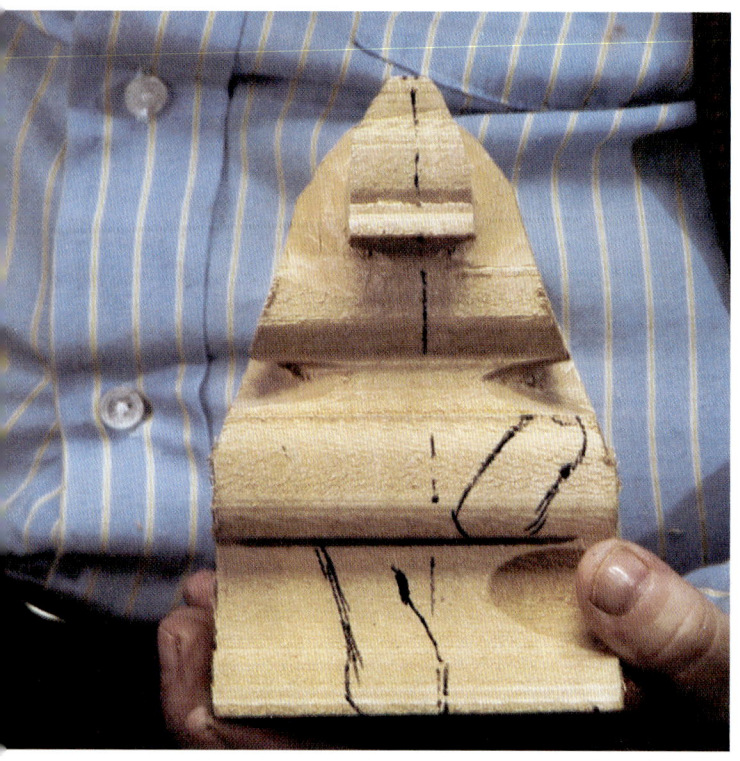

Repeat the process on the other side of the head until you get to this shape.

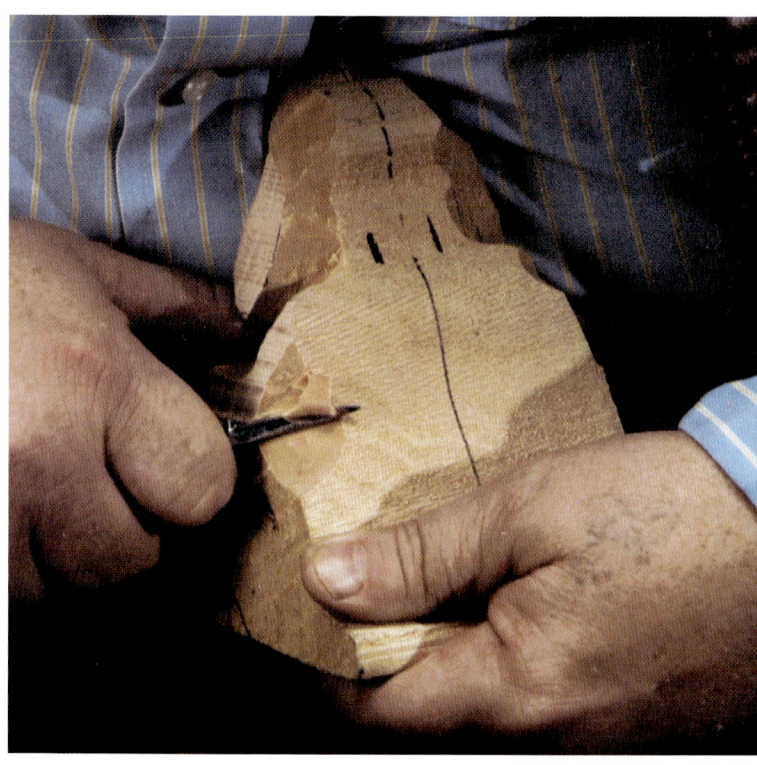

Round the back, shoulders, and neck to the mark. Begin with the saddle. Note: when carving, your thumbs should either be hidden or used. If you aren't using them, get them out of the way.

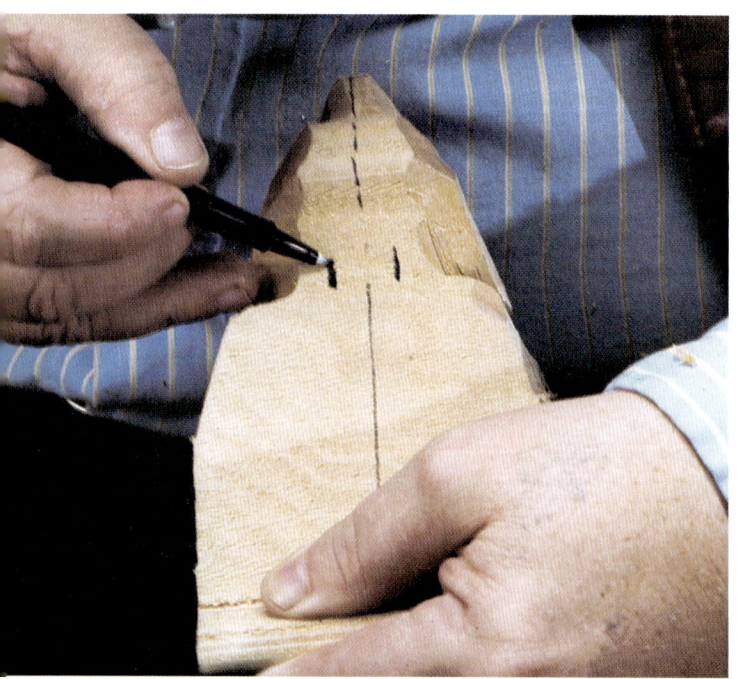

The neck will come into the points marked.

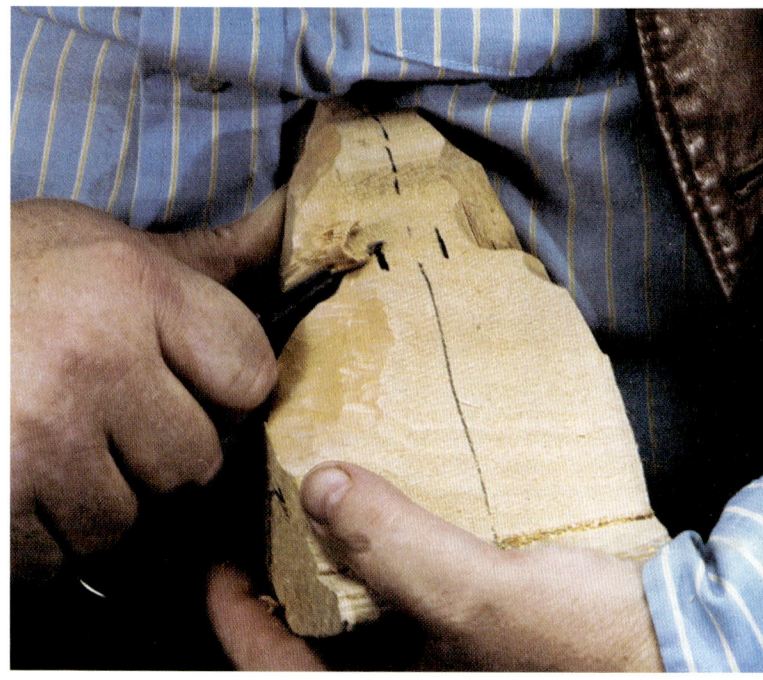

Continue up toward the neck.

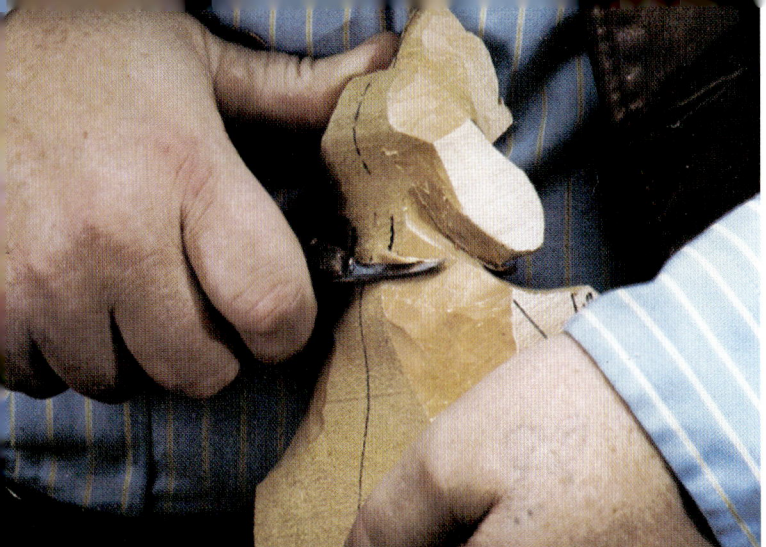

Do the same thing on both sides of the back and neck.

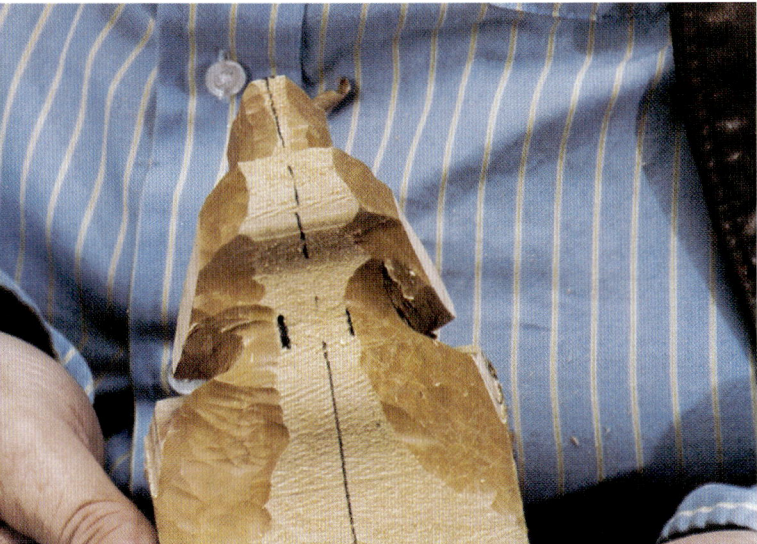

This is the shape of the back and neck so far.

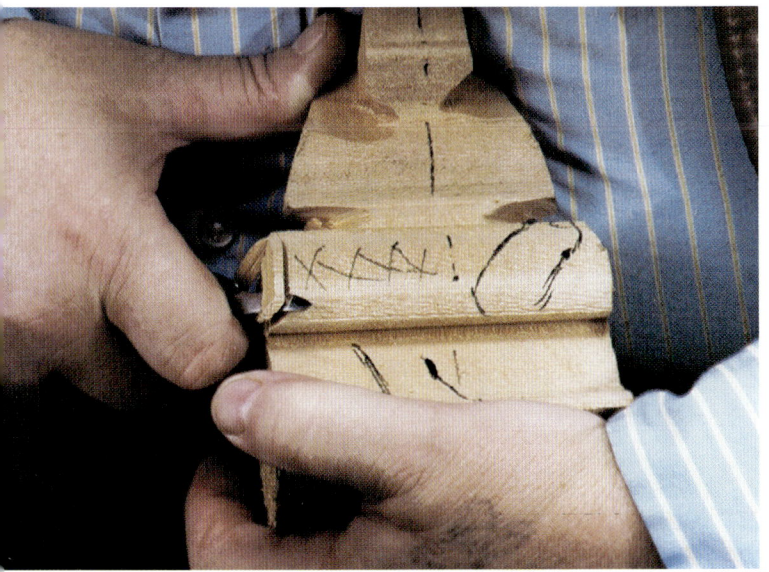

Remove the excess wood in front of the leg that goes to the floor. If the grain is good this will pop off easily with a knife.

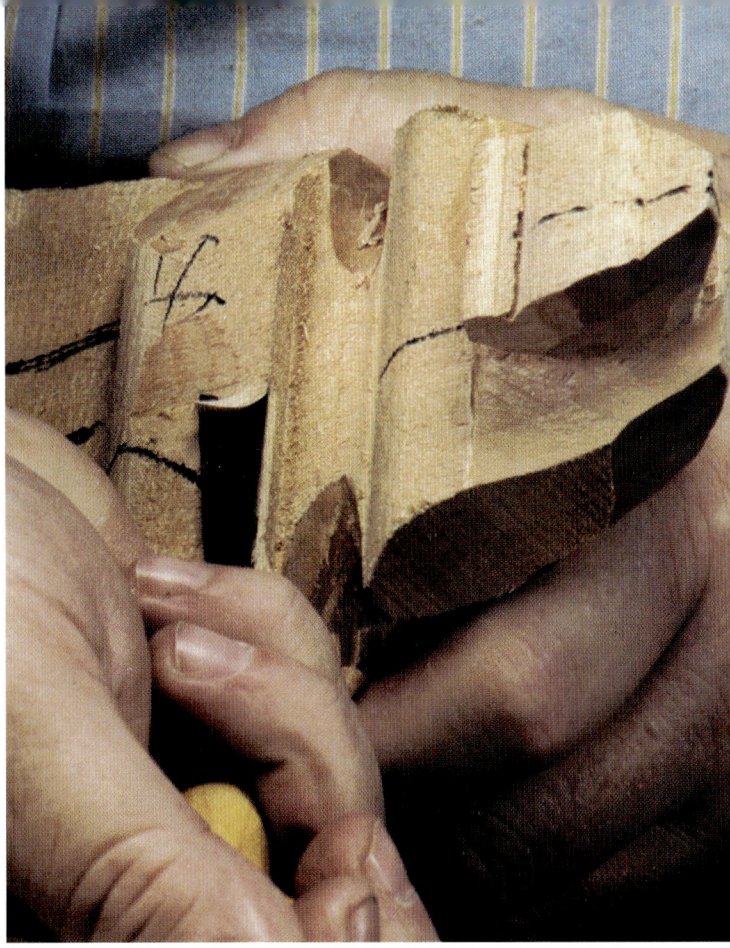

Sometimes it is better to use a gouge. I use a gouge in my lap, which is not the orthodox way. It is not particularly safe and sometimes leads to cuts. The safest way to use a gouge is with the piece in a vise. I work in my lap, and use finger and hand positions as a system of locks to minimize the danger. In this position the push comes from wrist action.

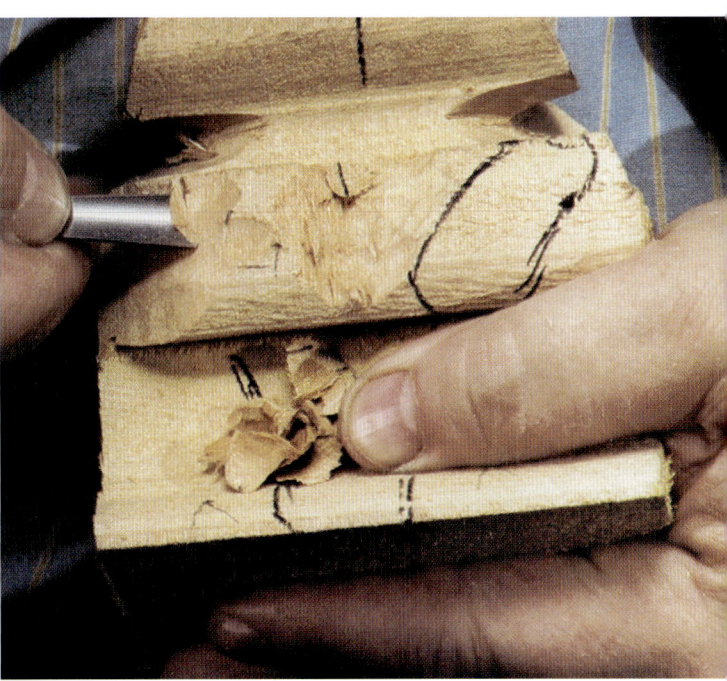

In this position the forefinger acts as a depth gauge/stop to keep the gouge from going too far into the carving.

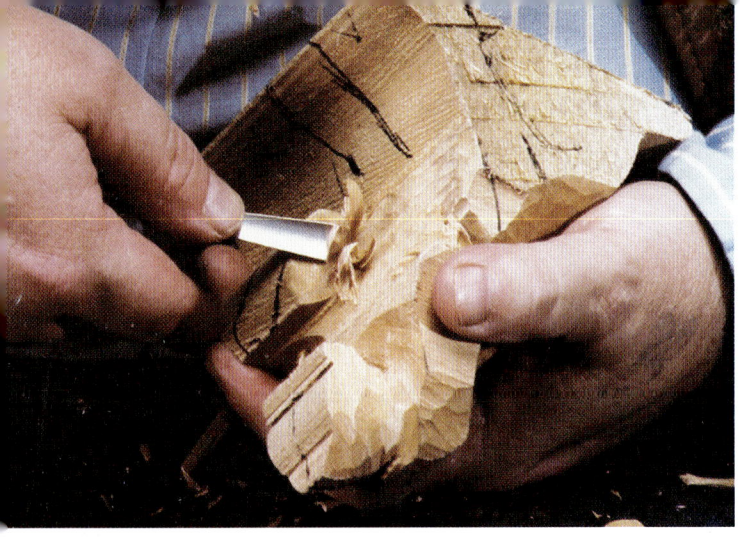

Various widths of gouges may be used.

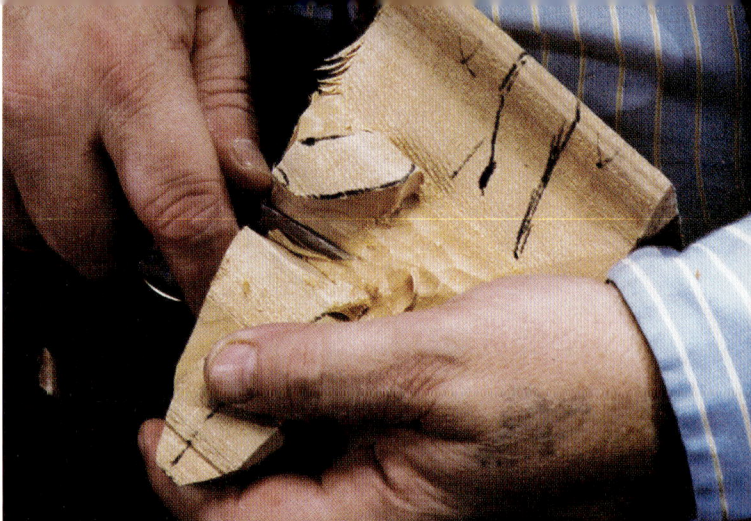

Trim all around the left leg, bringing it out.

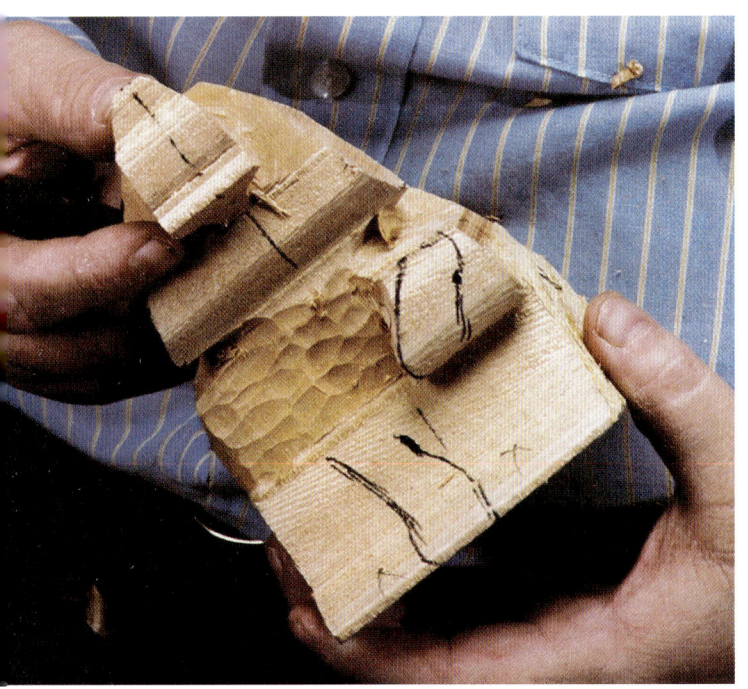

The excess removed.

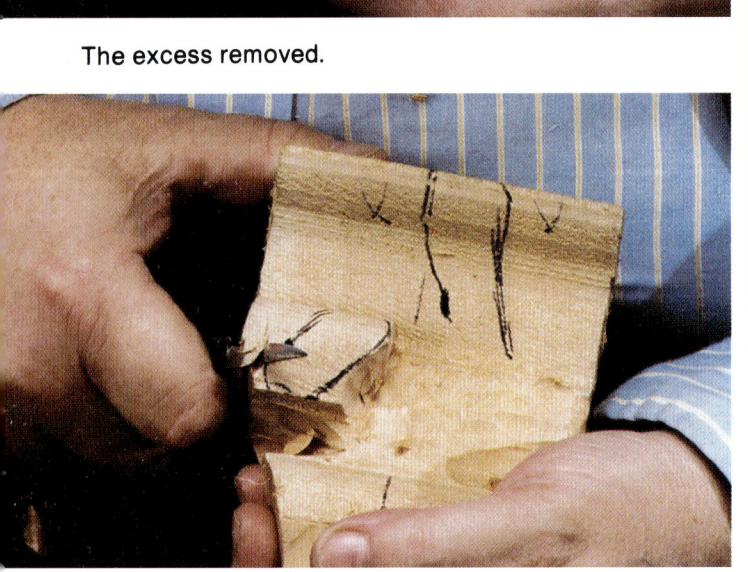

Carve away the excess on the outside of the left, raised leg.

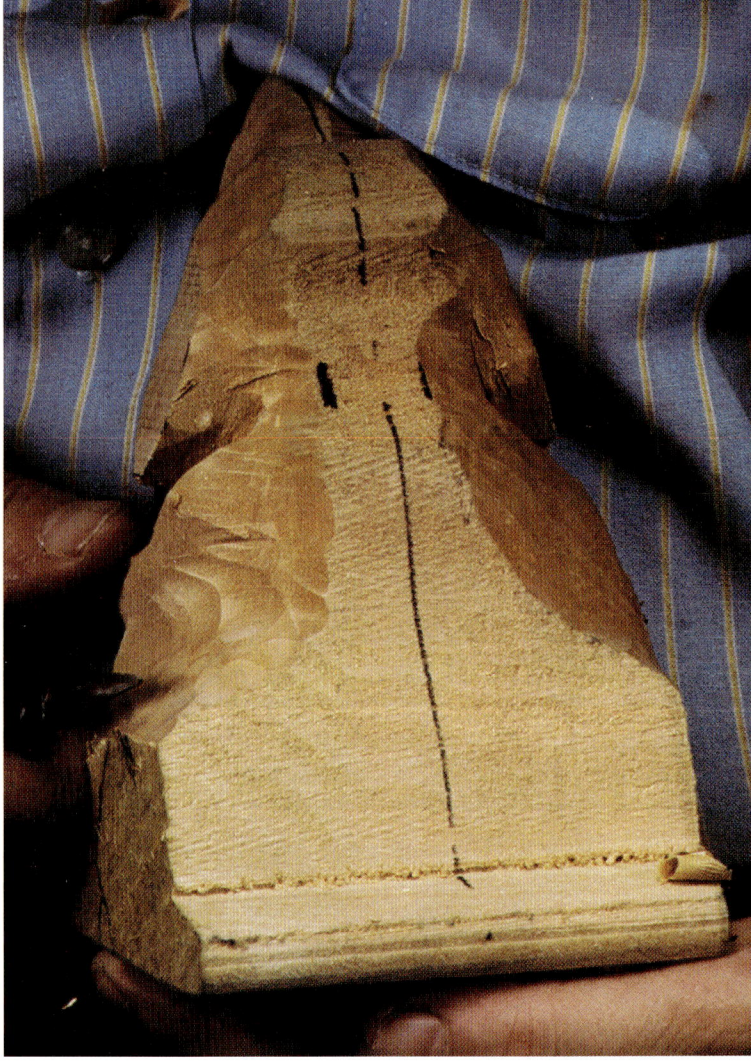

The blank is made so wide because when a hound dog sits down he tends to spread his legs real wide.

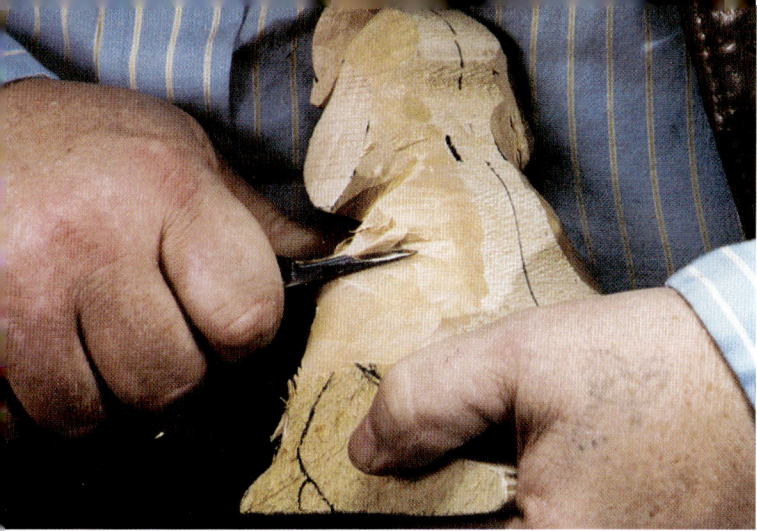

Shape the left shoulder, bringing it back to the neck.

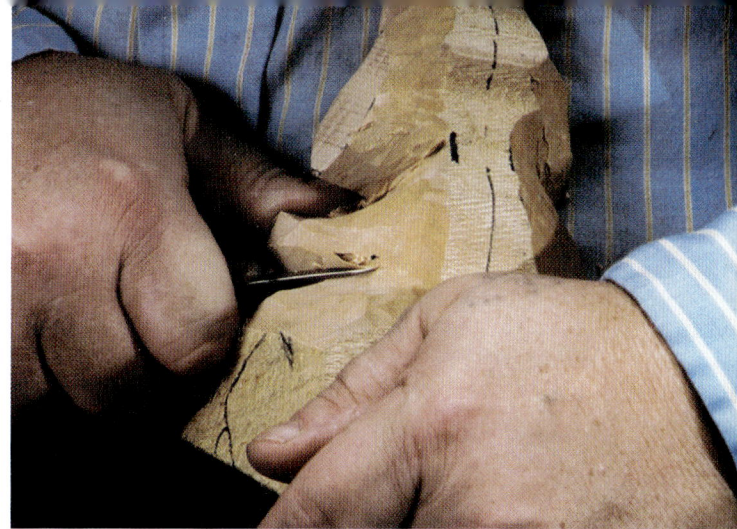

trim back to it from the body.

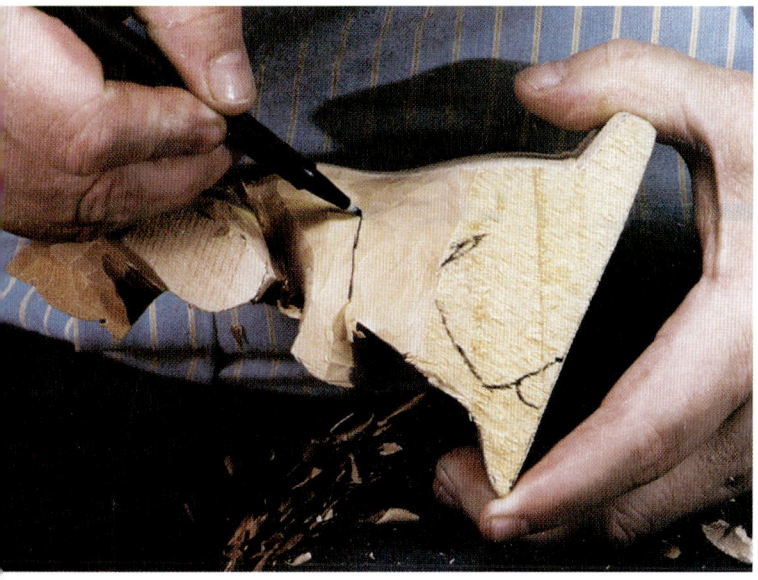

Mark the line of the underside of the leg.

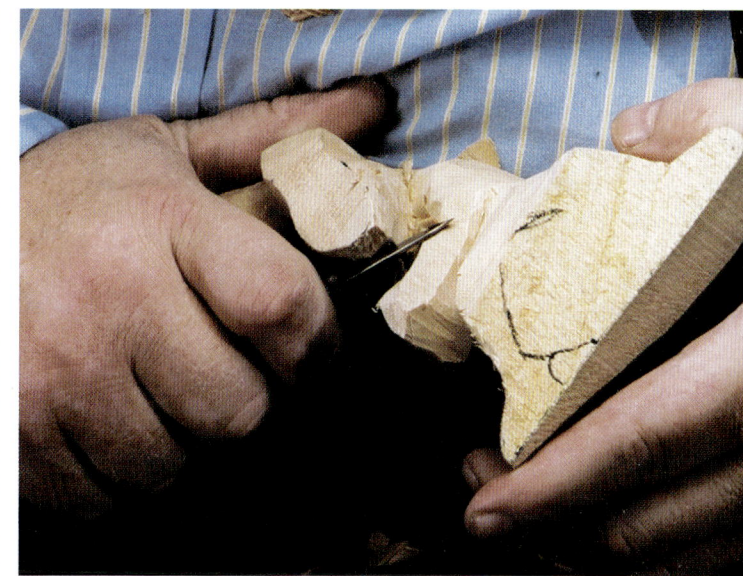

Begin to shape the left leg.

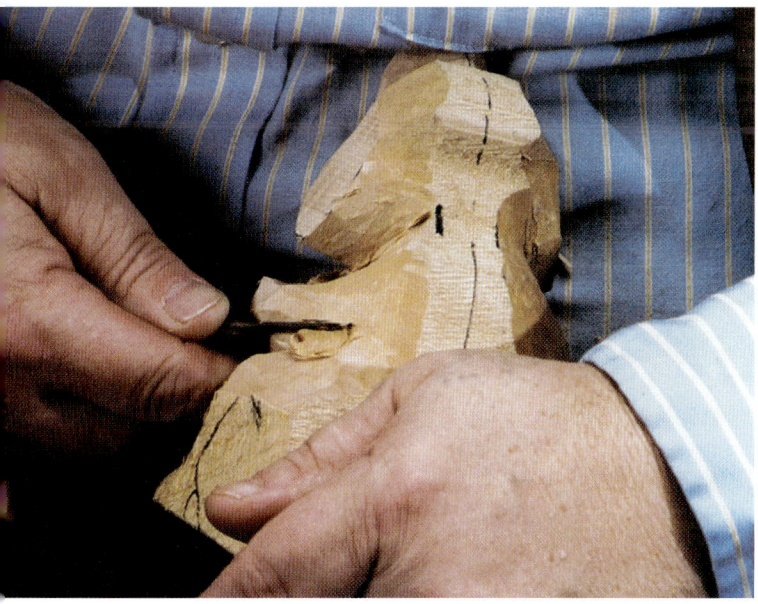

Cut a stop along the line and...

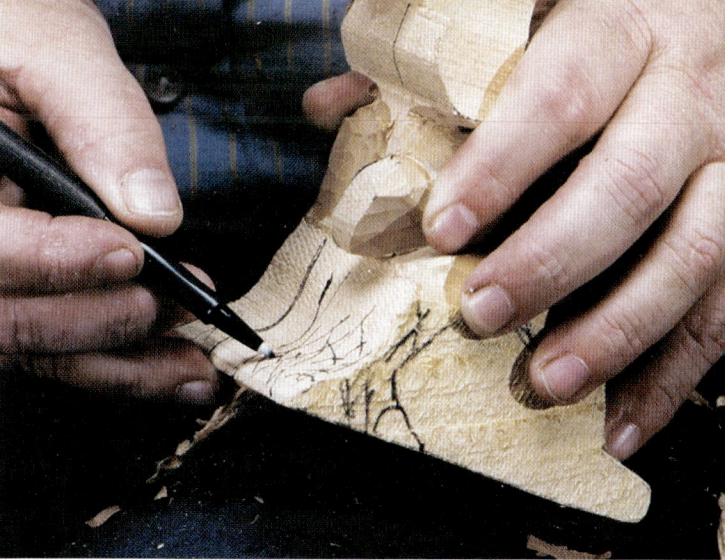

Mark what is to be removed around the right front leg, first on one side...

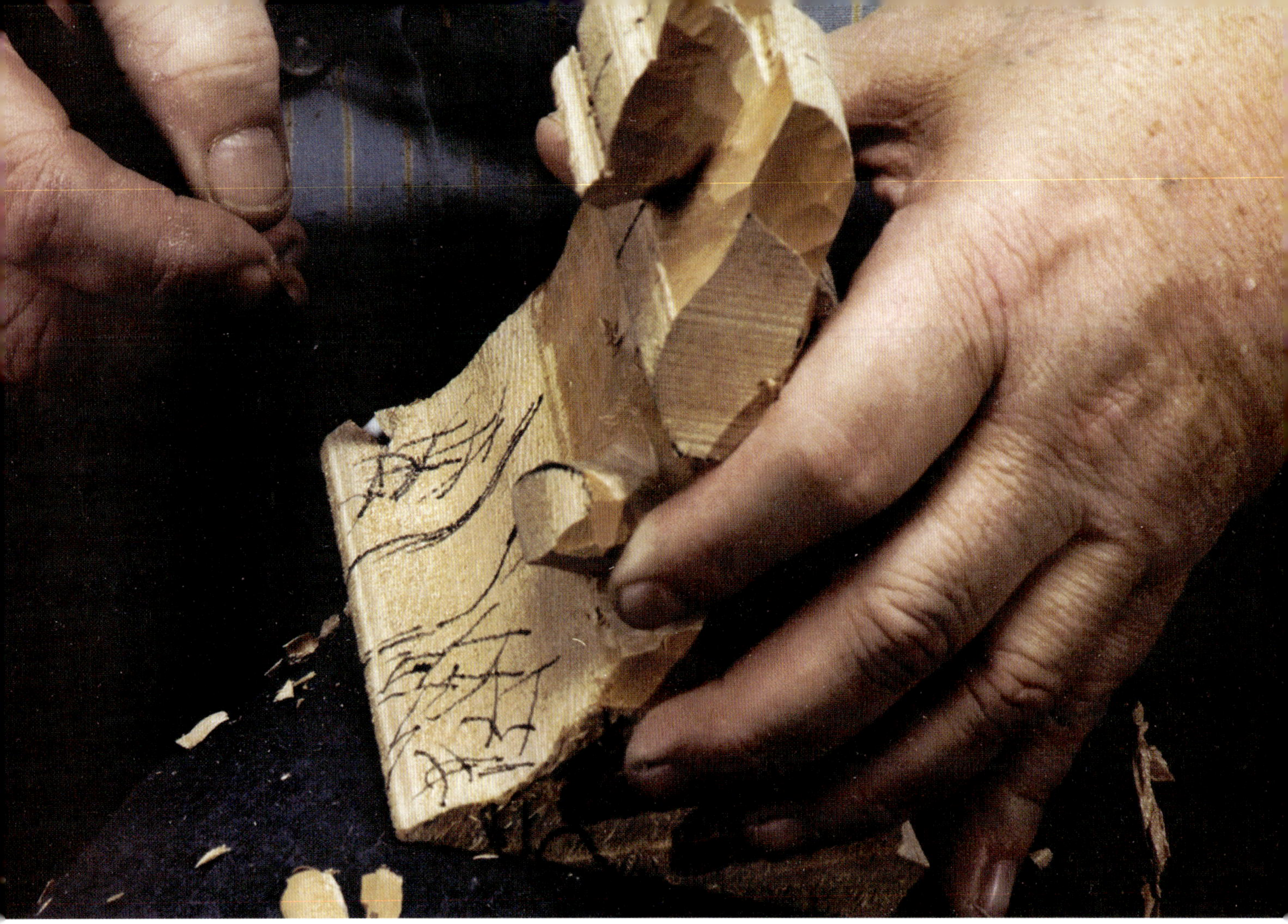

then on the other.

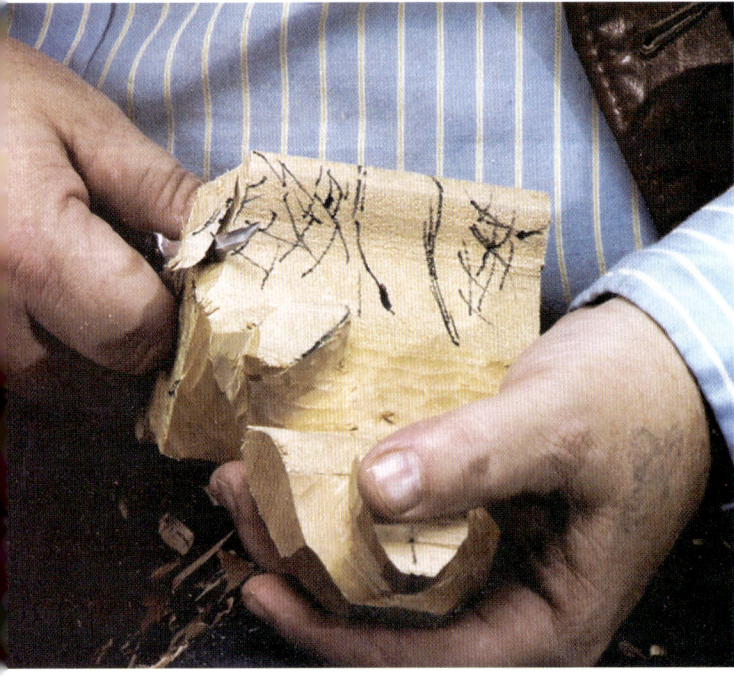

If the grain is right, most of this area will just pop off with a knife.

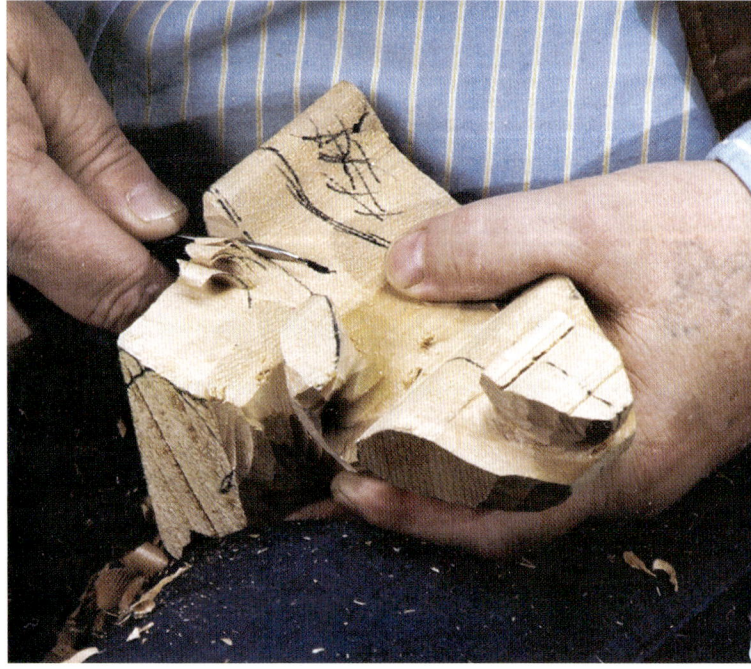

When you get closer to the leg carve more carefully, taking of several thin slices.

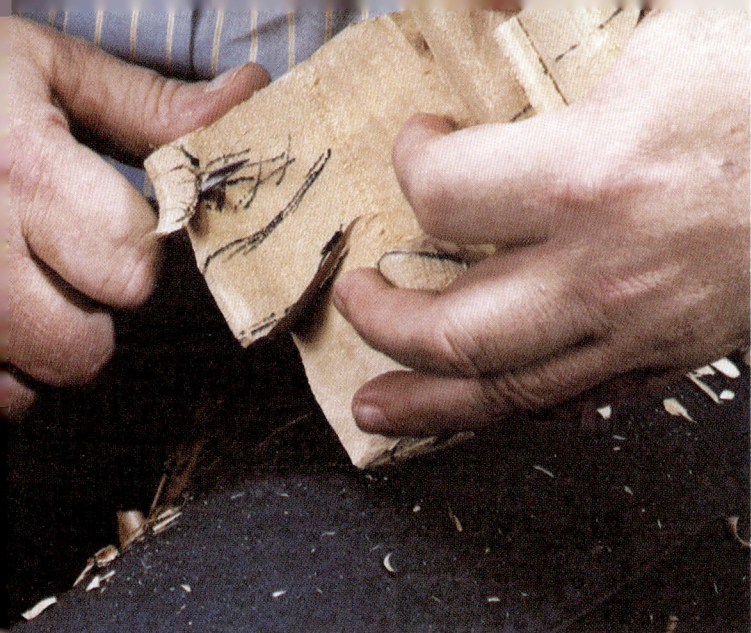

Do the other side in the same way.

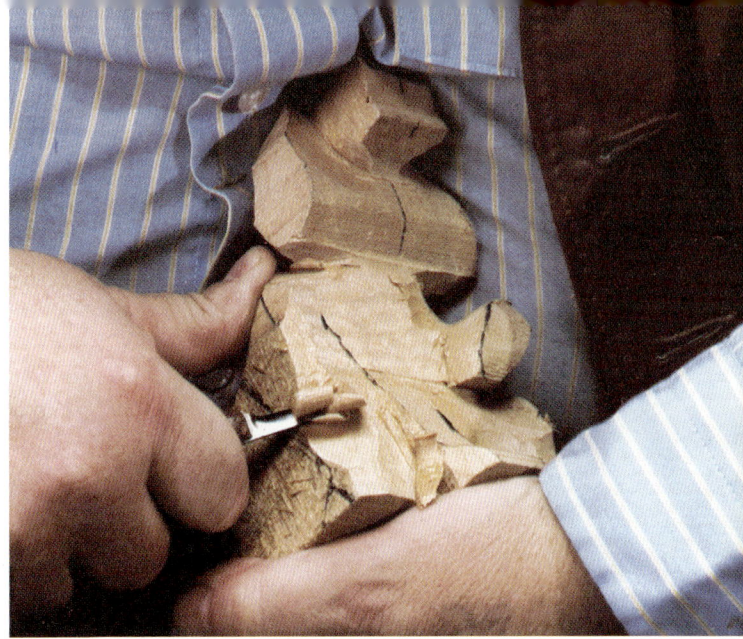

Remove the excess around the hip, using a knife or a gouge depending which works better for you.

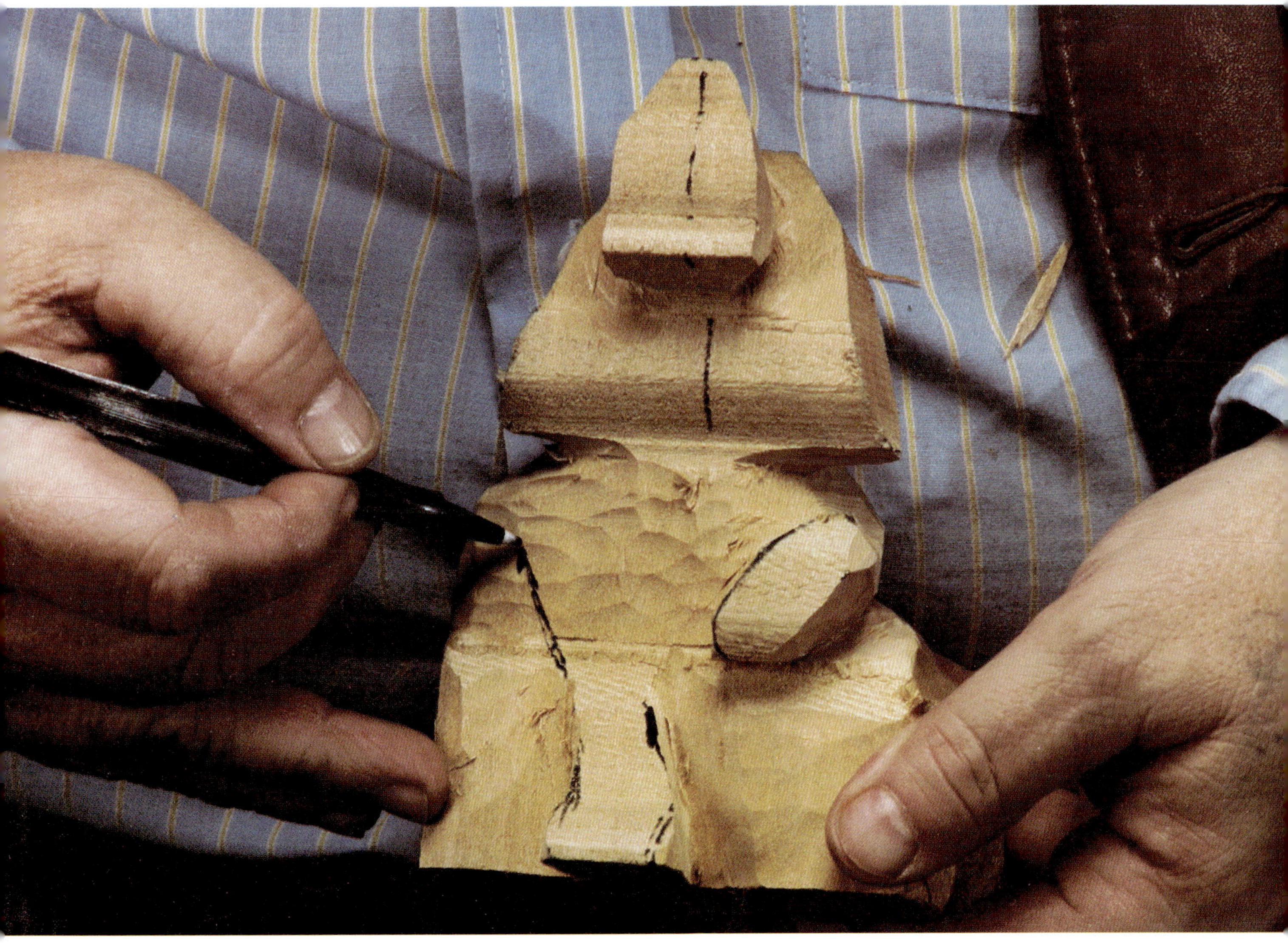

When the right front leg is defined redraw the line from the paw to the shoulder.

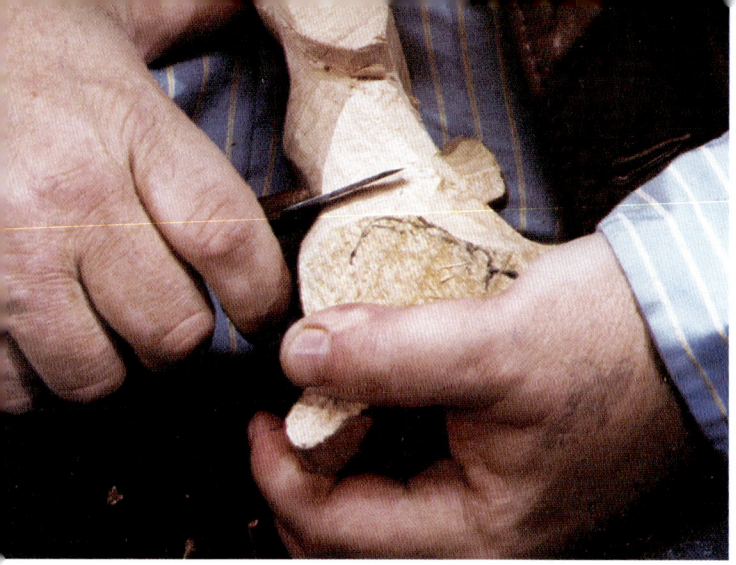

Continue up the shoulder...

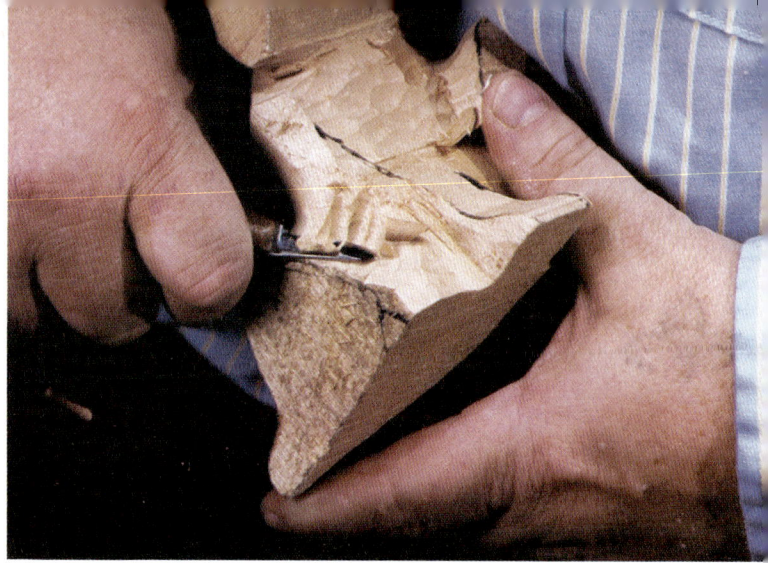

A knife will work, too, but not quite as well in this situation. Tools are often interchangeable, but the better the tools the better the carving. If the tool is working well, it is probably right. If it isn't you should change to a tool that does.

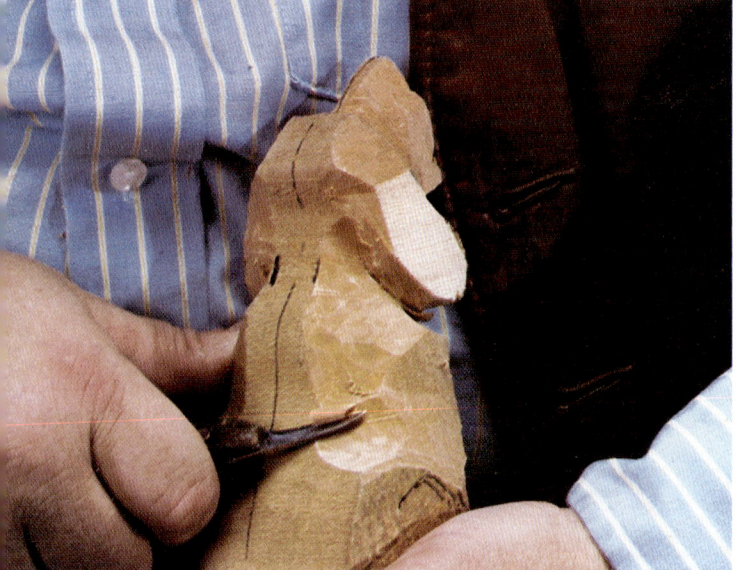

and around the back.

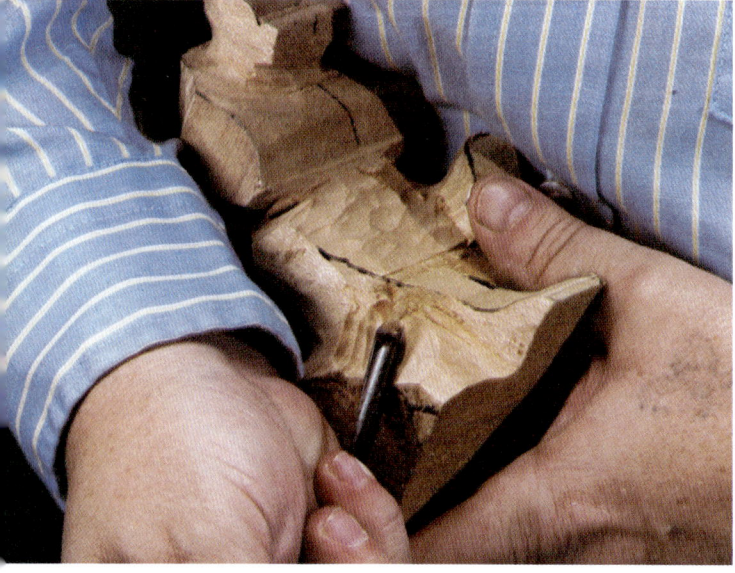

Use a gouge around the haunch, to bring it out.

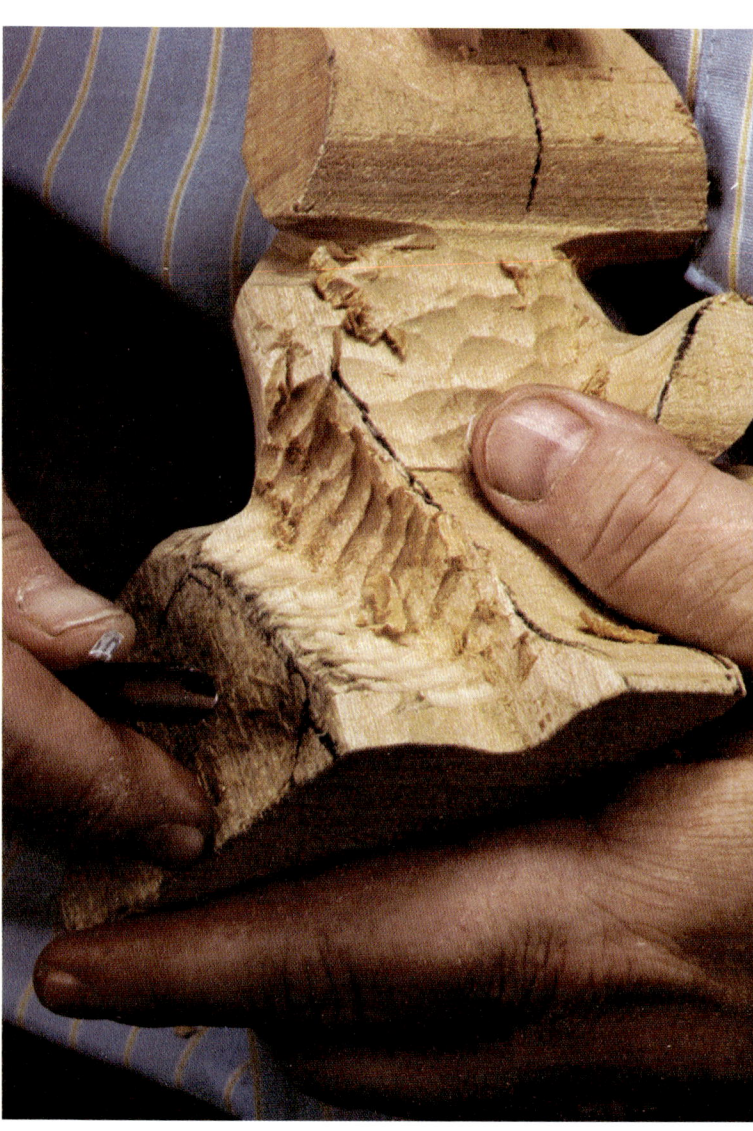

The smaller gouge is good for roughing out a shape.

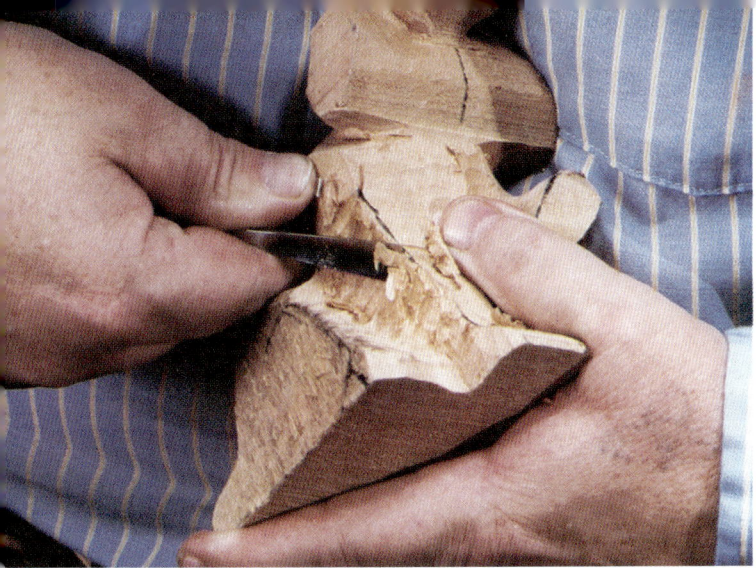

Then a flatter gouge will smooth everything up.

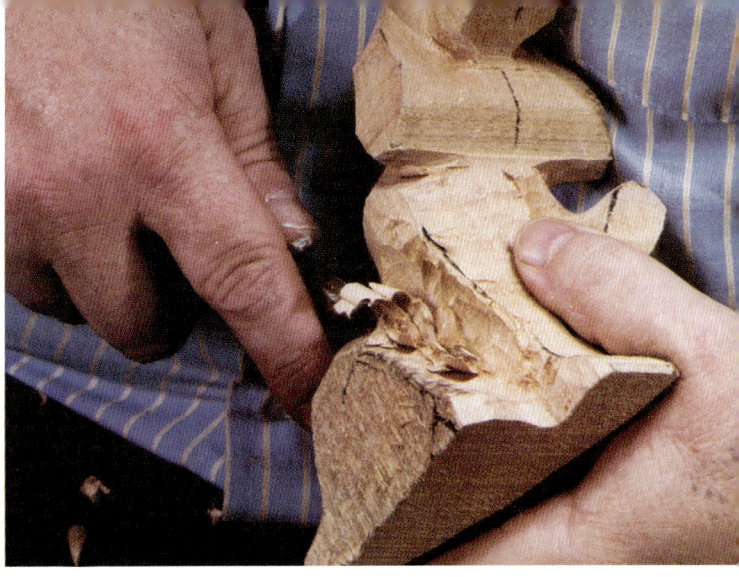

The same smoothing action can be had with a turned up knife.

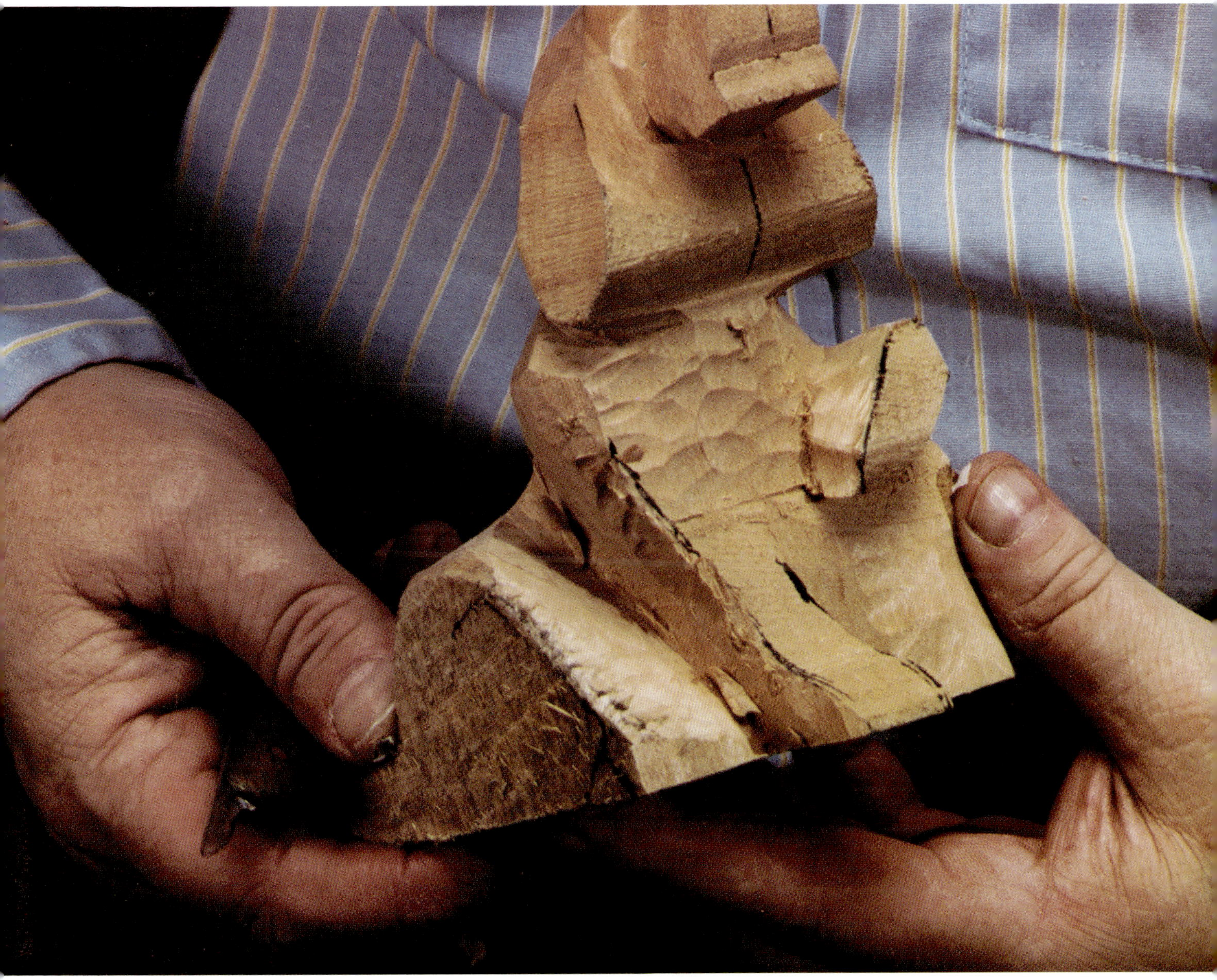

The roughed out leg.

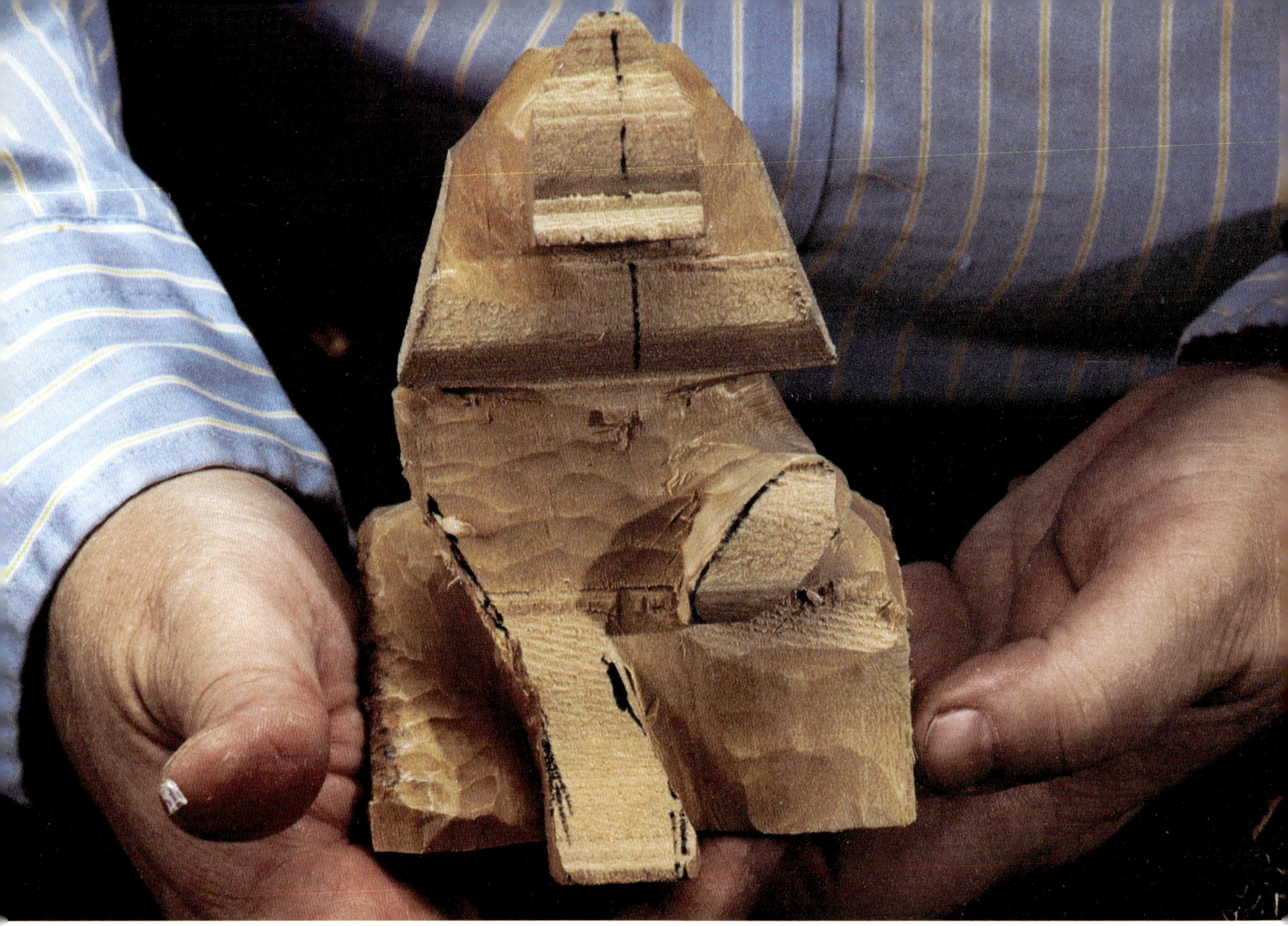

About now you need to decide where the tail is going.
With the right leg forward....

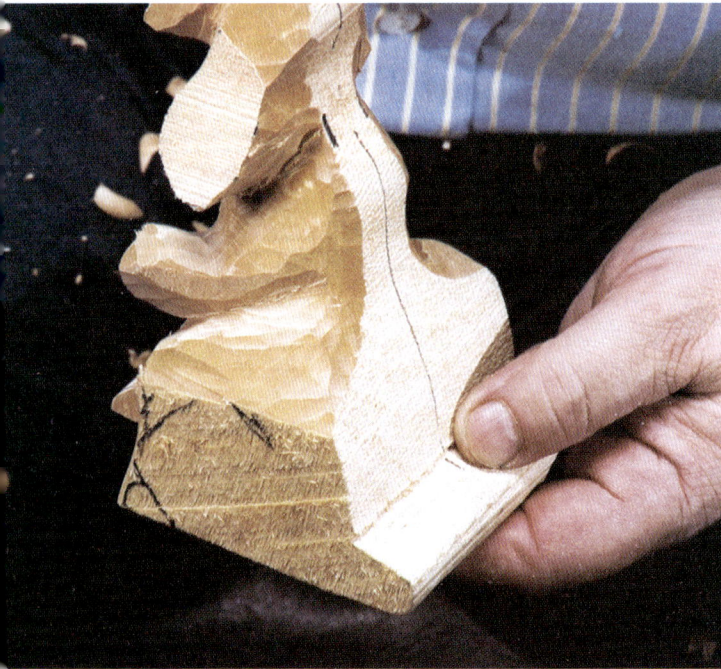

it will balance the figure to bring the tail around the left
side.

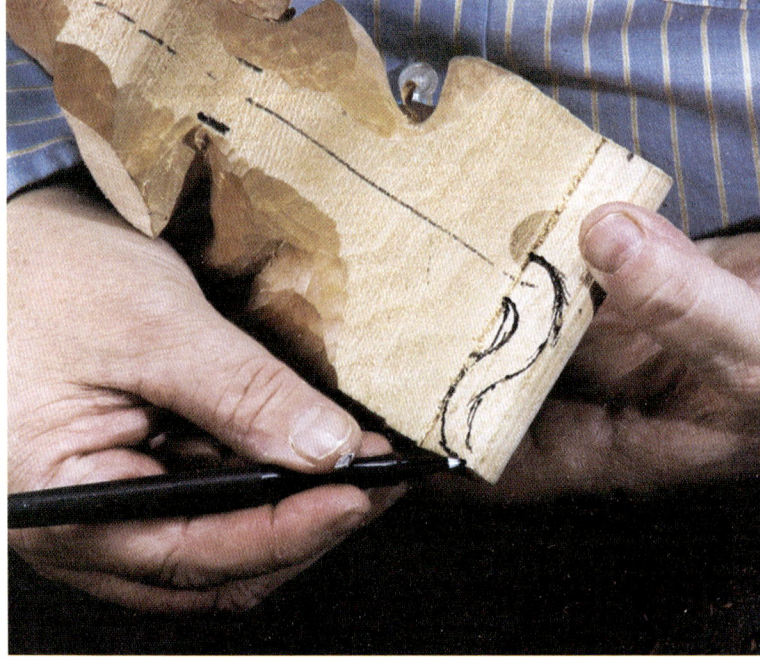

Mark it. This area is fragile, but if something happens we
can bring the tail into the body more.

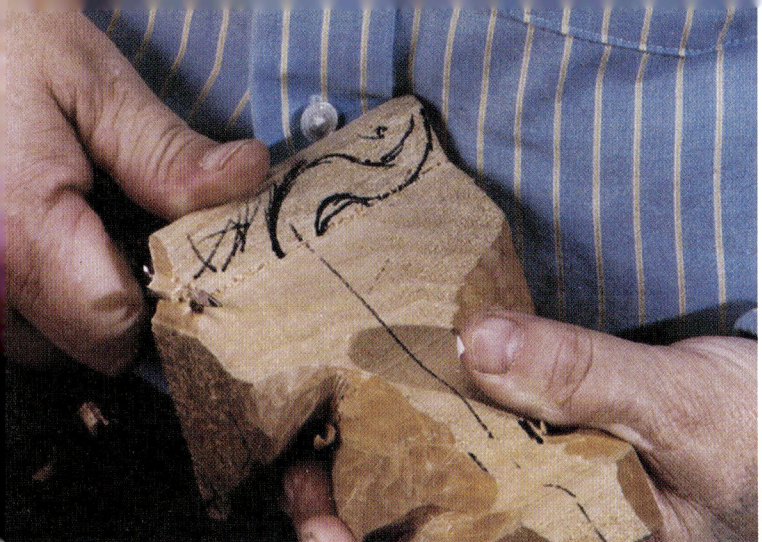

Mark the area to be removed and chip it away.

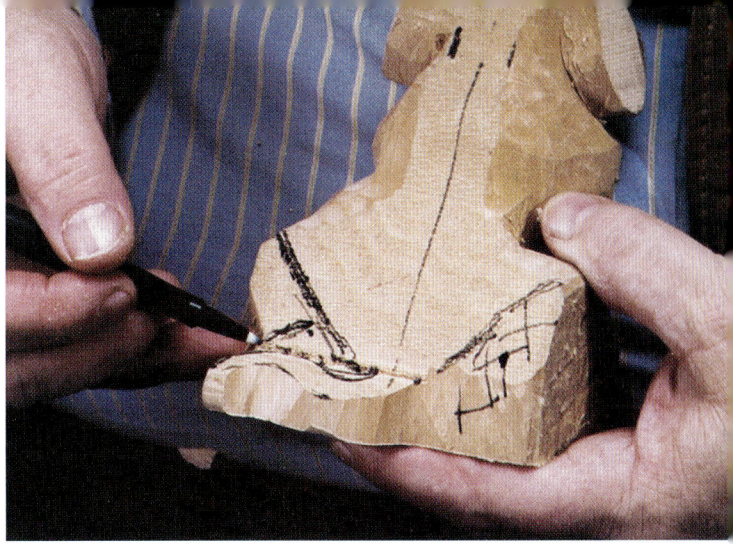

On the tail side remember that the tail has to connect with the hip. I've marked it to remind myself. I'll keep modifying it as I go.

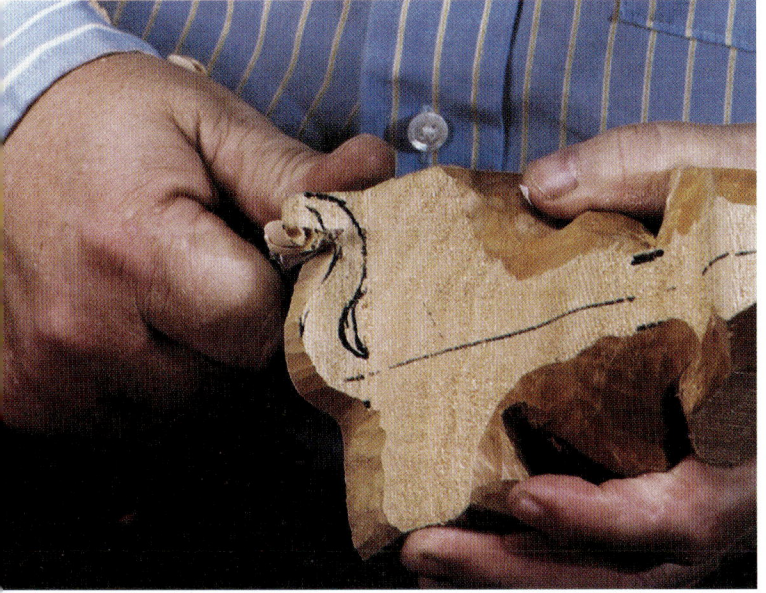

I do not take special care around the tip of the tail. Instead I carve normally to see how strong it is. If it breaks there is still time to redesign it.

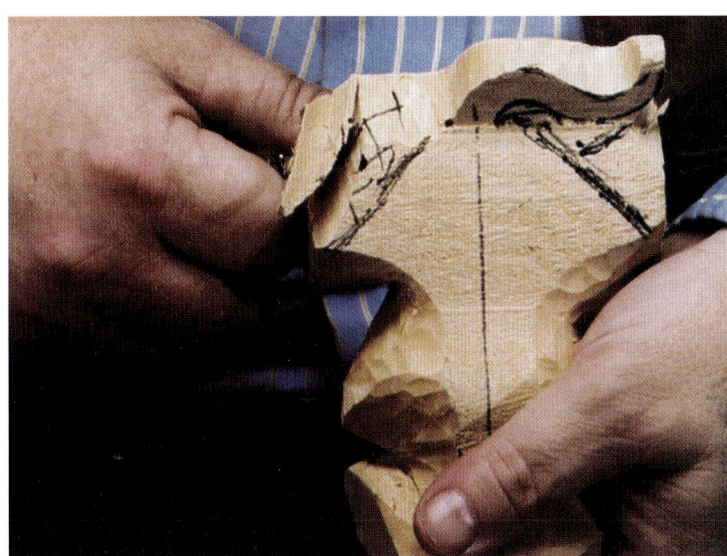

Chip away the excess...

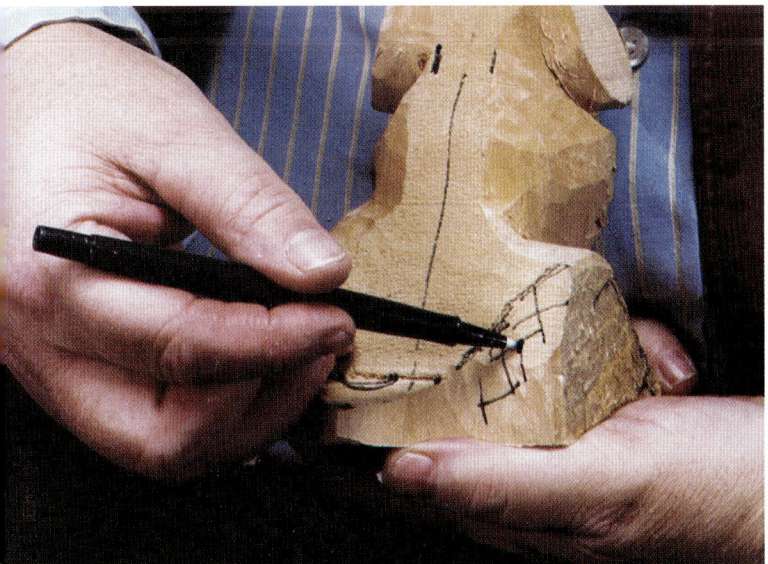

Mark the hips from the tail up.

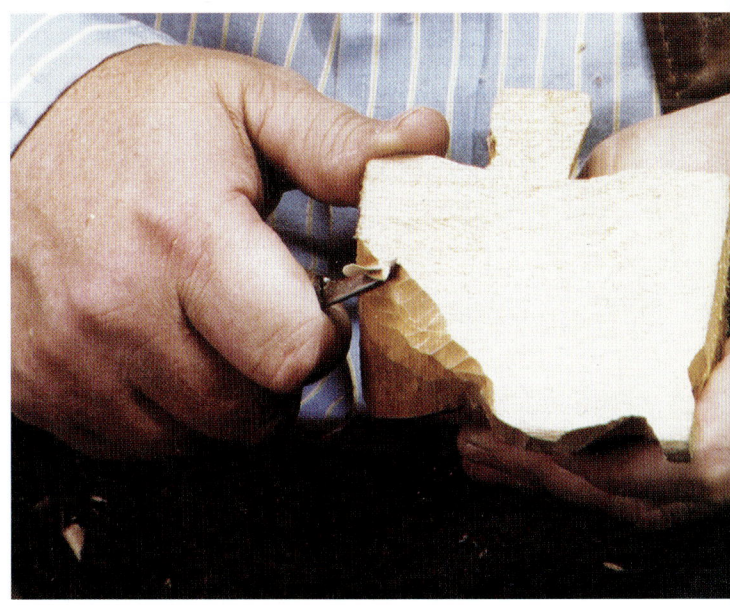

and round the haunch down around the rump. Looking at the bottom often gives you a good perspective.

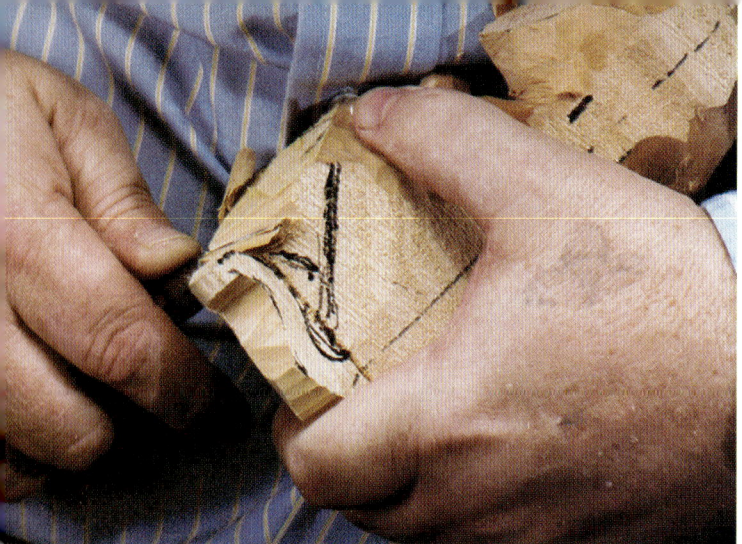

On the tail side, work the hip and tail at the same time.

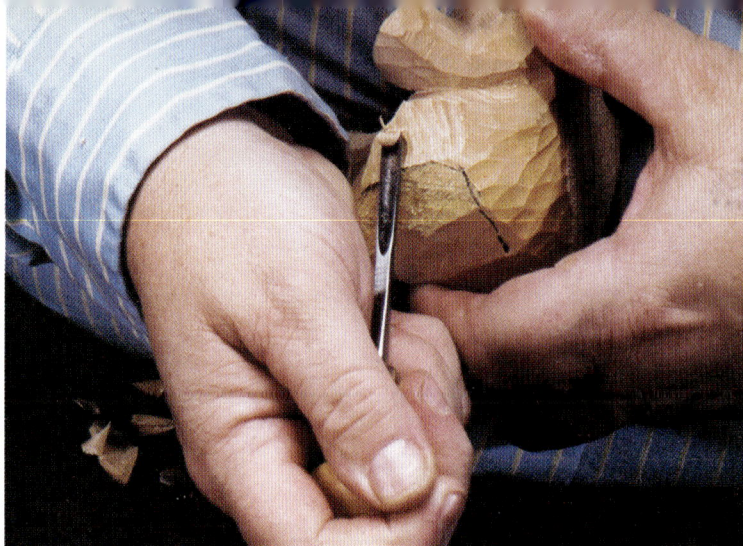

Use a palm gouge to shape around the front of the haunch and into the body.

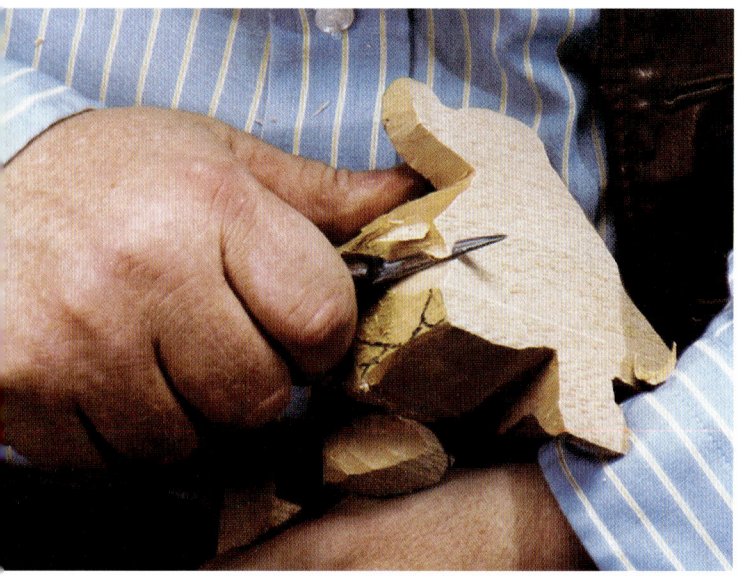

With the exception of the tail touching the body, this side is done like the other side.

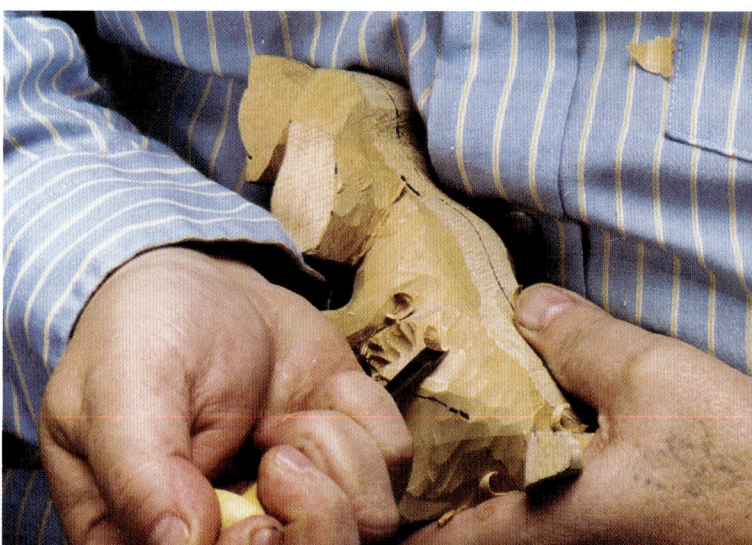

Use a little flatter palm gouge to shape around the back of the haunch. The exact size of the chisel will depend on how it works. If it chatters and cuts inefficiently, try another size.

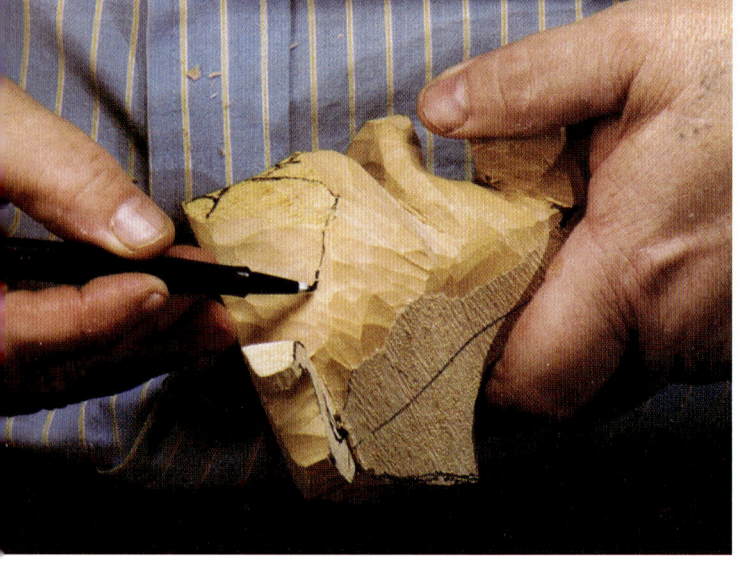

After rounding off the haunch, redefine the line of the hind leg.

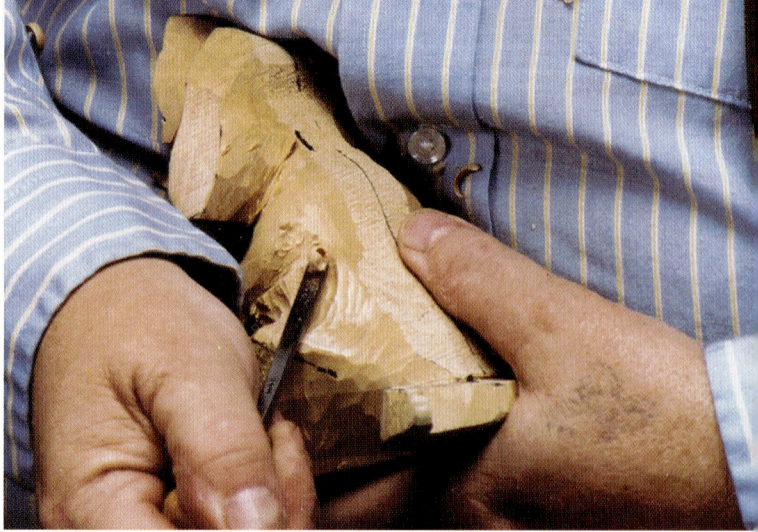

Continue the rough work with the gouge...

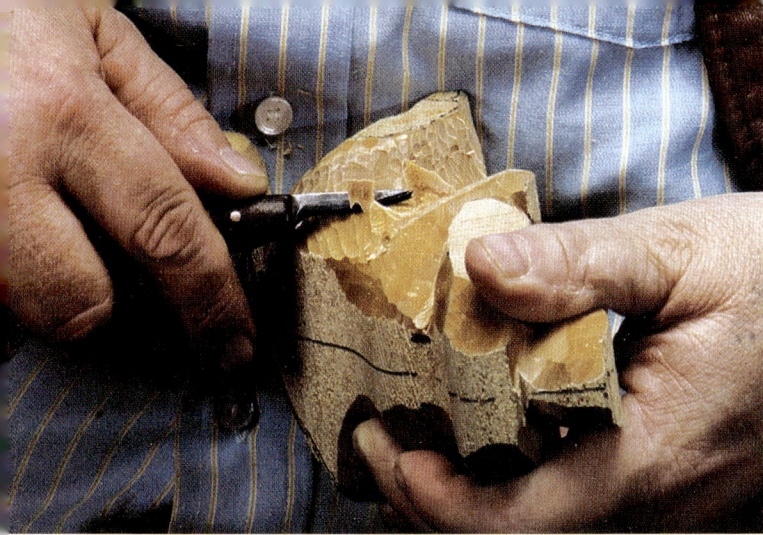

then smooth things over with a turned up knife.

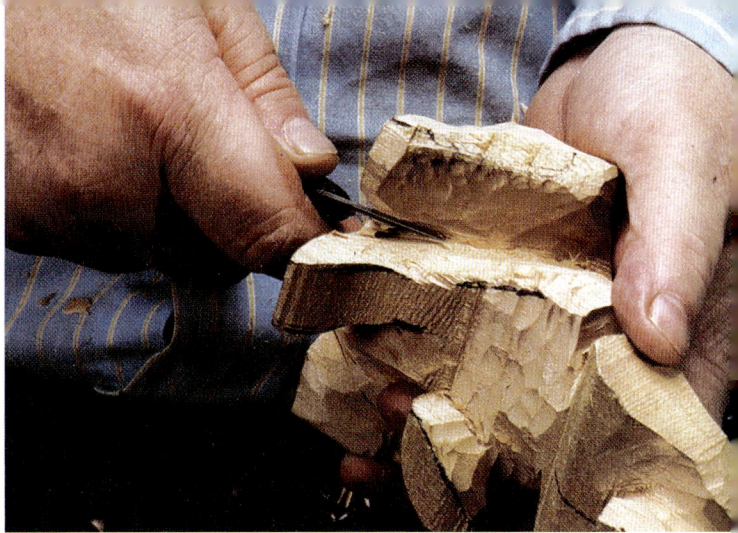

Begin to free the front leg from the hind leg.

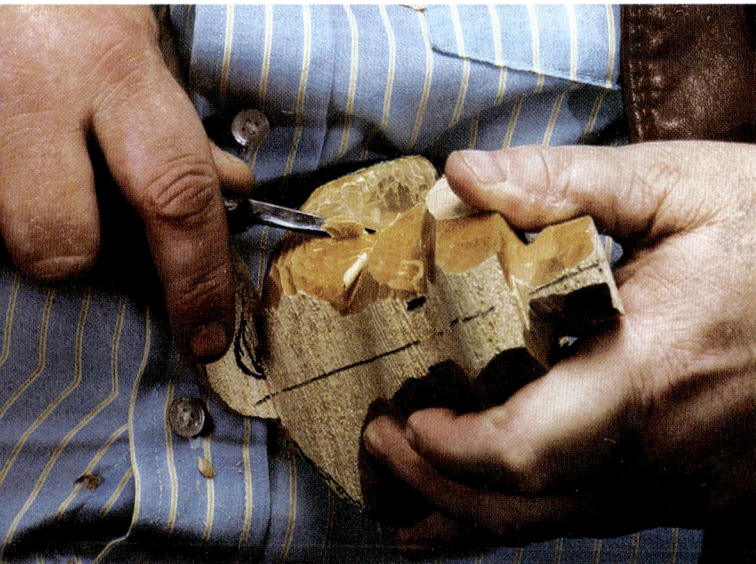

The turned up knife allows you to push into the work and get into harder to reach places.

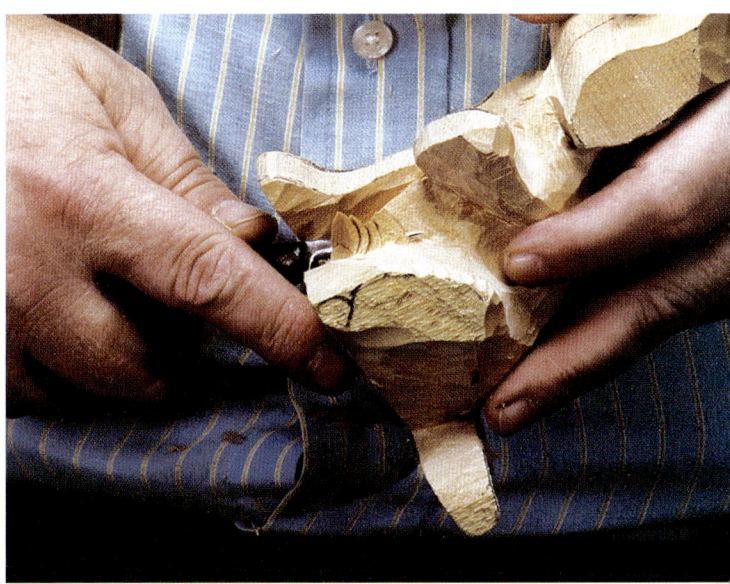

The area between the legs is hard to get at, but the knife seems to work pretty well. You are trying to get that sucked-up look of the dog's stomach.

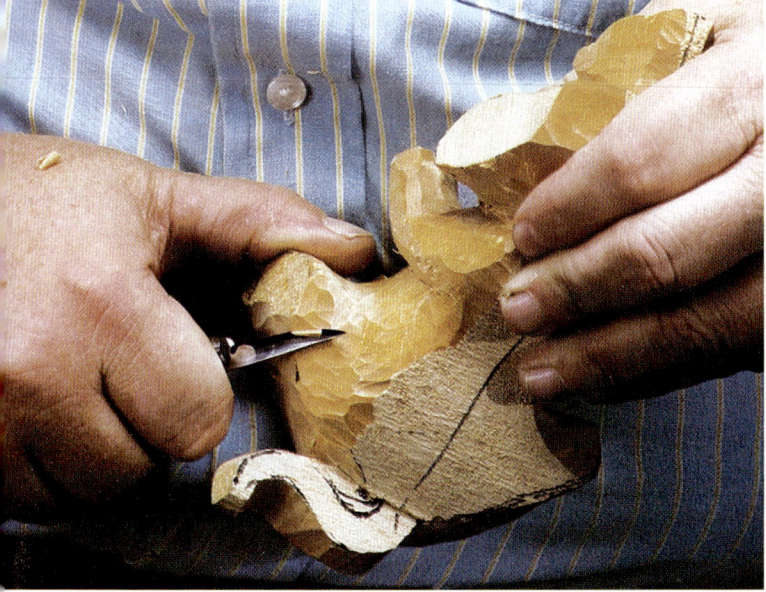

Dress things up and refine with the knife.

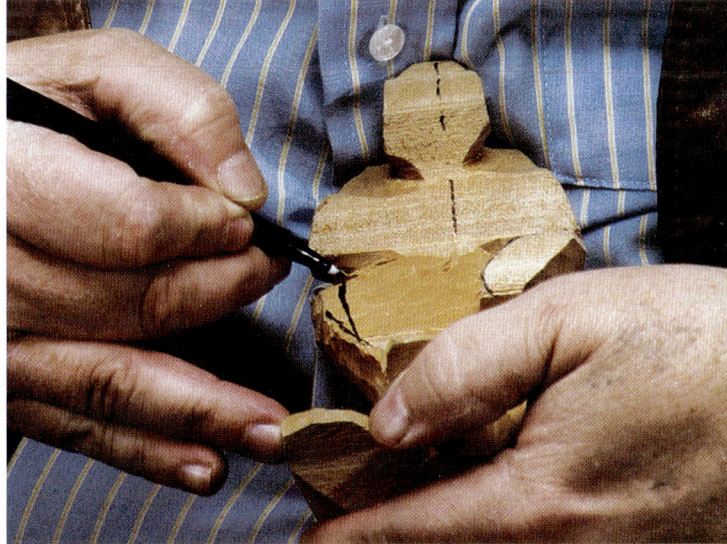

The right shoulder is a little broad. Mark it to be more proportionate...

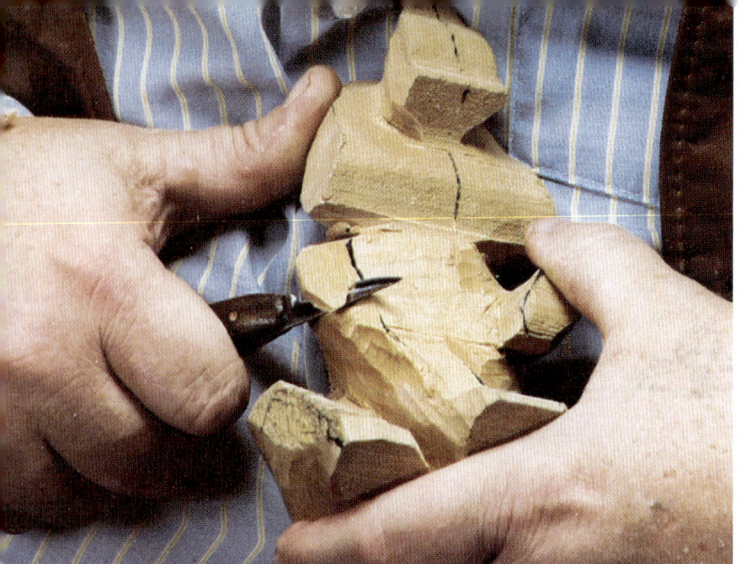

then trim it off.

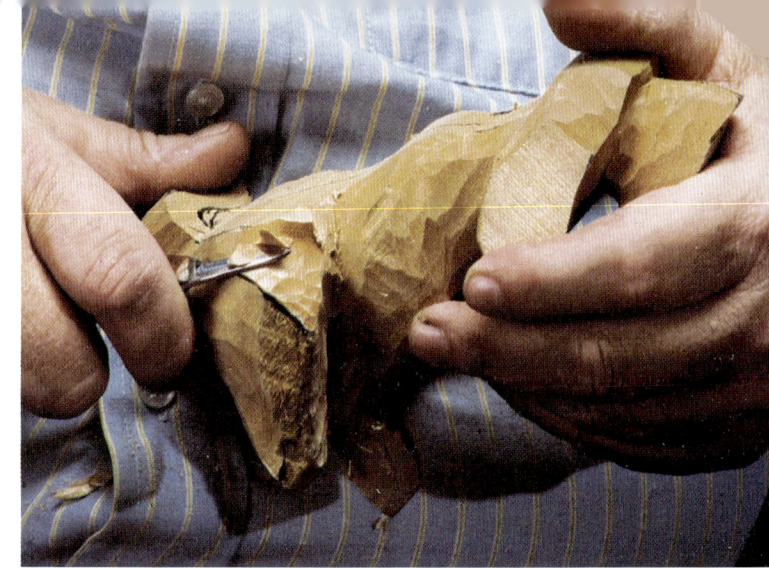

and trim it down.

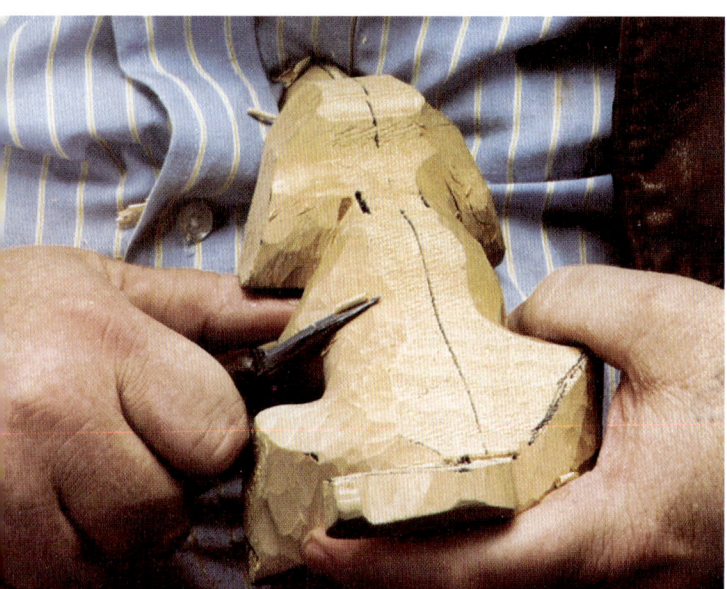

Refine and shape the back.

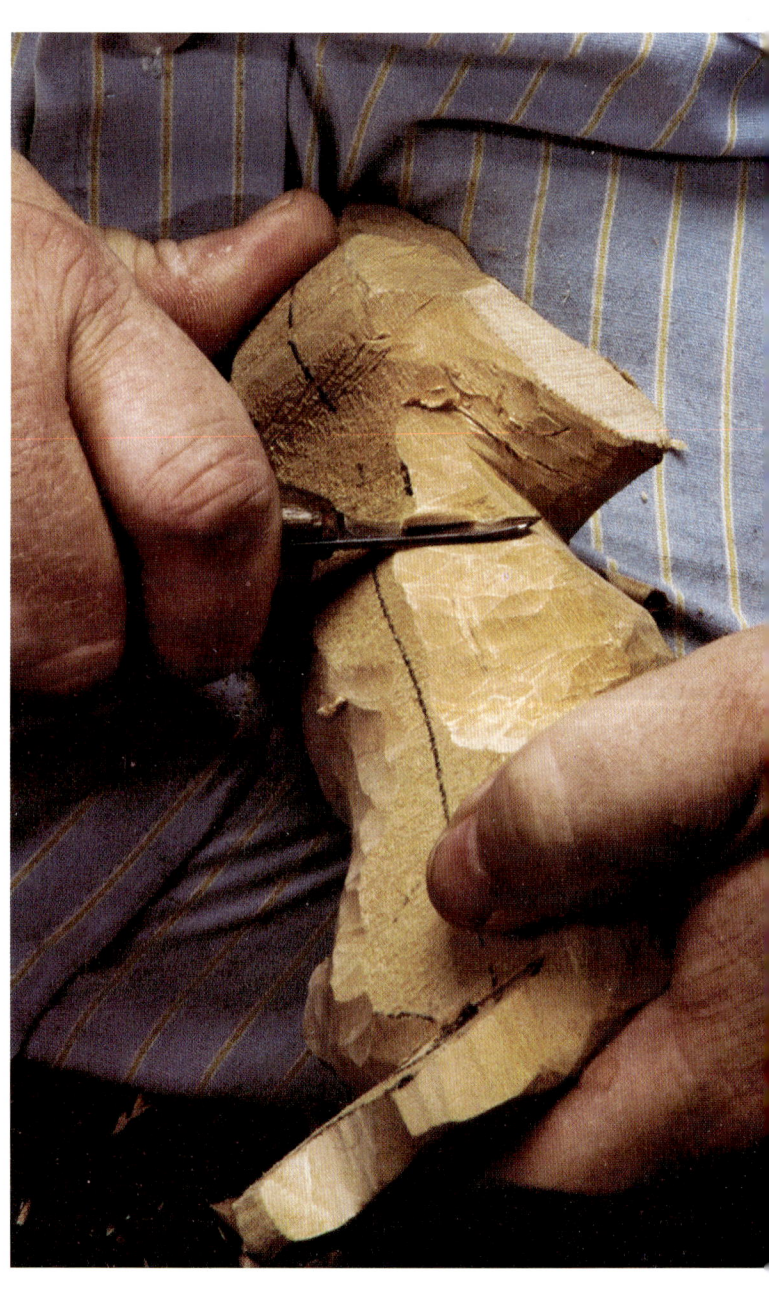

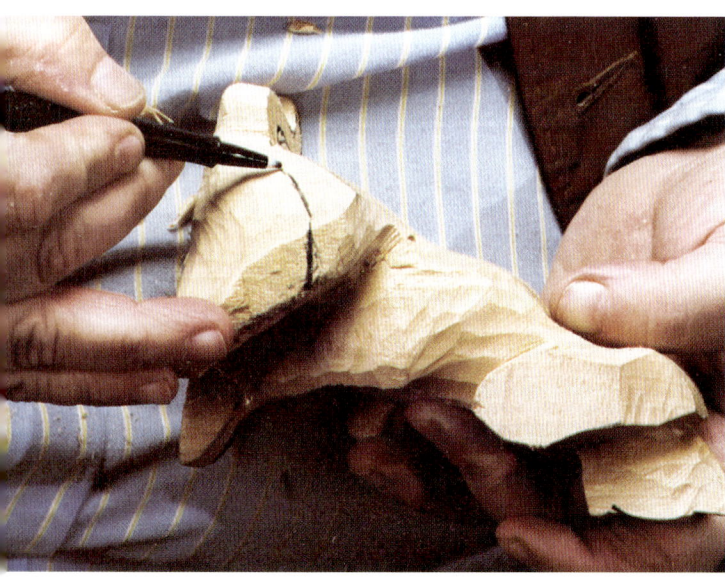

The right haunch is a little too tall, so I mark it shorter...

Continue rounding up to the neck.

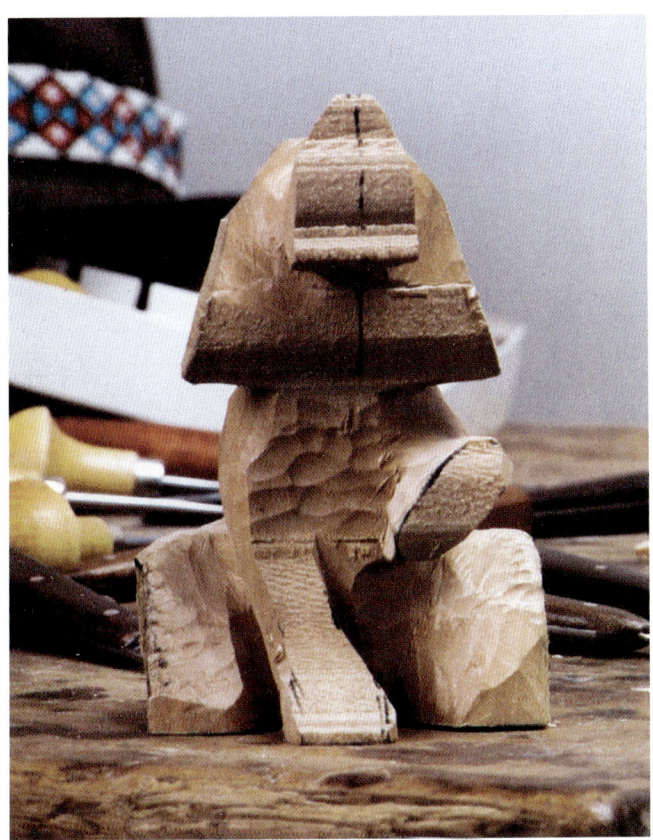
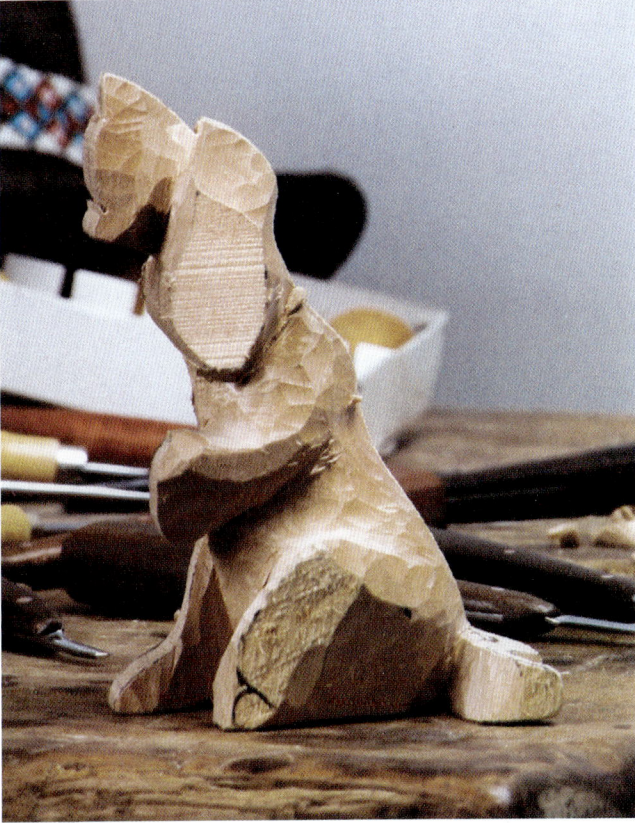
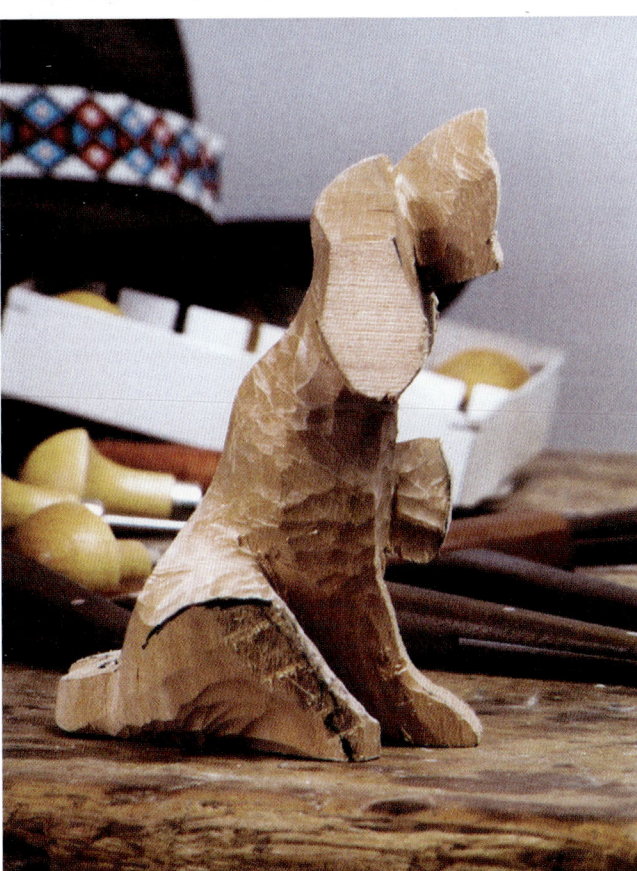
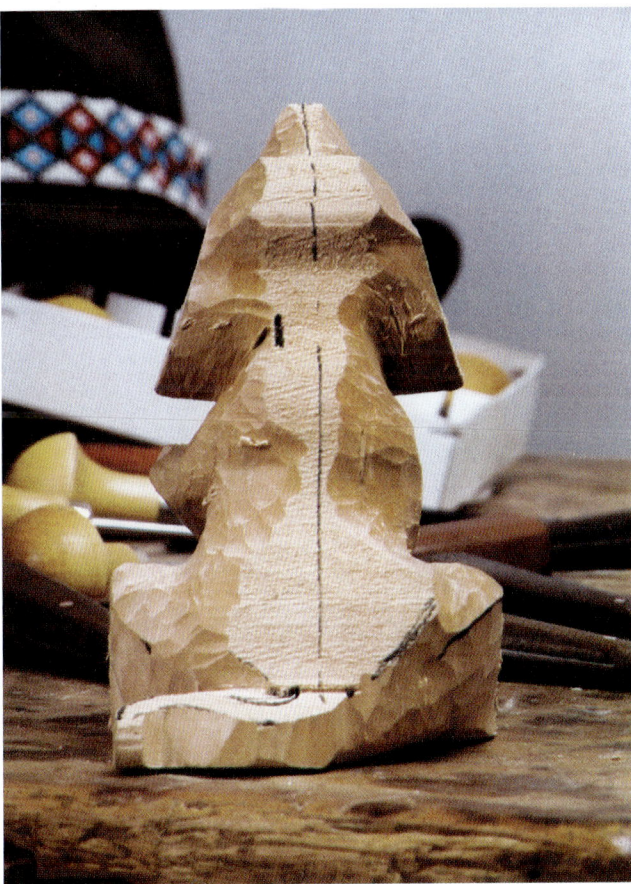

As you can see the basic dog shape is there. Now it is just
a matter of going over and over the piece to refine it,
before adding the details.

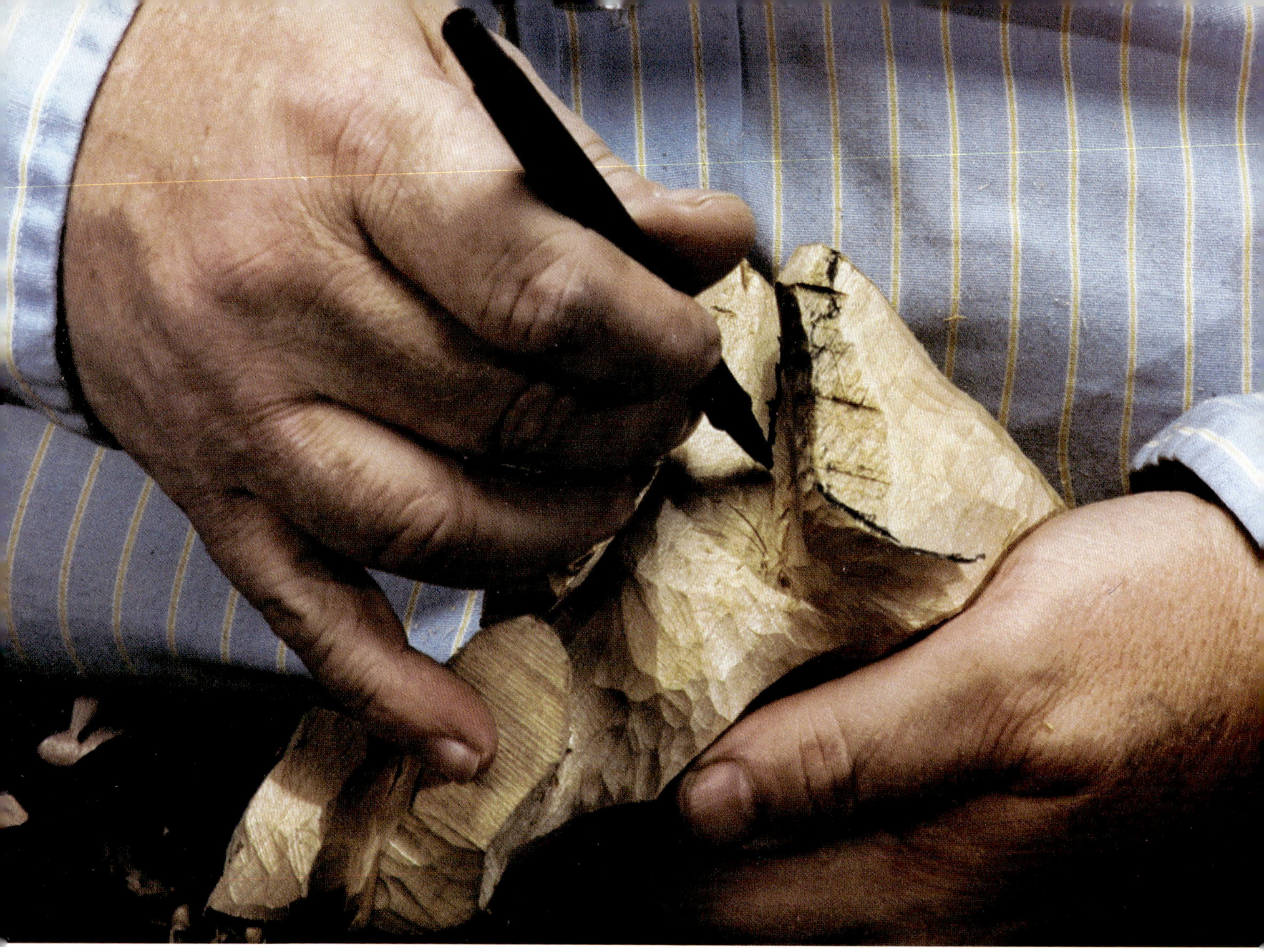

Draw the line to define the back of the front leg.

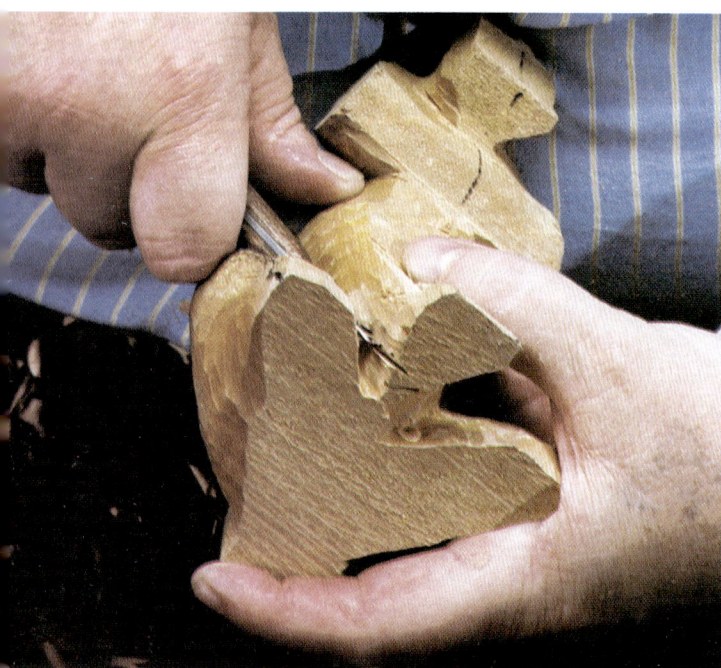

Cut a stop along the line...

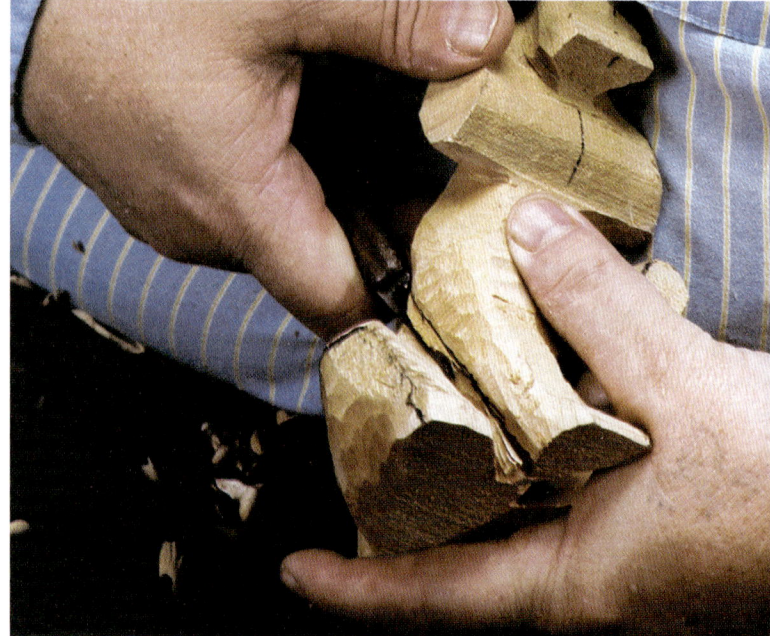

and trim back to the stop from the body, using a thin, turned up knife.

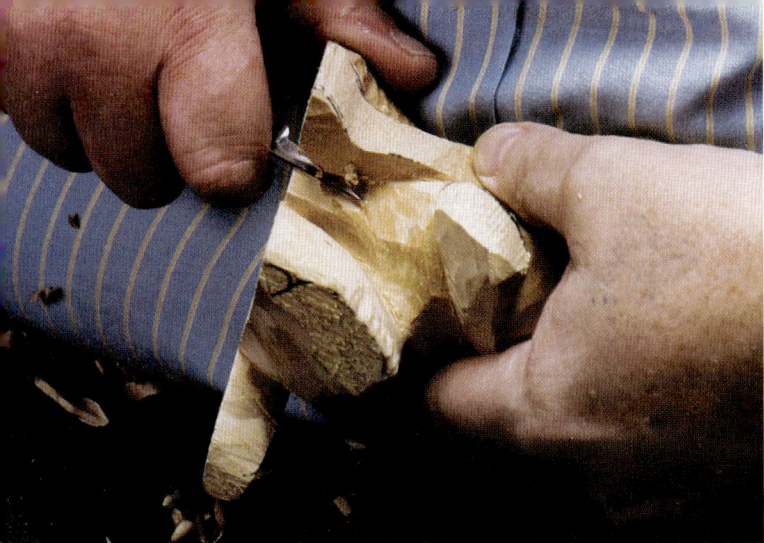

Use the same knife to remove excess wood behind the leg and to refine around it.

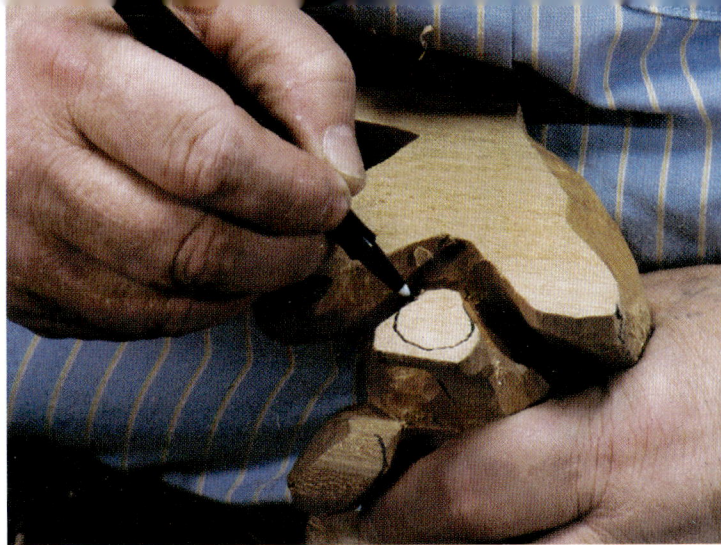

On the bottom of the piece, pick one foot and draw a circle to mark its size. This will serve as a guide for the size of the other feet when you get to them.

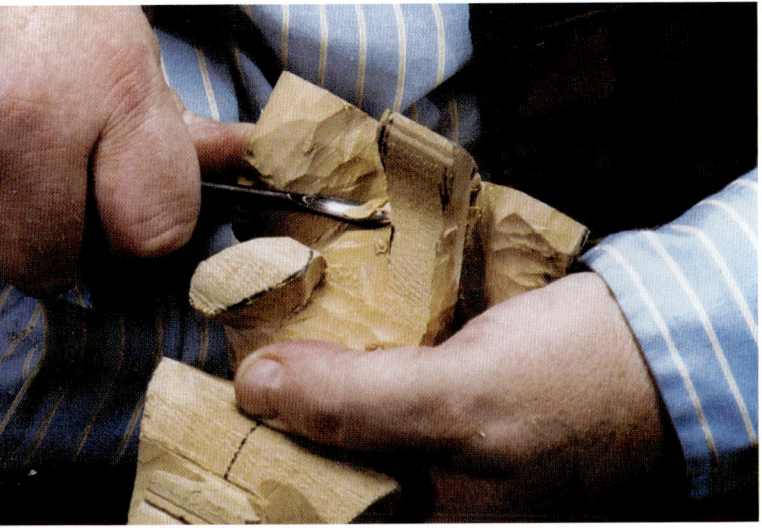

When every other tool seems to chatter and skip, it is a good time to use a spoon gouge. You could use a knife here, but it would take longer.

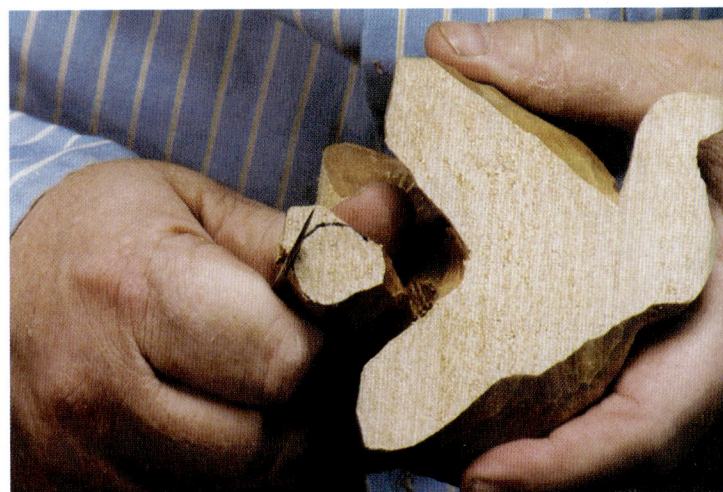

Cut around the foot to get it to the size you have drawn. Carving the bottom of the paw like this now helps keep the carving straight.

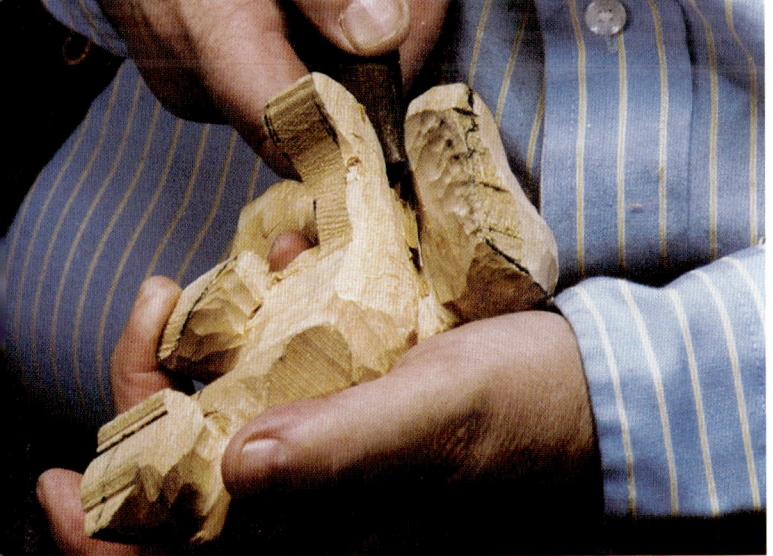

In this tight space the only thing that will work is a turned up knife with a long, thin blade.

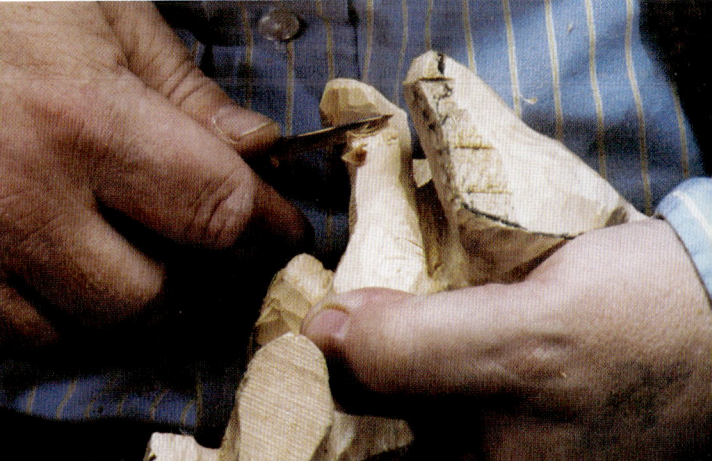

Carve the leg down to the foot. Setting the size of the foot first also helps keep the leg the right size. When carving a leg never carve in the same spot too long. If you do, before you know it you'll end up with a board instead of a leg.

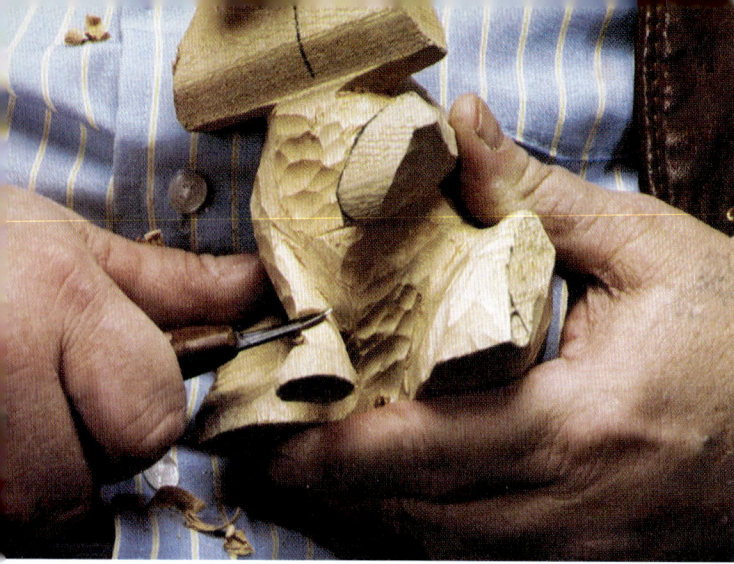

Keep going around and around on the leg until it looks to be about the right size.

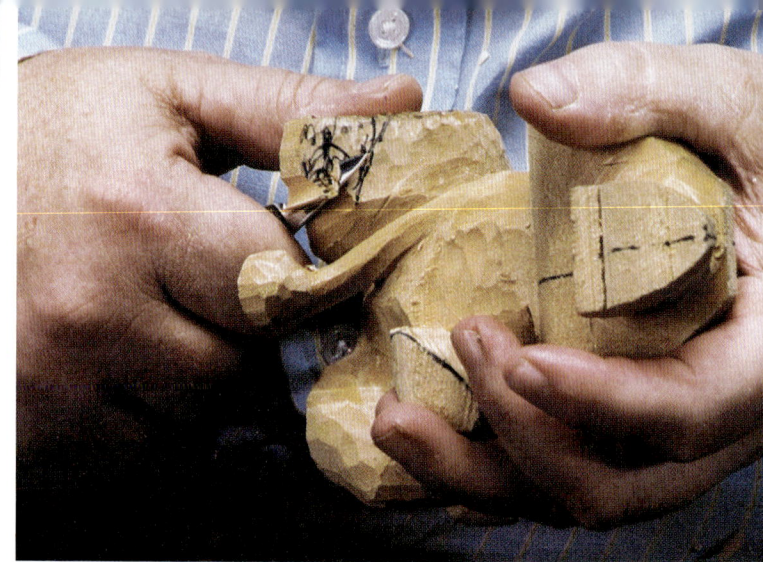

and pop off the part to be removed.

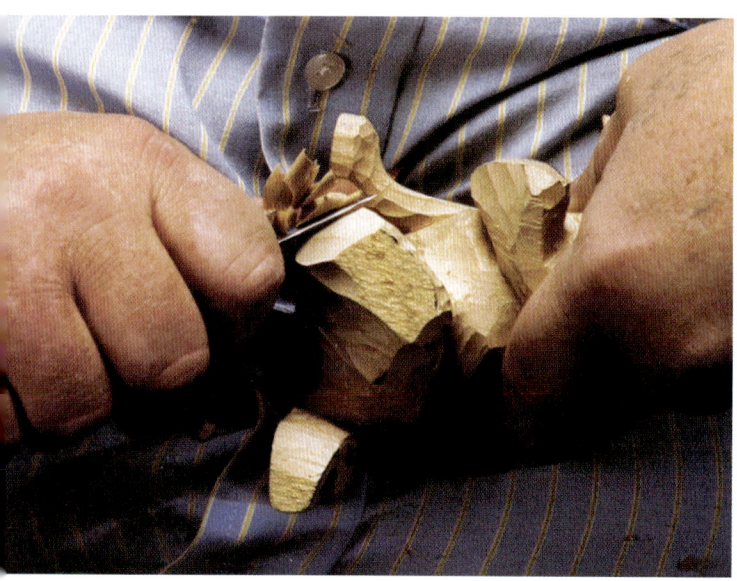

Round down the front edge of the hind leg toward its foot.

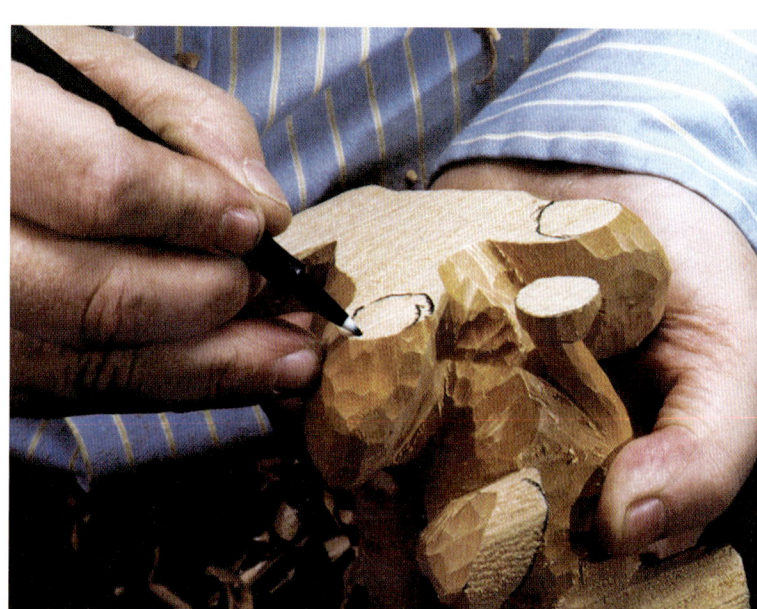

After carving the rough shape of the hind legs, turn the figure over and mark the pads of the hind feet. The feet will just peep out from under the hind legs.

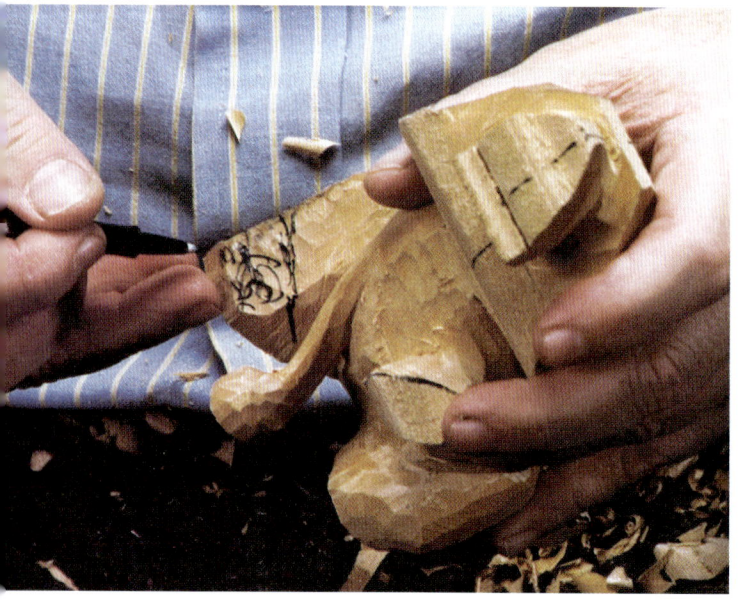

Mark the front edge of the other hind leg...

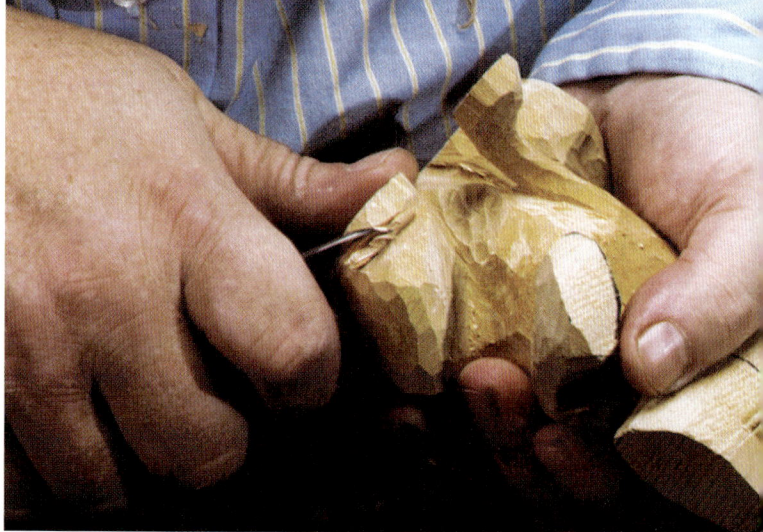

Define the top of the rear feet.

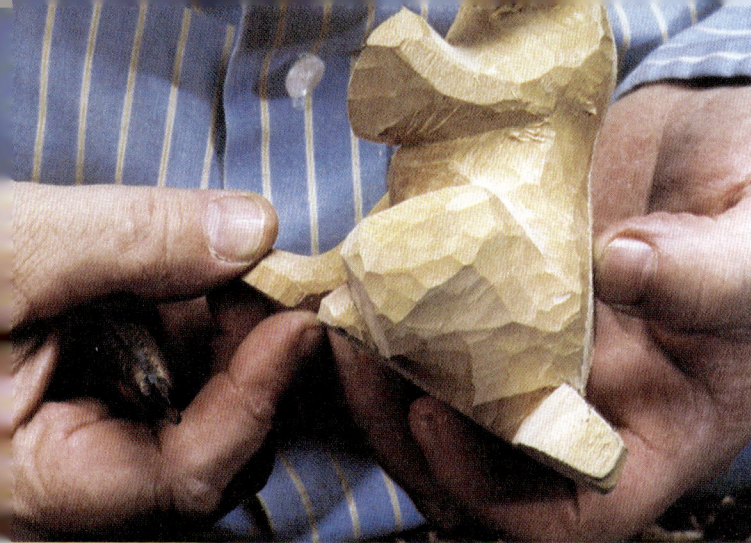

This is a profile shot of the defined rear foot as it comes out from under the haunch.

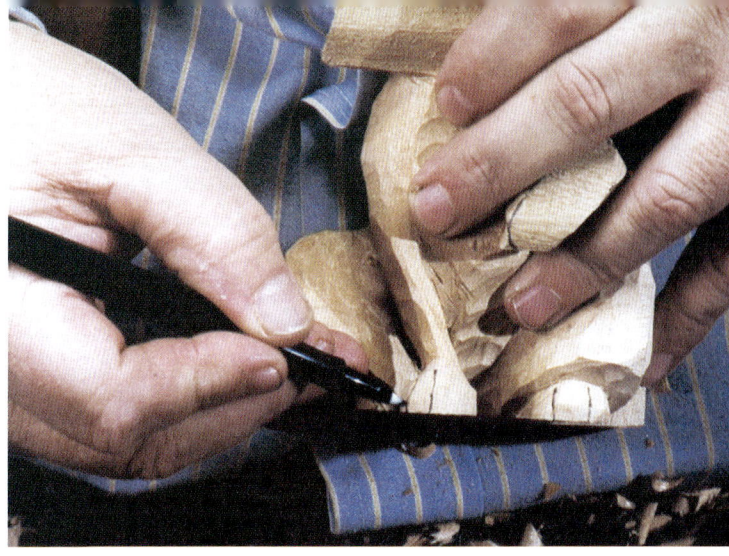

and the front. Three lines give you four toes.

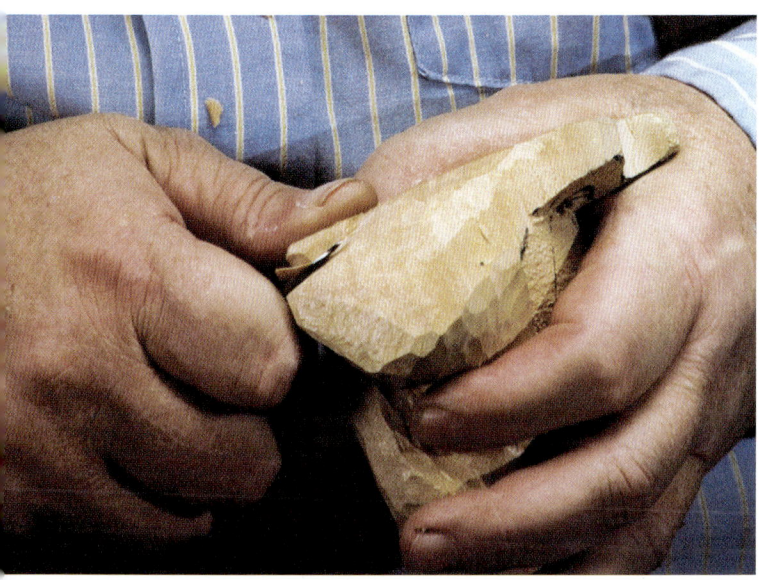

Repeat the process of the other leg.

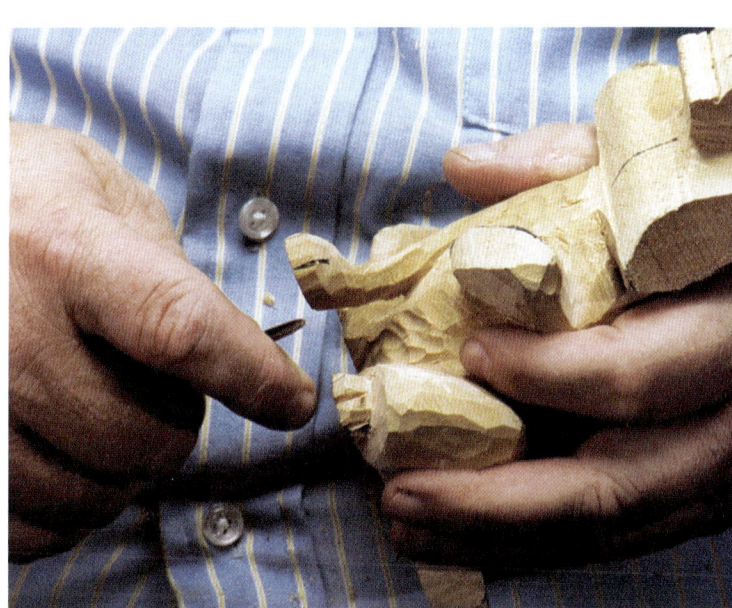

Use a small veiner or a v-gouge to define the toes.

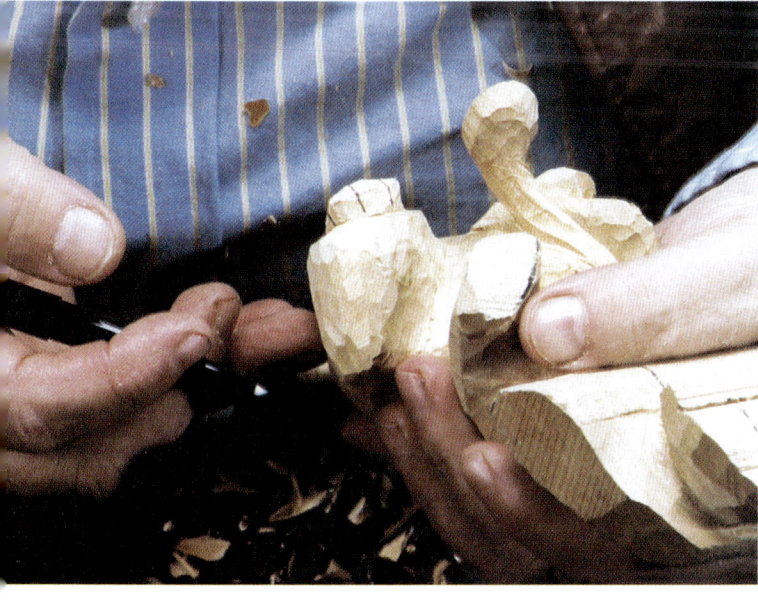

Draw in toes on the back feet...

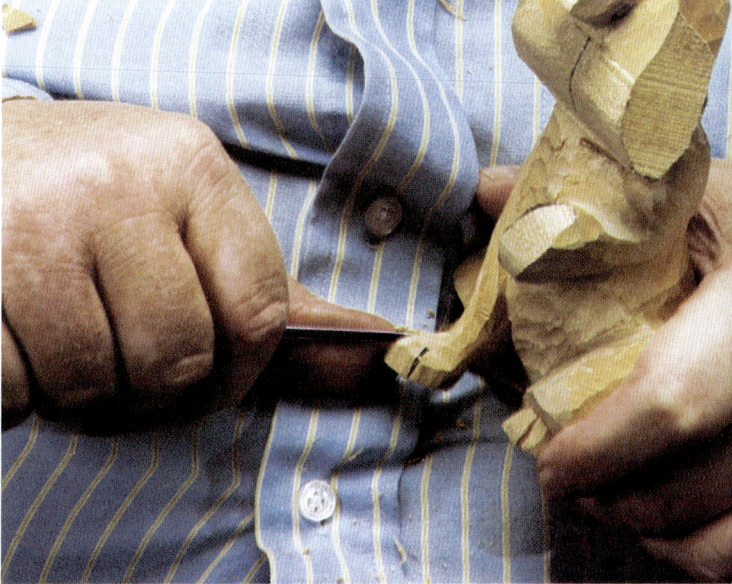

Simply follow the line with the tool.

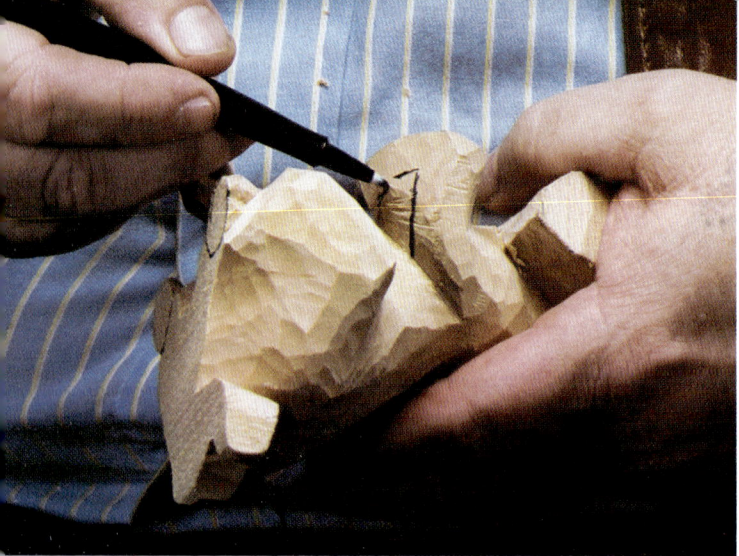

Mark the raised front left leg.

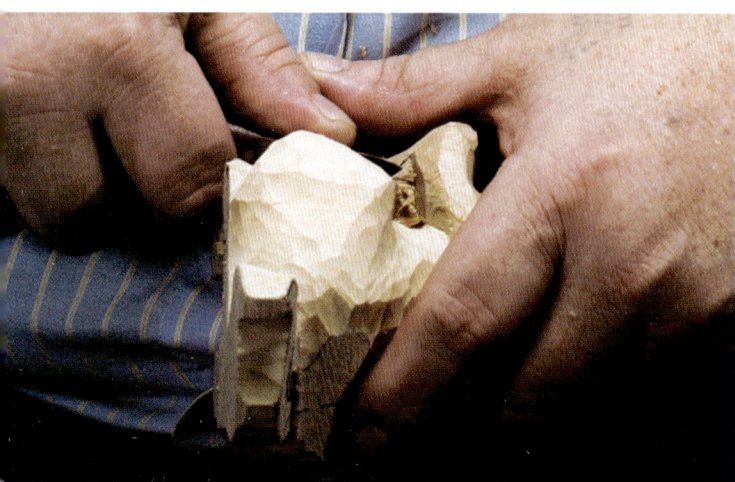

Open the space between the leg and the body, first from below...

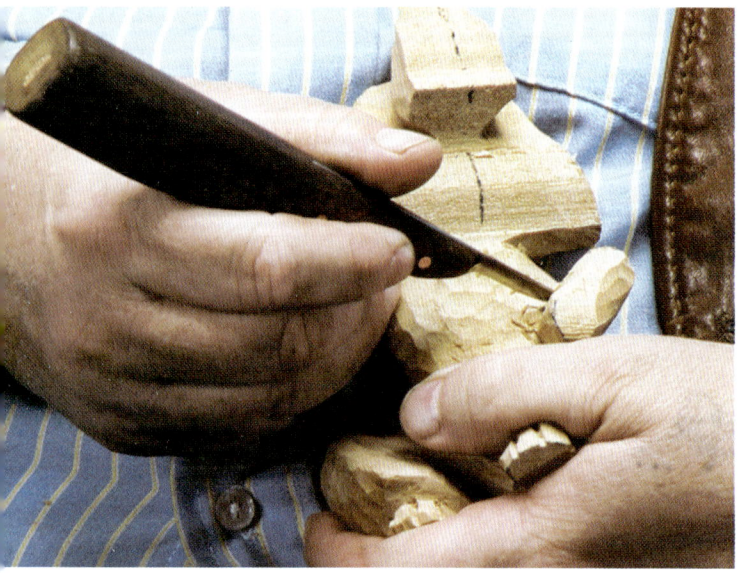

and then from above. The object is to create open space between the body and the leg while leaving the paw attached to the body for strength. This is made harder by the small space in which we have to work.

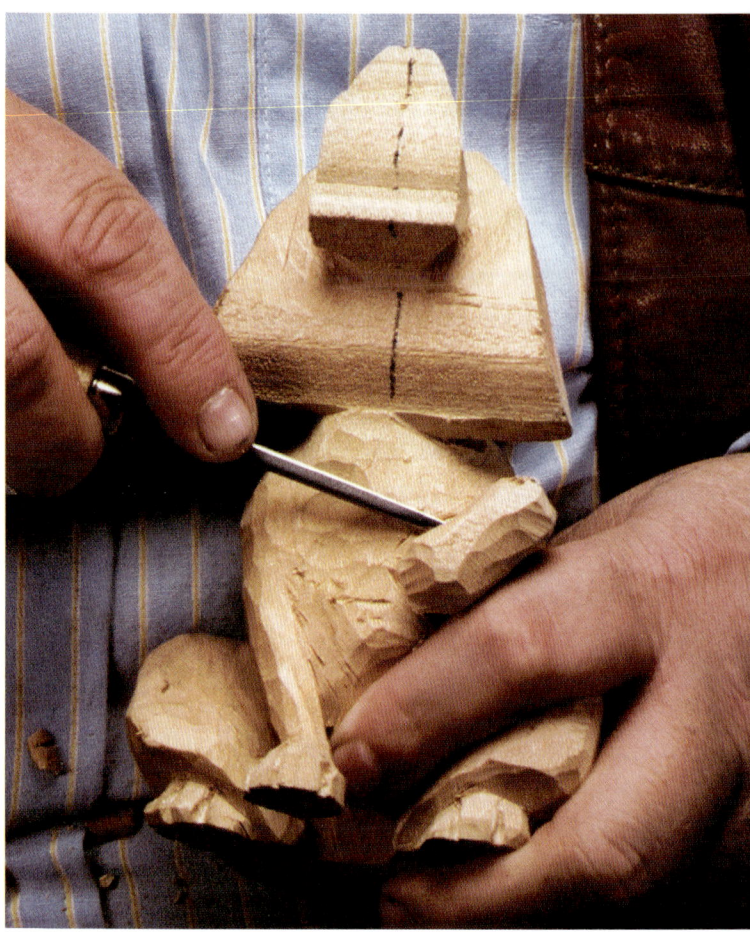

After beginning to form the space with a knife, switch to a gouge and slowly open it wider.

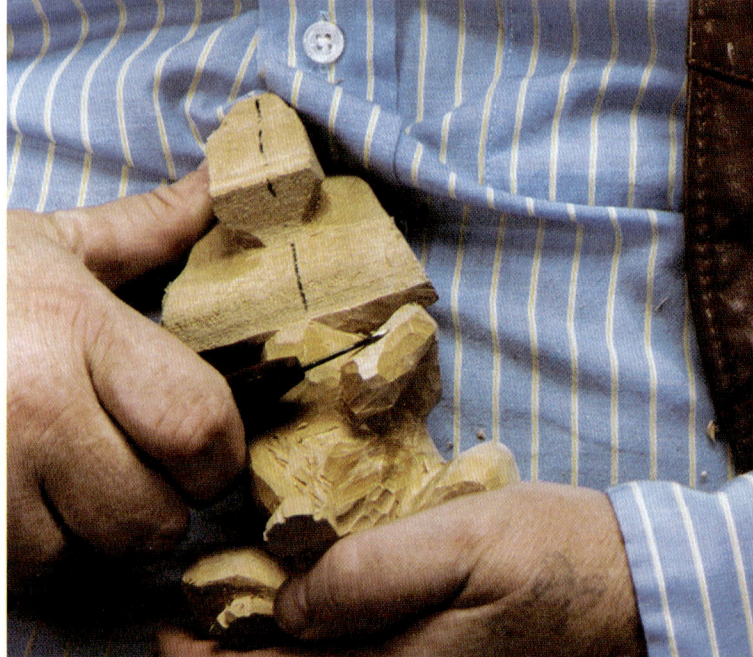

The raised leg is a bit meaty when compared to the other front leg. Use a knife to trim it down. It is always good to keep moving the piece around and comparing various perspectives.

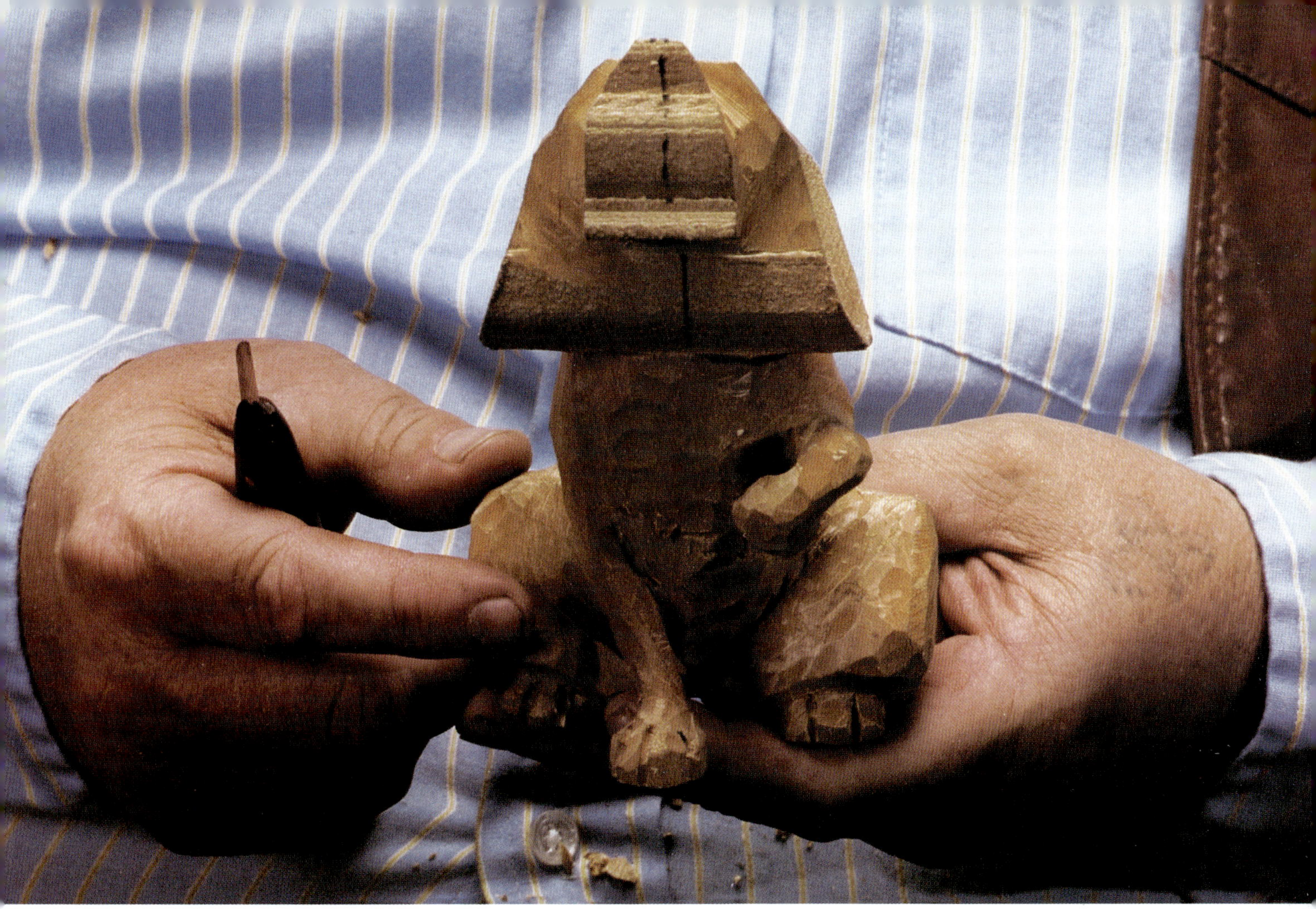

It occurs to me that the way the raised paw is being held looks as though it may be injured. I think I'll add a bandage for a touch of the comical. These opportunities sometimes arise and you should take advantage of them.

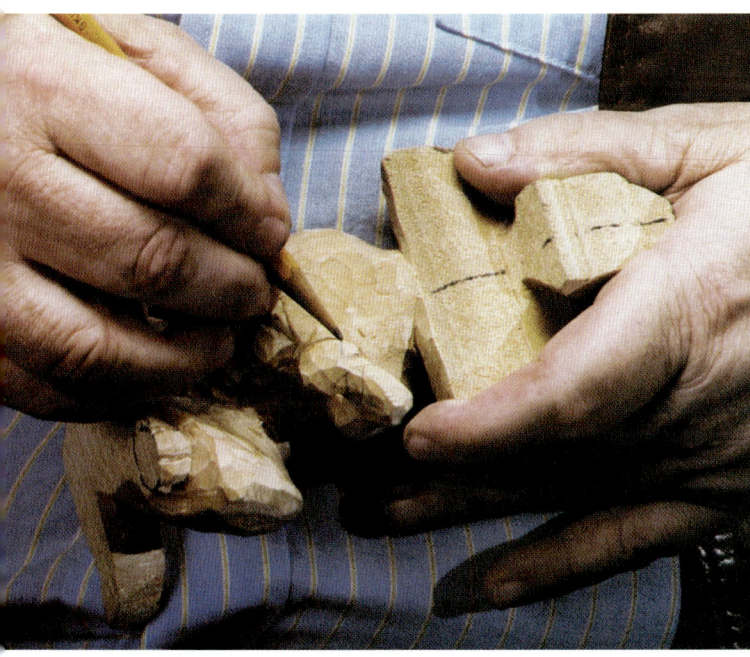

I'll mark the bandage in pencil so the marks won't soak into the wood.

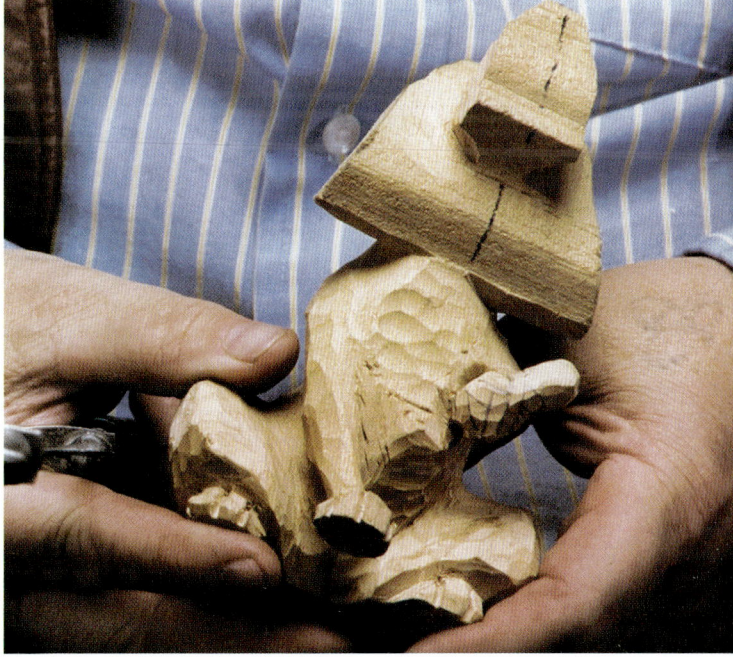

The paw marked. We'll return to it later.

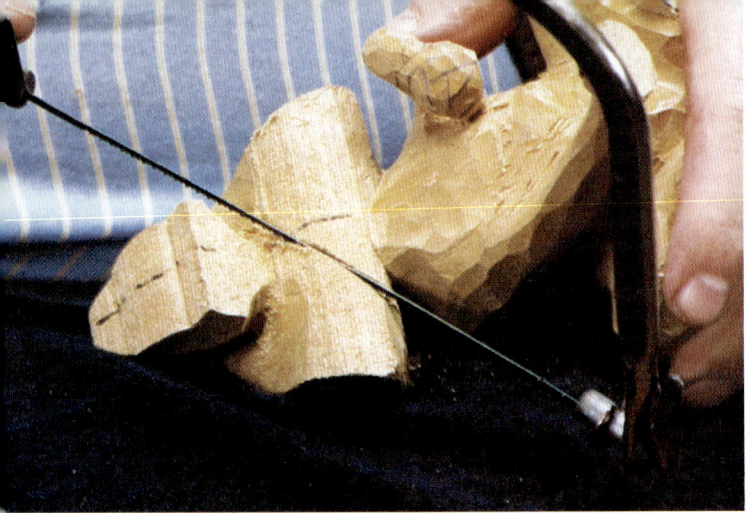

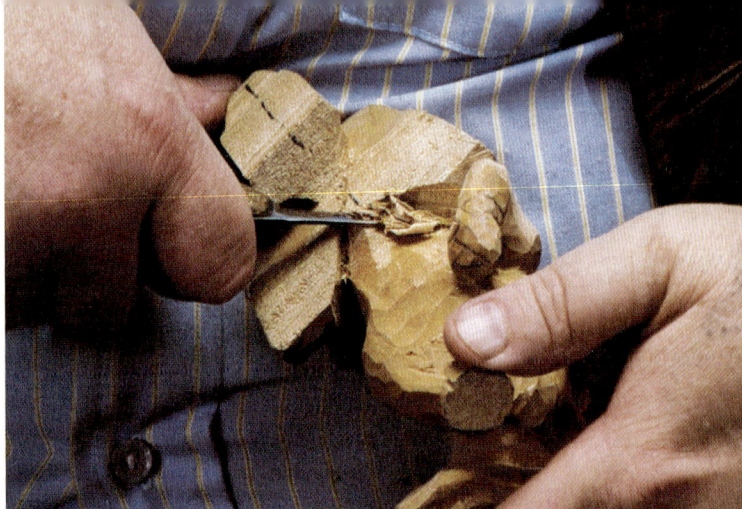

Returning to the head, I use a coping saw to open it up under the ears. This will make it easier to carve, but it is a place where you can overcut quickly, so be careful!

Gradually the material between the ears is removed.

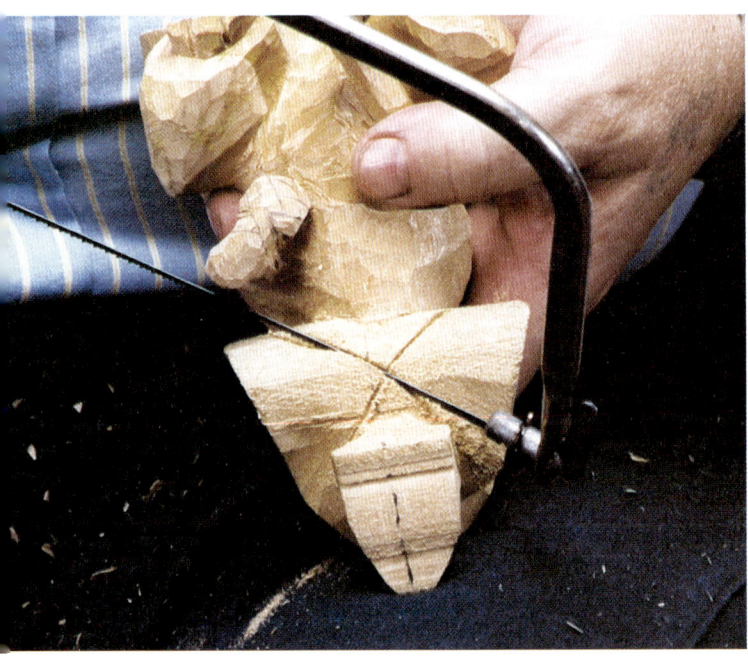

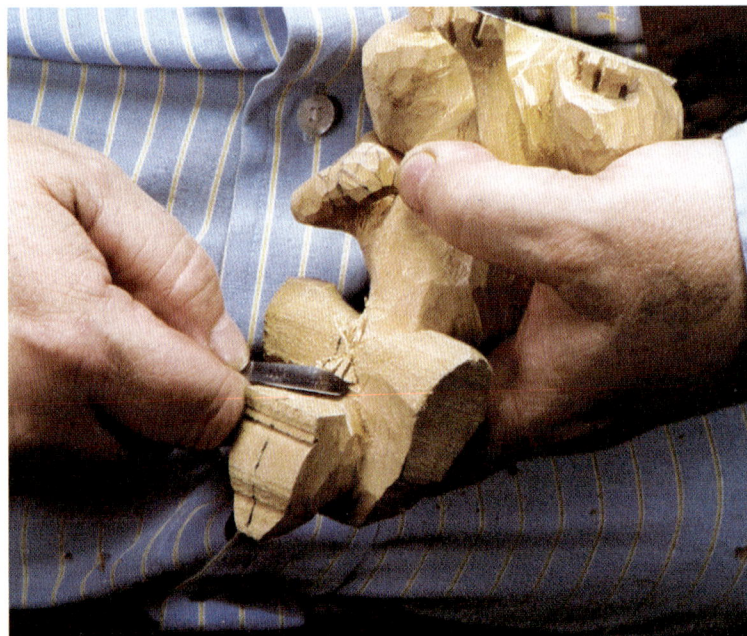

Cross the first line with a second. I always put my blade in the coping saw backwards so the cut is on the pulling stroke. This gives me more control.

A gouge works well in this spot to chip away excess wood.

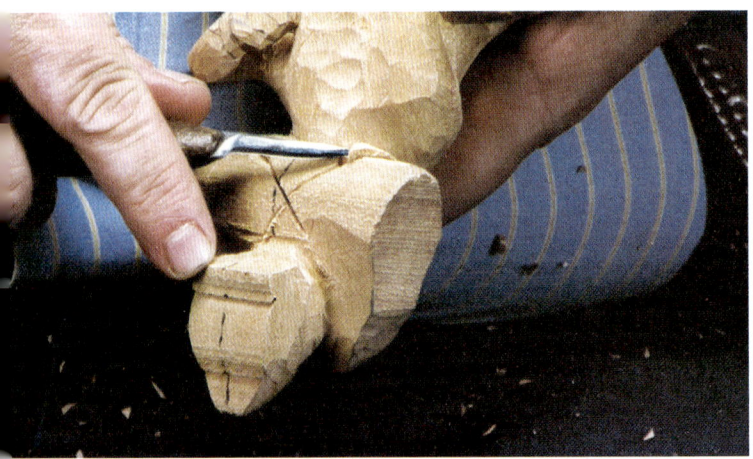

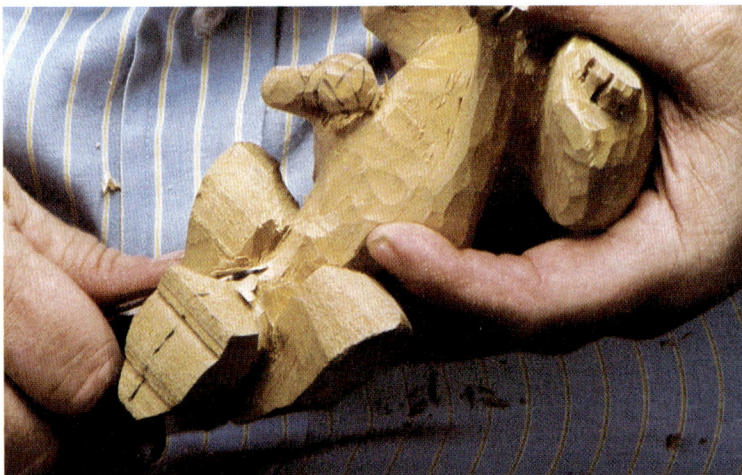

The coping saw cut acts as a stop, allowing you to use your knife to remove excess wood more easily.

Clean the area between the ear and the neck with the knife, defining the neck as you go.

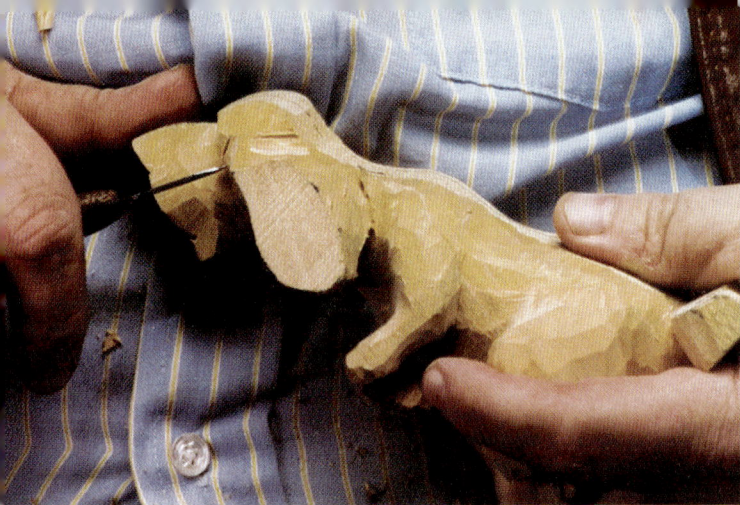 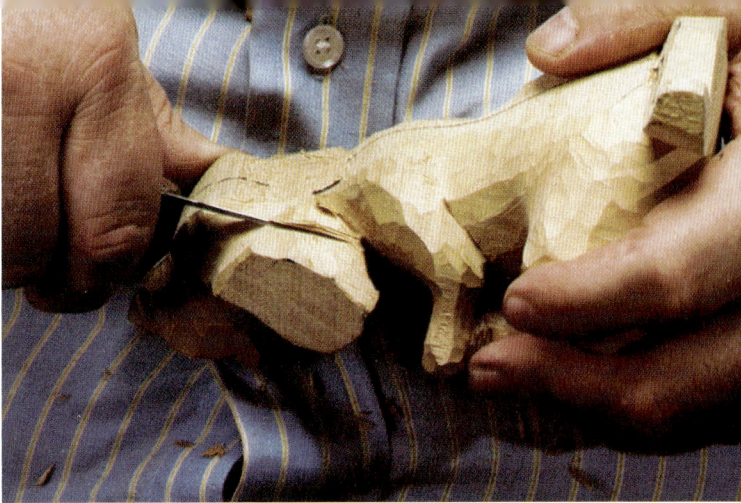

The most common mistake in carving animals is making the ears come too high on the head. The top of the ear should be level with the back of the jaw.

Cut a stop behind the ear.

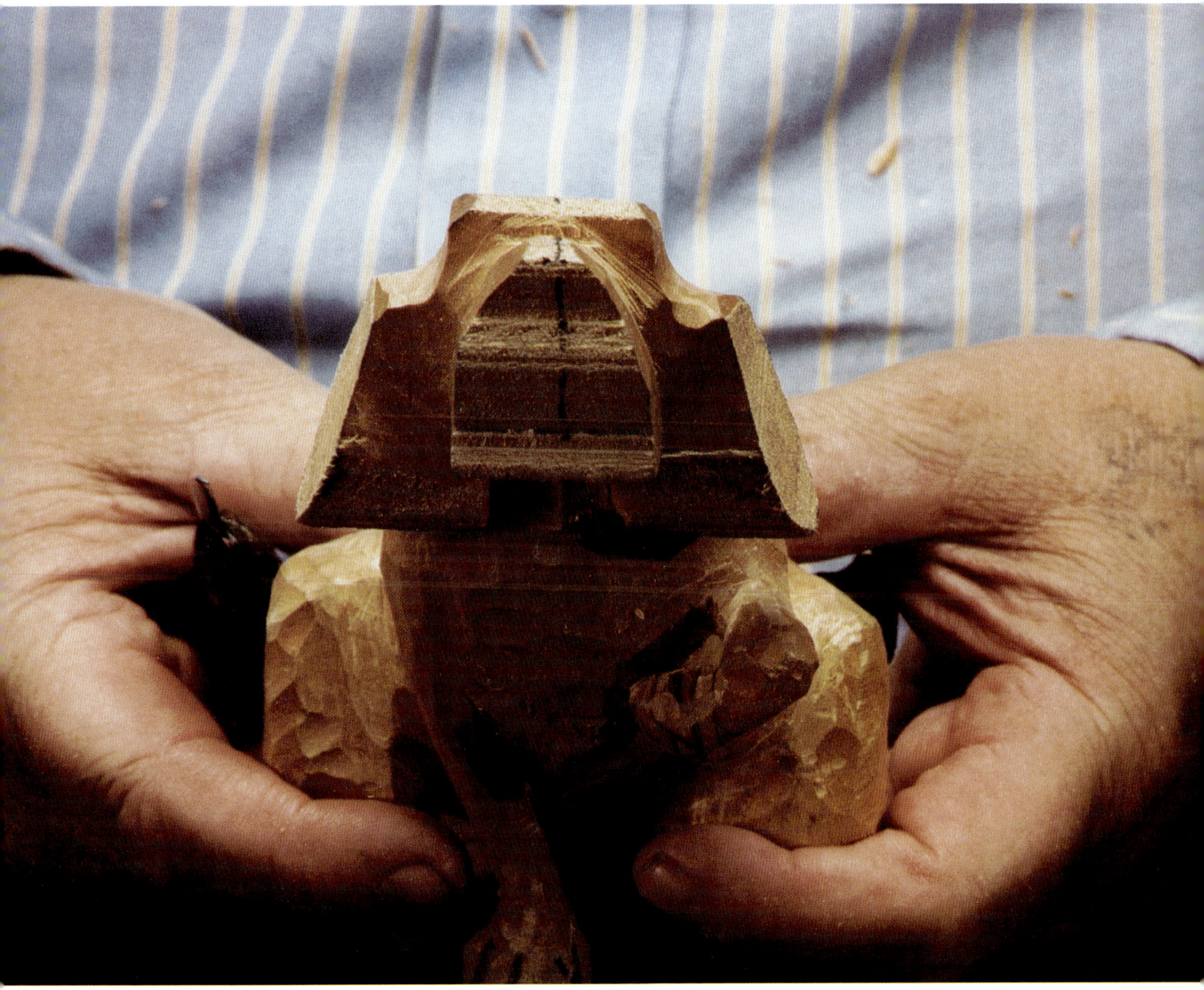

Use the knife to trim the top of the ears to this position.

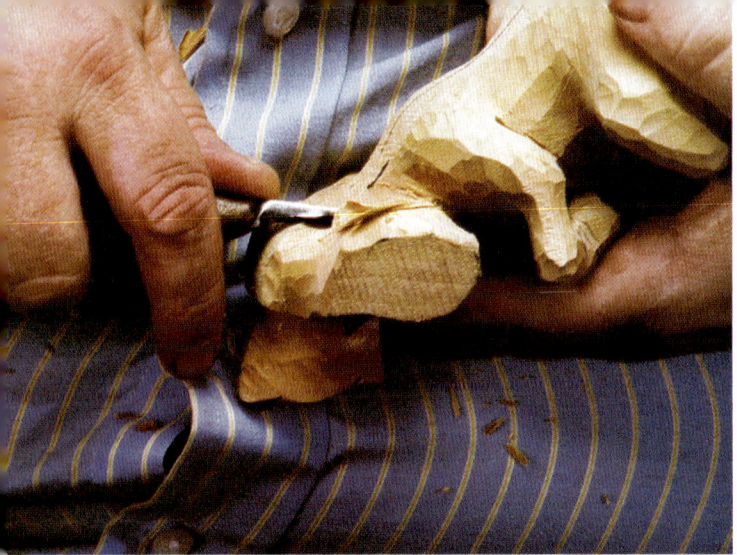

Cut back to the stop from the neck and the back of the head.

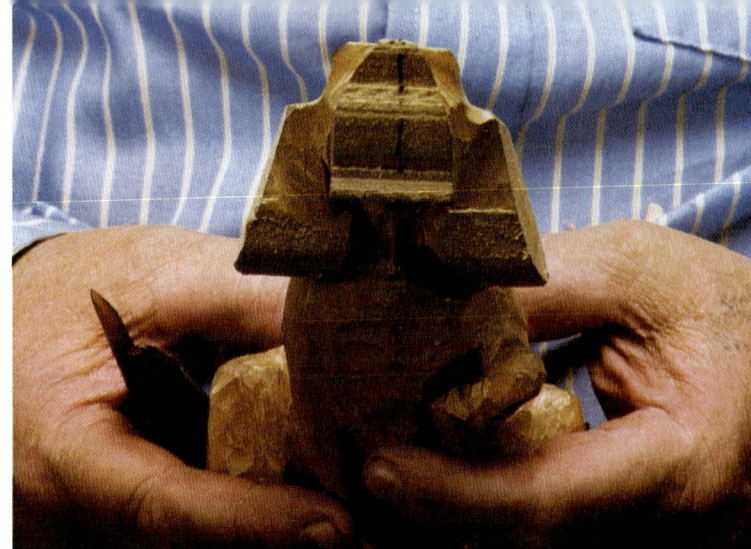

Don't make the ears too thin at this point.

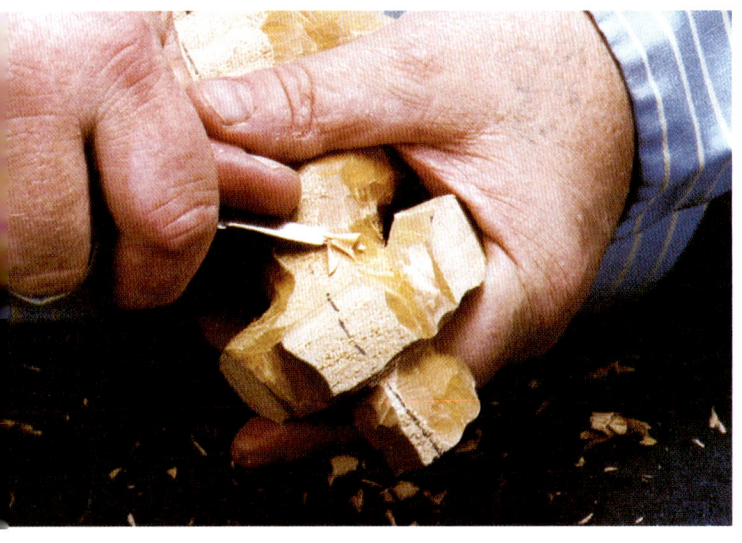

Refine the neck.

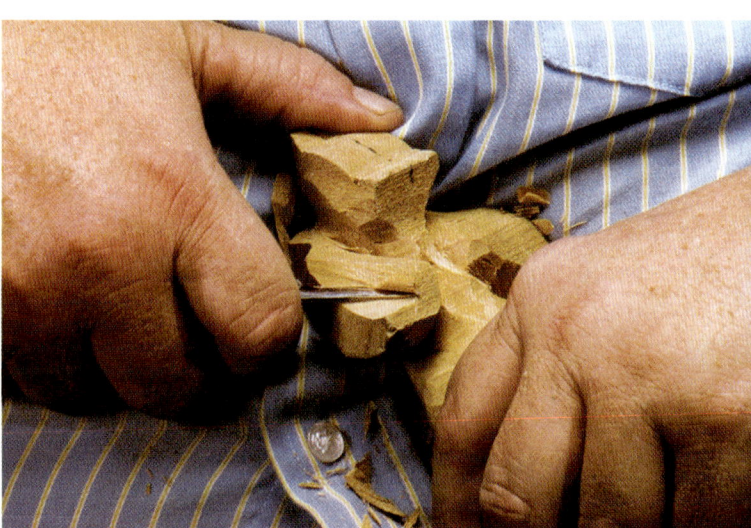

The thickness gives you a lot to play with. To place a fold in the ear, begin by trimming the outside front surface...

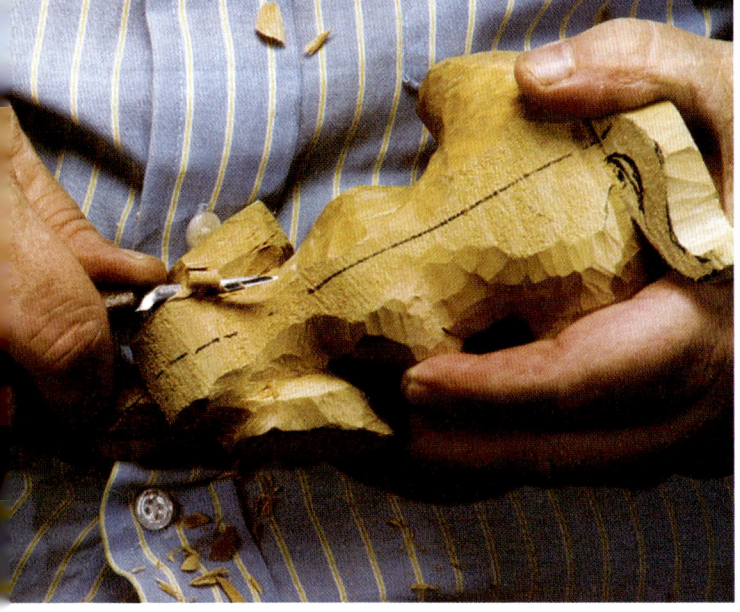

Carve the other ear in the same way.

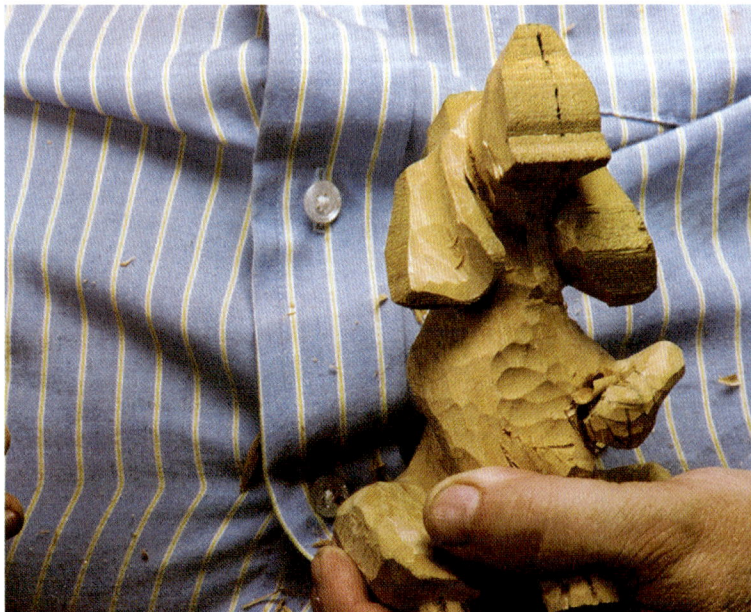

to look something like this.

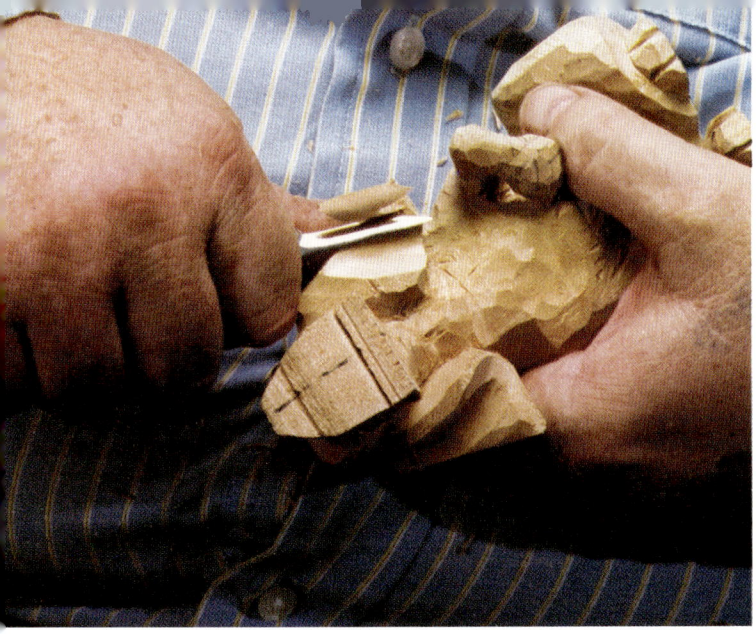

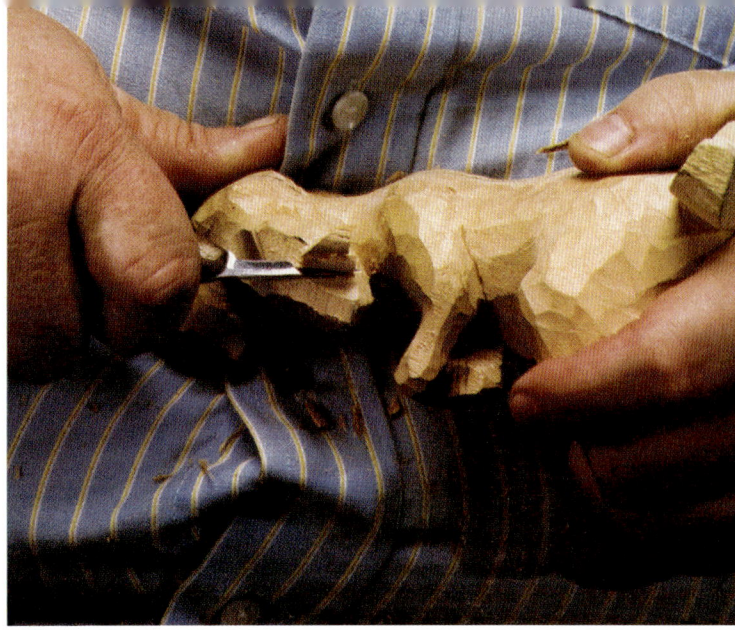

Do the same thing with the other ear.

Carve another fold down the backside of the ear.

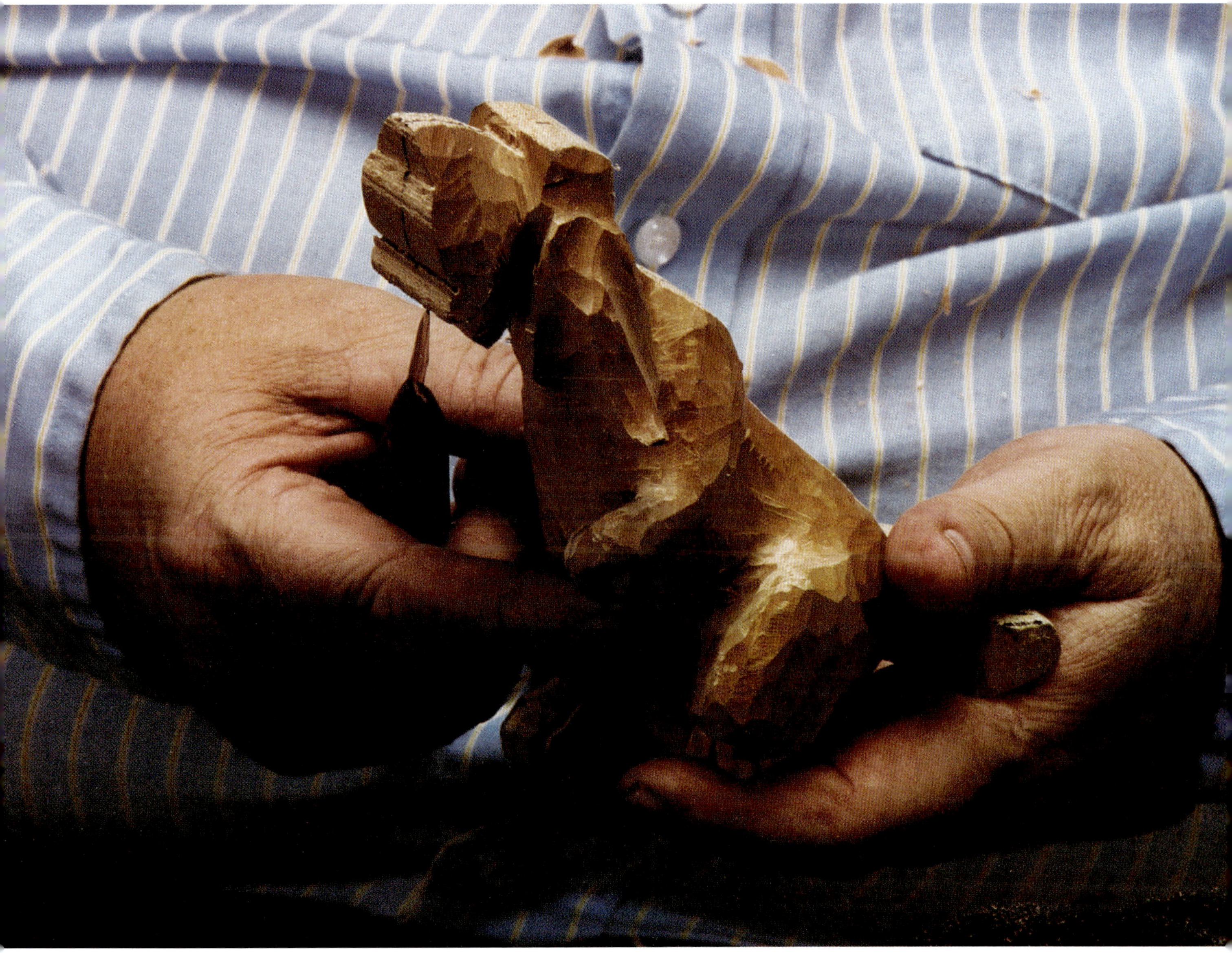

The object is a groove in the front and a grove in the back.

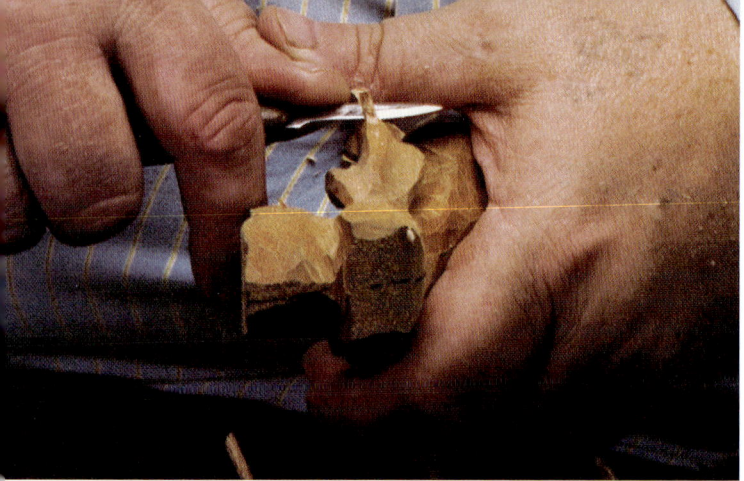

Next trim the ear back into the head.

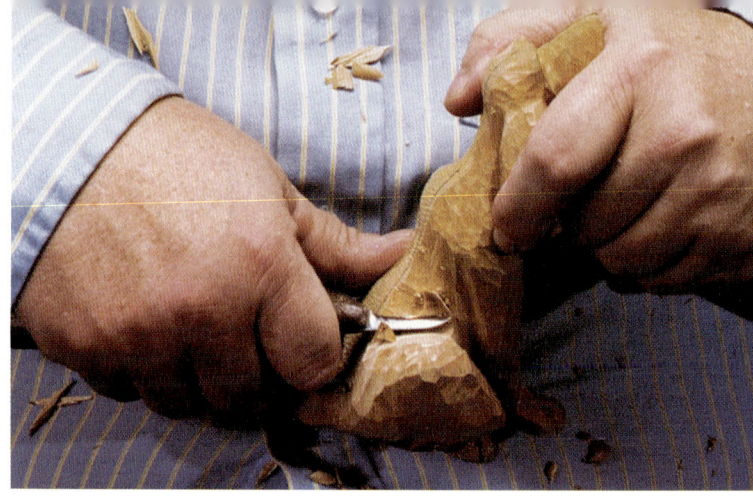

and he needs a trim.

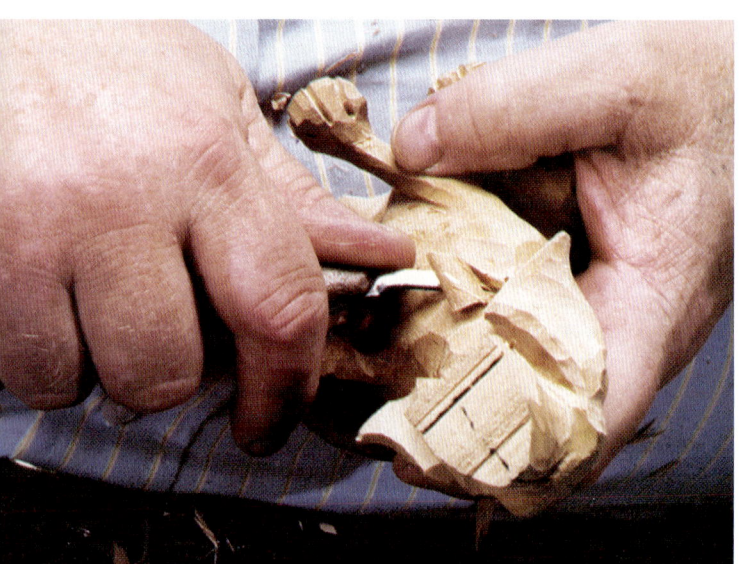

Go all around the carving, looking for things that need straightening up. I like to do this often to keep the work in perspective.

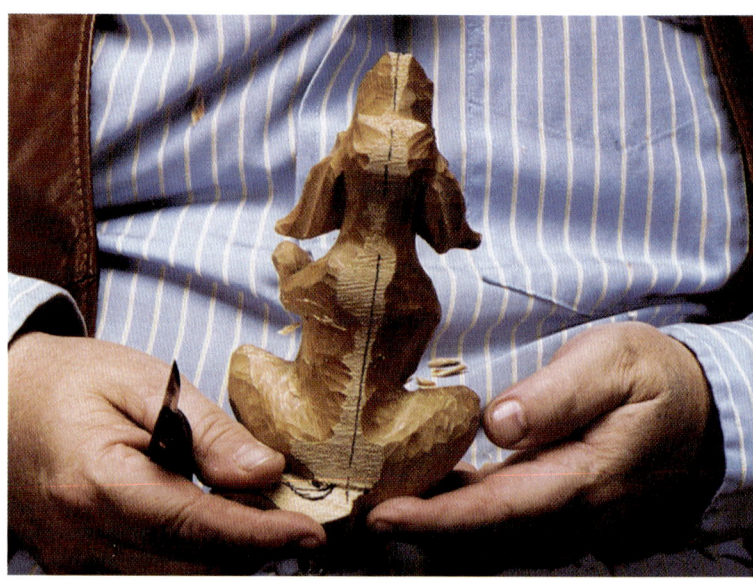

The waist line is better, but now the shoulders protrude and need some reduction.

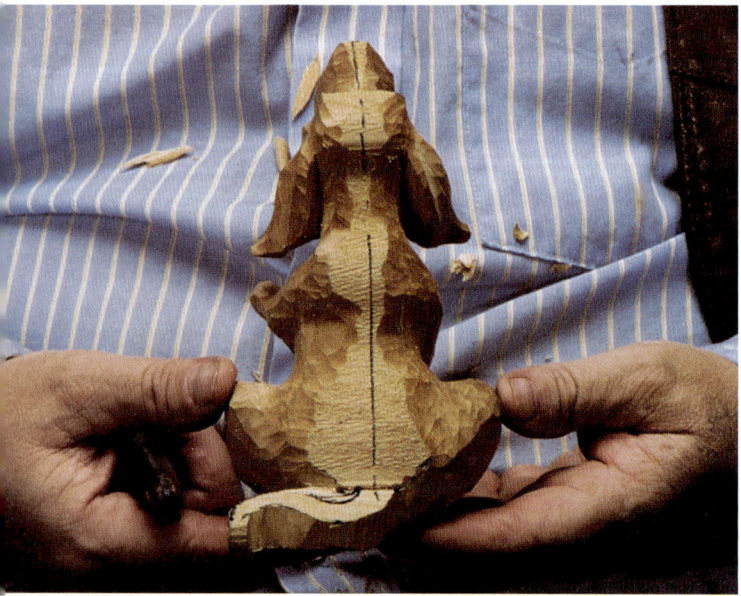

He's a bit too fat. If he were a puppy this would be alright. But this is a mature dog...

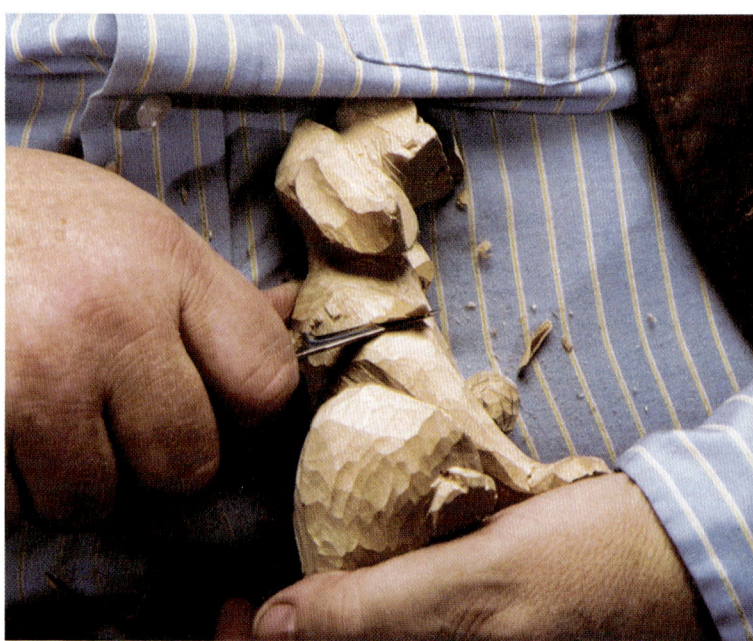

Thin the shoulders with a knife.

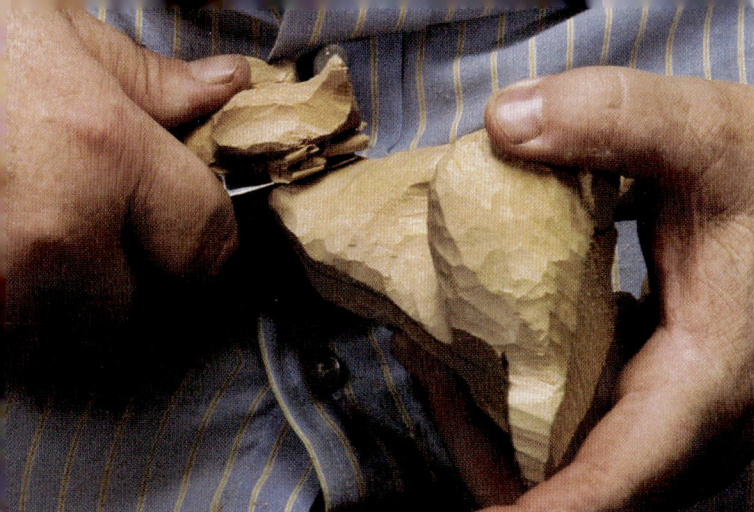

The neck, too, needs thinning.

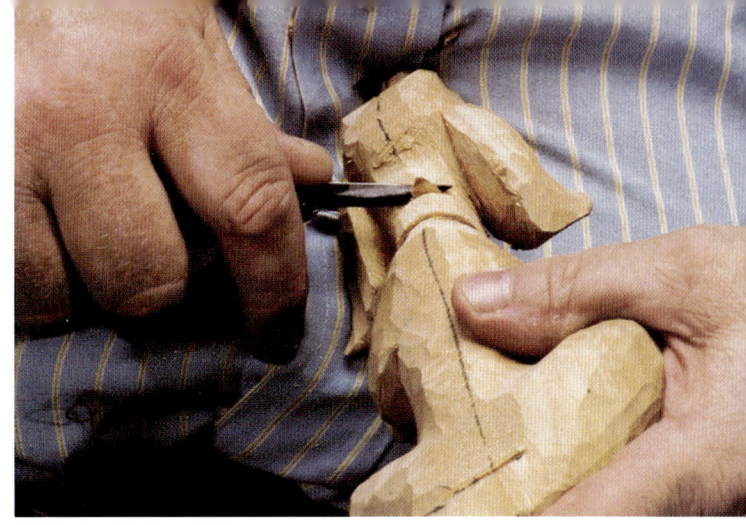

Do the same around the top, cutting a stop and carving from the neck back to it.

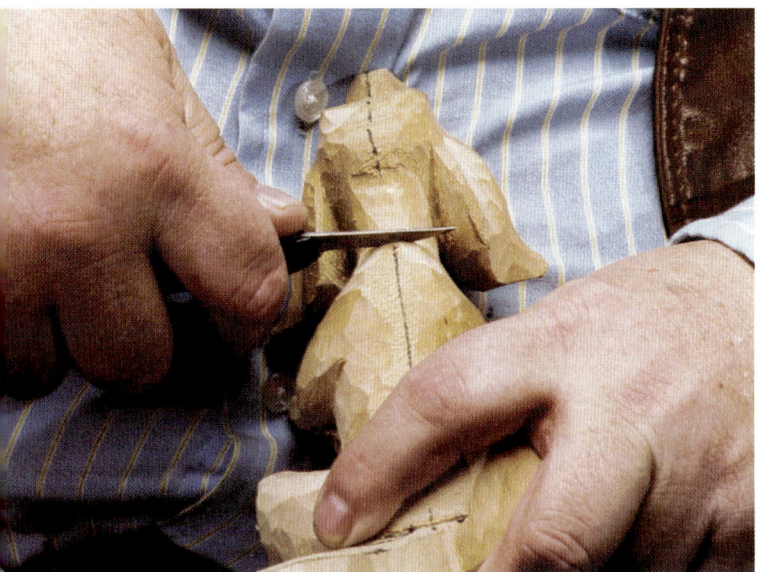

Cut a stop all around the neck. This will be the bottom edge of the collar.

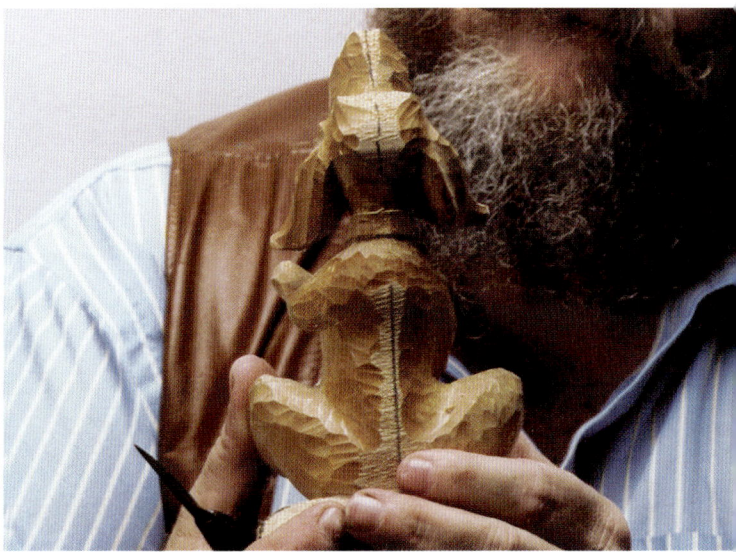

The diet has done its work.

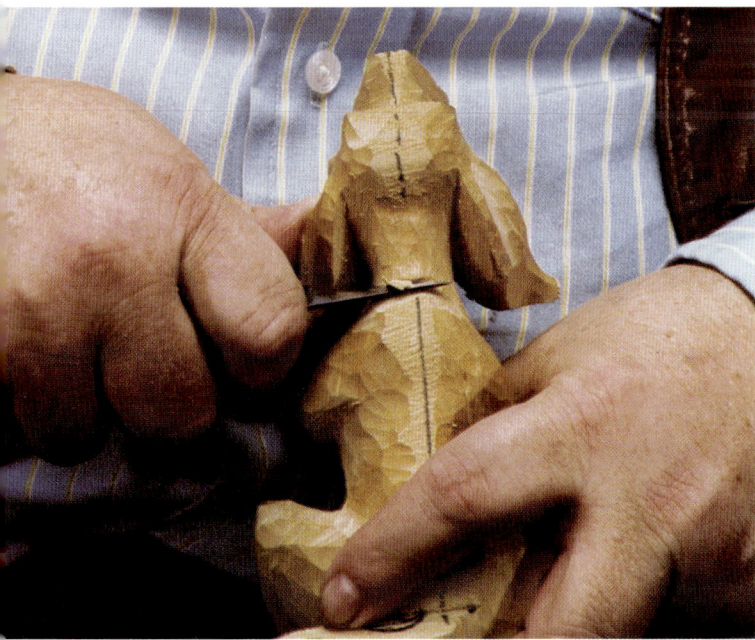

Trim back to it from the shoulder.

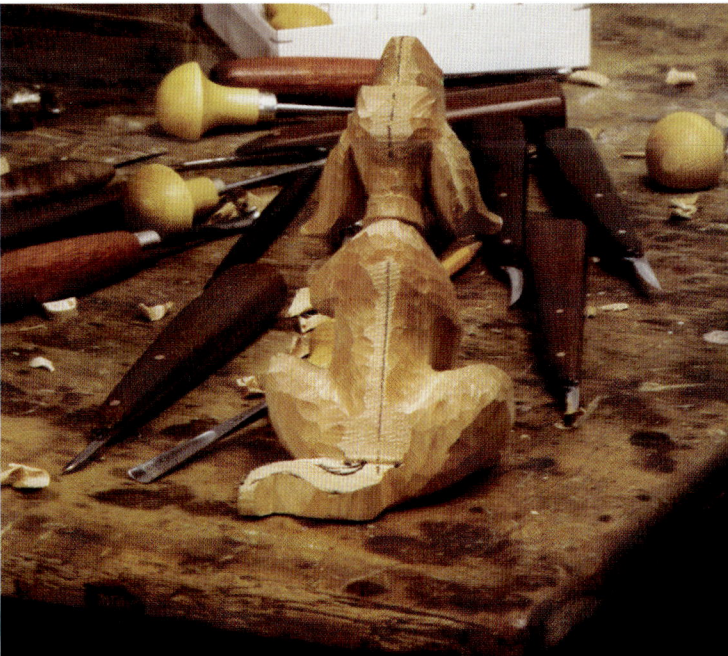

The tail needs some work.

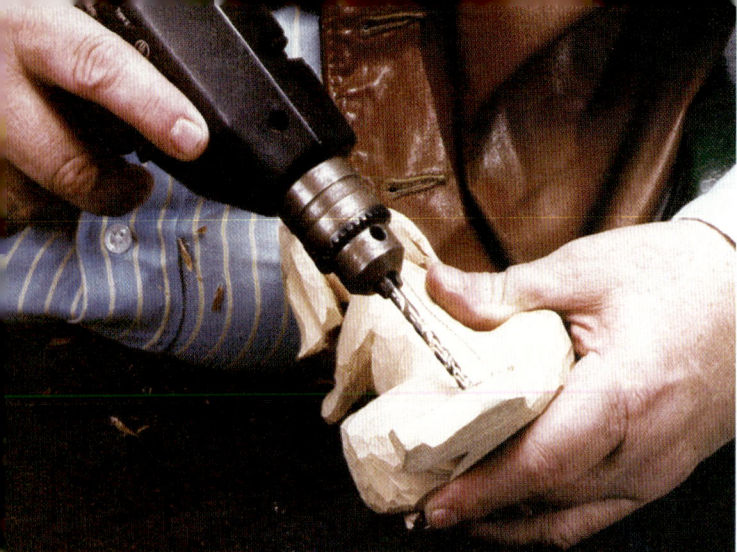

Begin by drilling a hole.

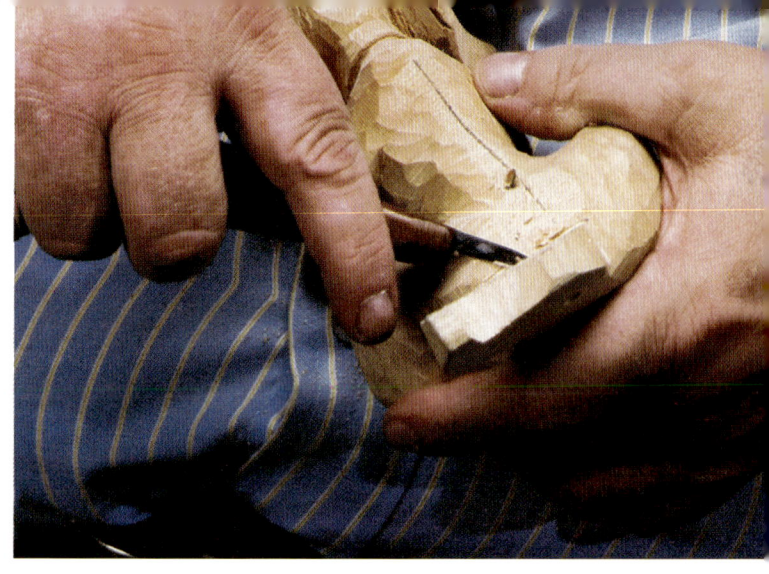

Use a knife to open the hole. The grain is such at this point that you must be careful or the piece may chip.

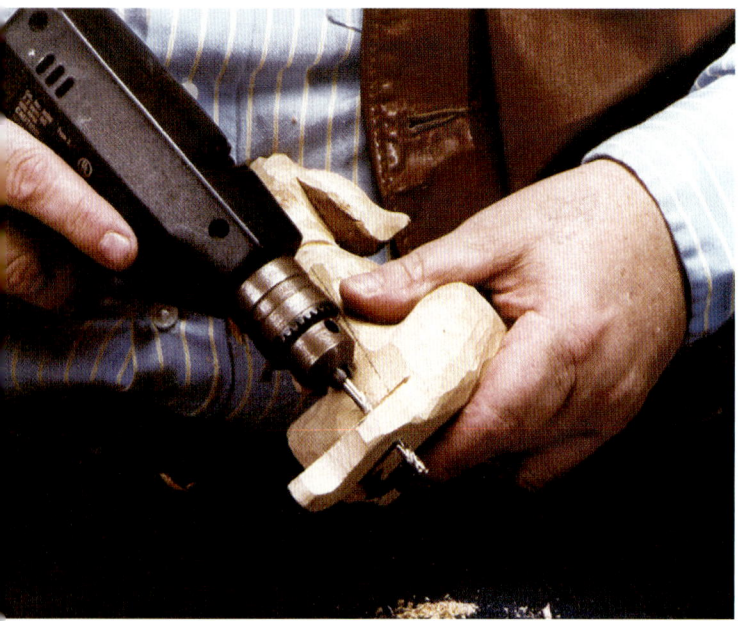

This will give a starting place for carving the tail.

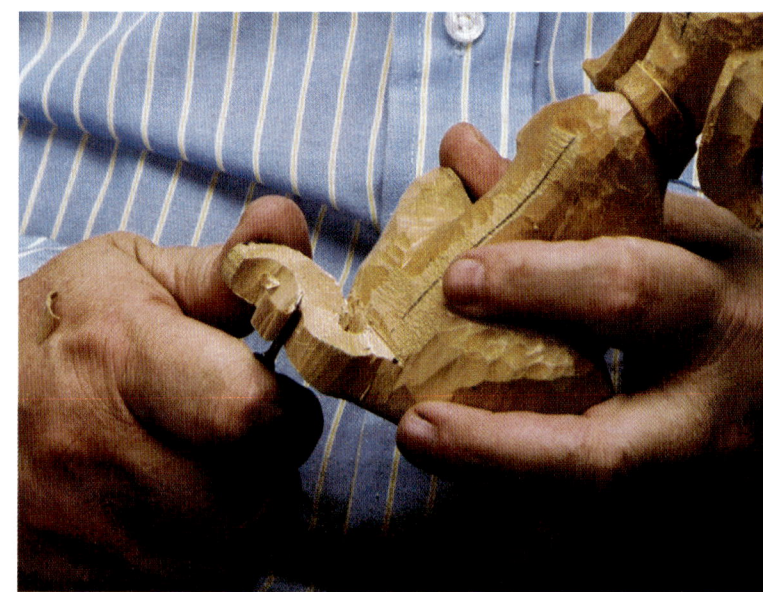

Thin the tail down and begin to shape it.

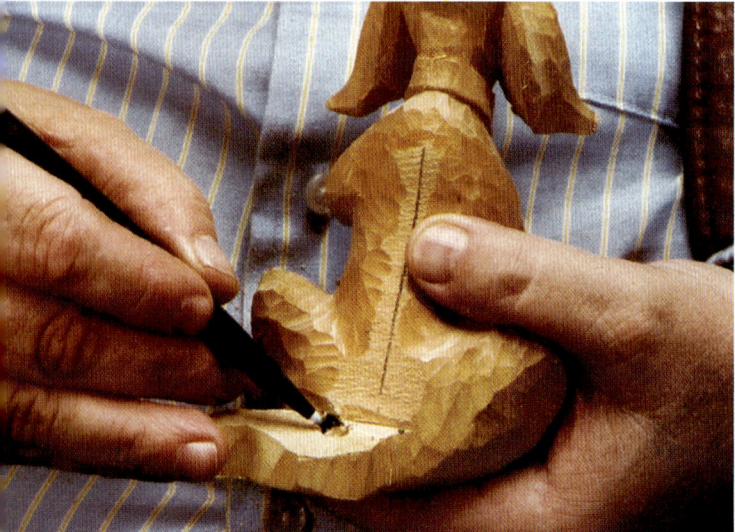

Keeping with the shape of the tail, extend the hole as shown.

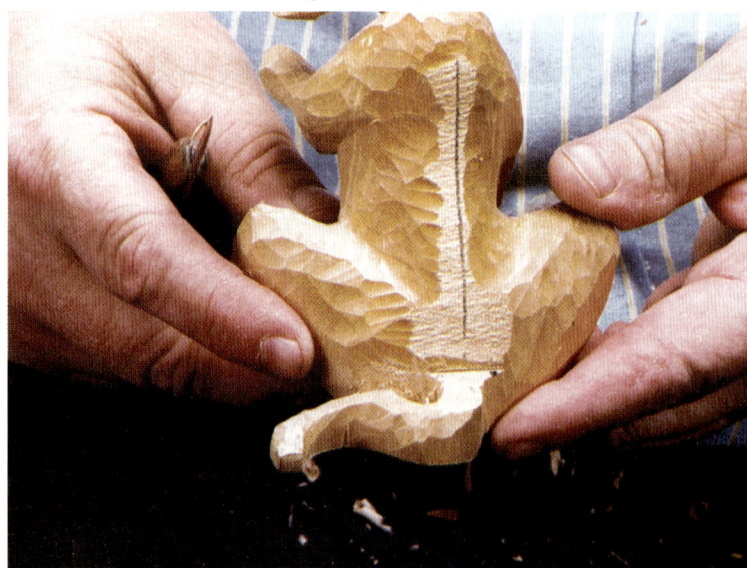

The tail to this point.

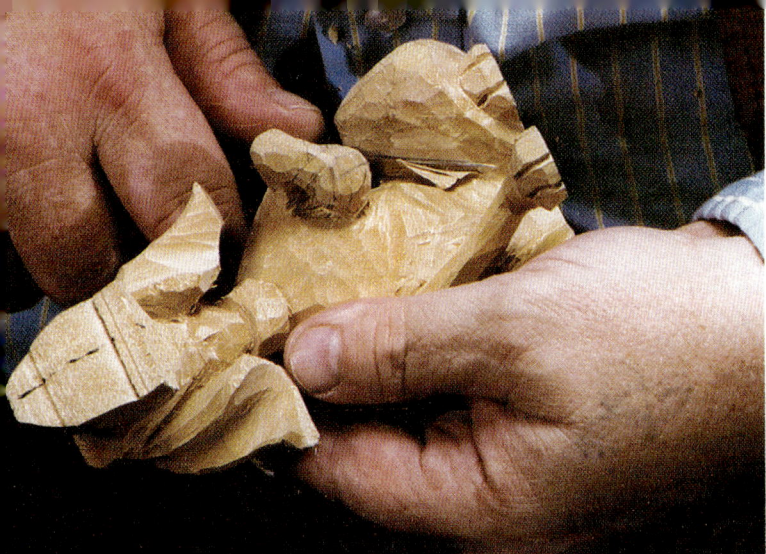

Return to front to trim the belly.

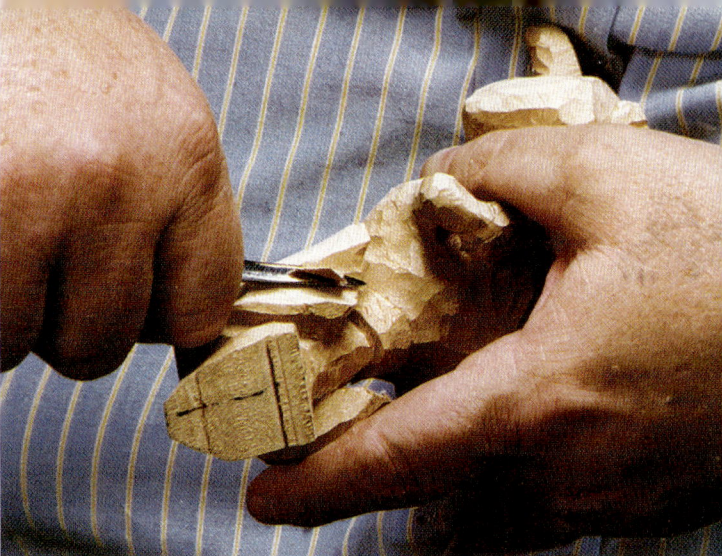

As before, begin by trimming the front edge.

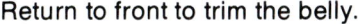

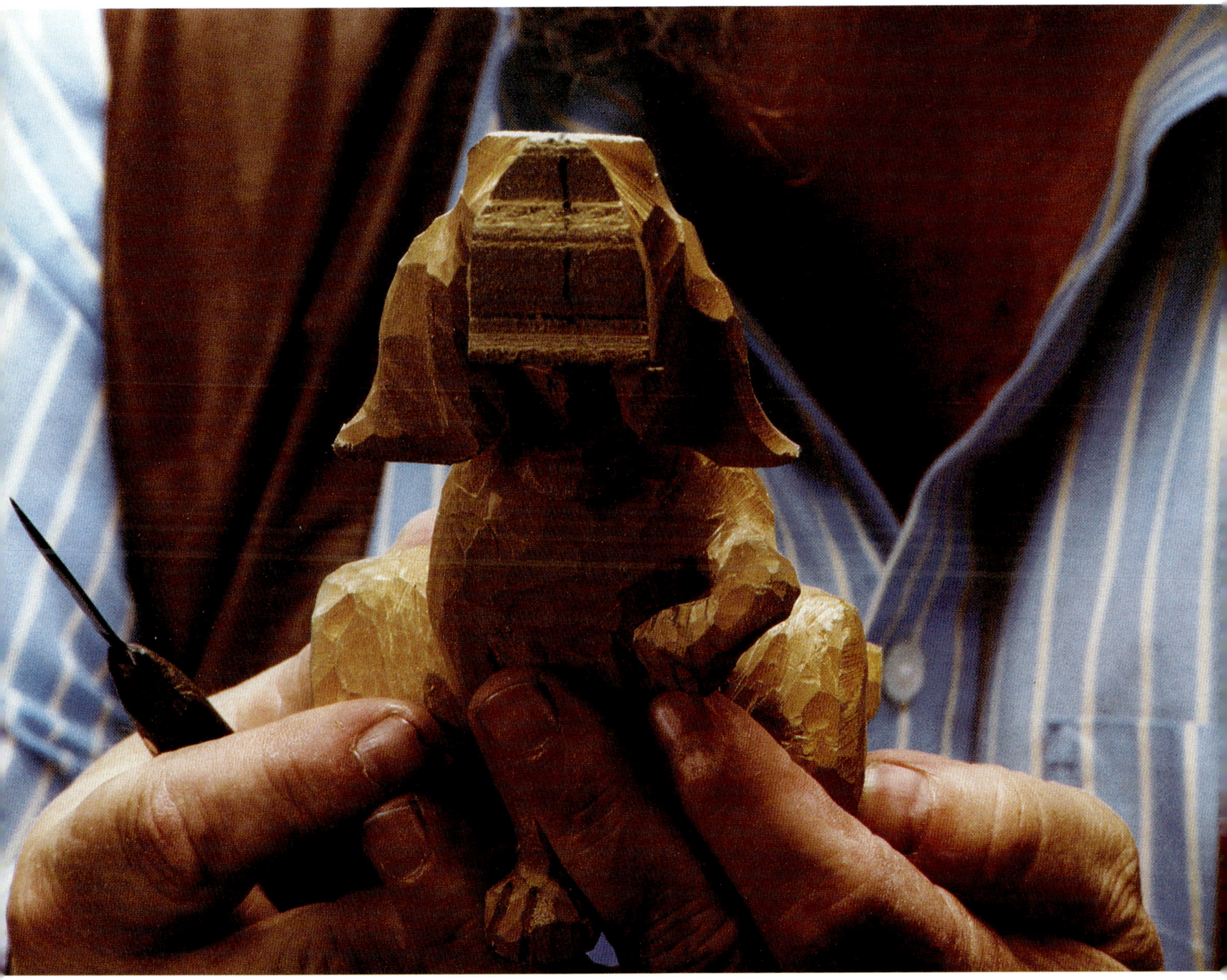

With the body thinned down, the ears appear too heavy.

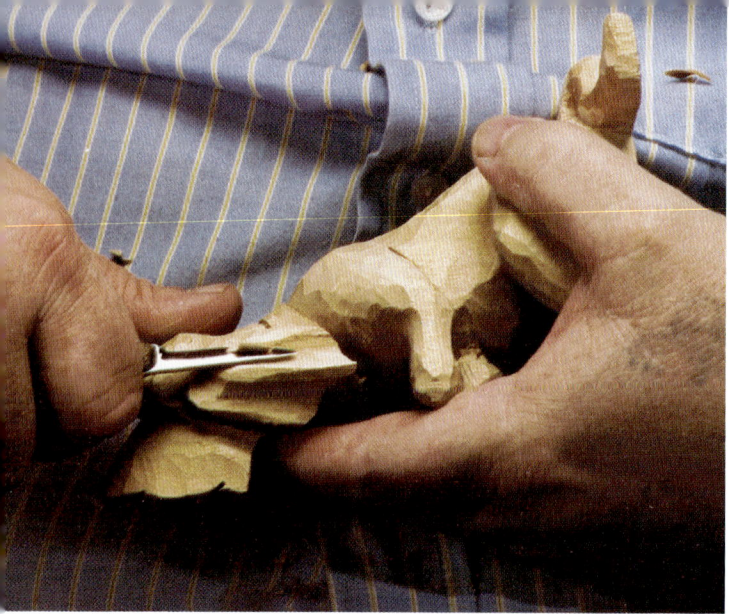

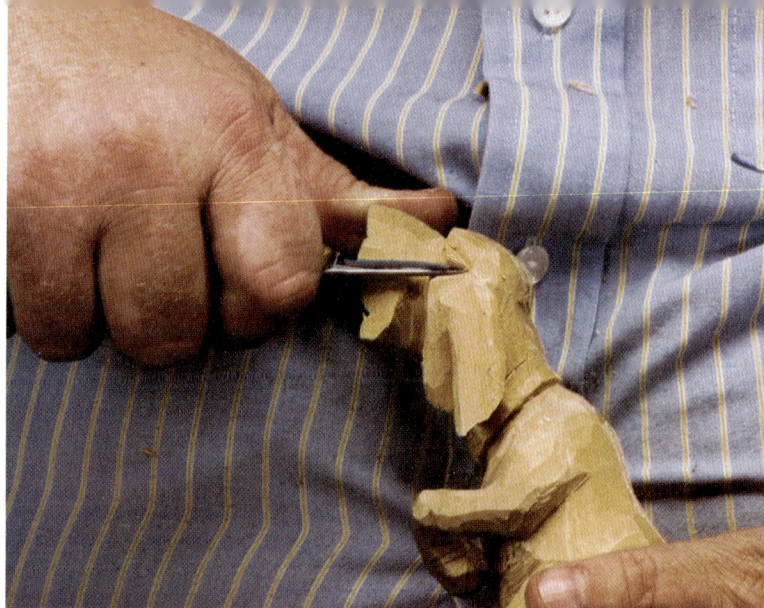

Then trim the back edge...

and from the ear to the head.

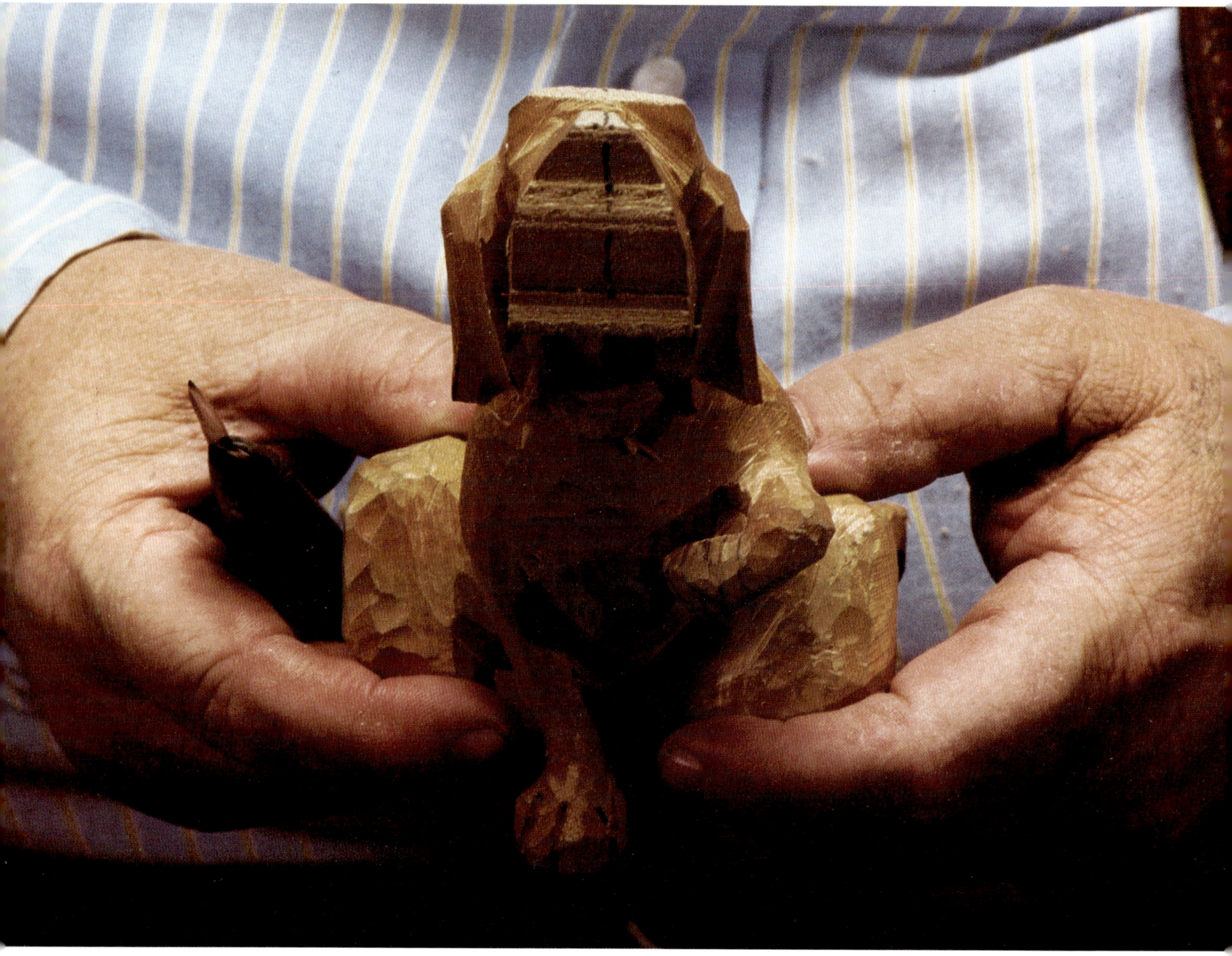

Do the same with the other ear until you are satisfied with the appearance of the ears.

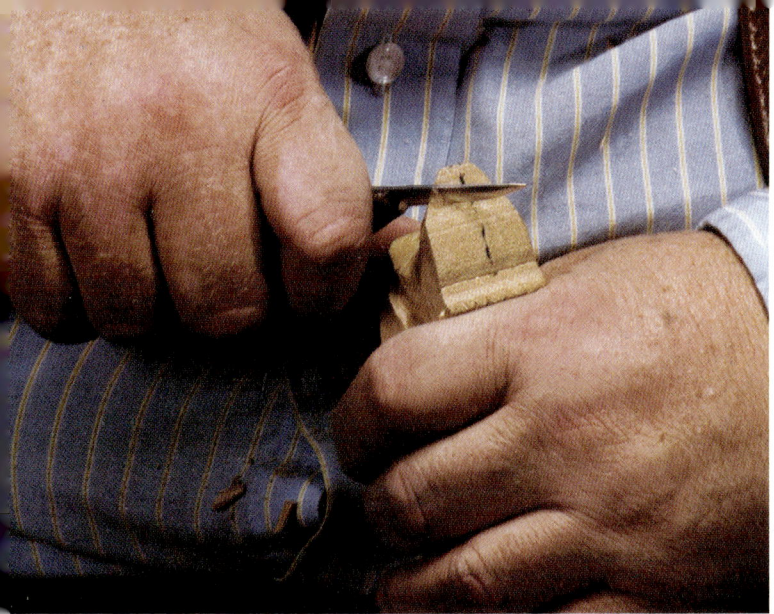

Begin the face by cutting a stop for the nose...

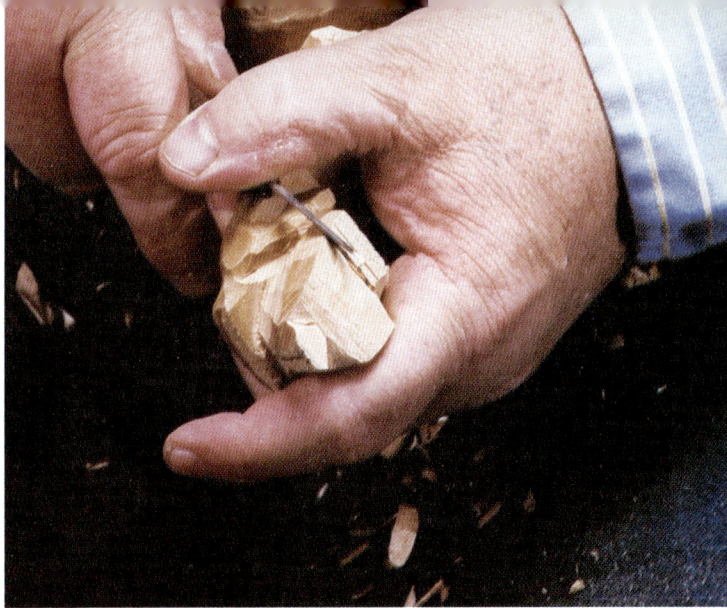

Cut a stop into the jowl line.

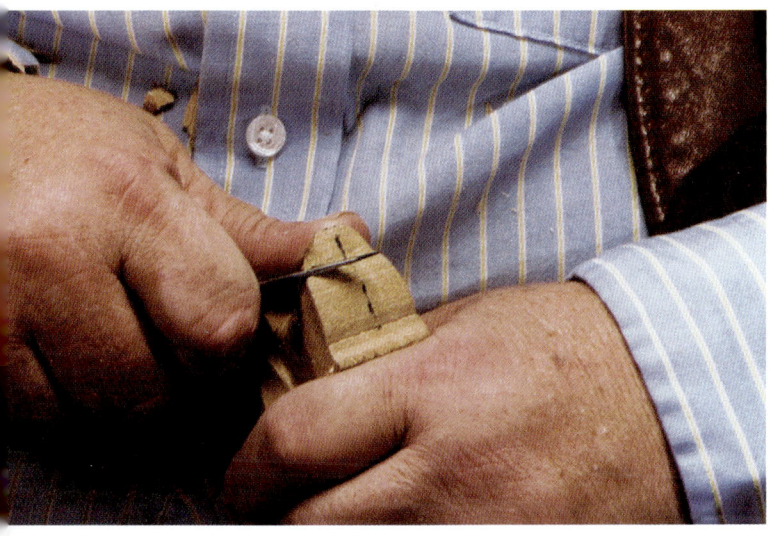

and notching it out.

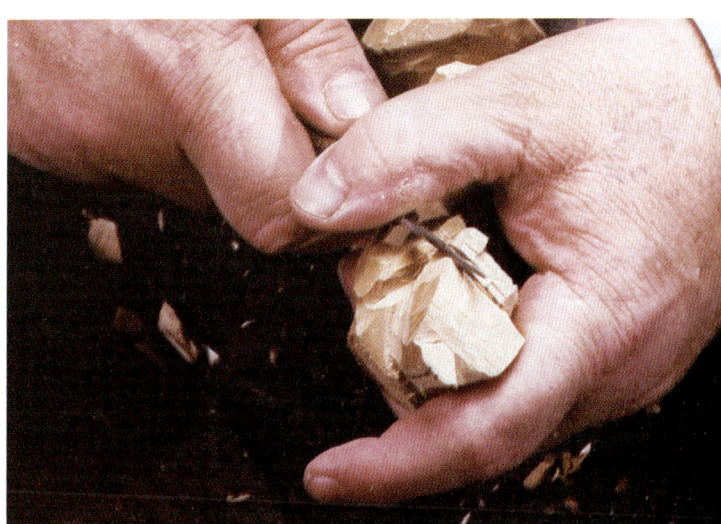

Cut back to the stop to narrow the jaw. This piece should just pop off.

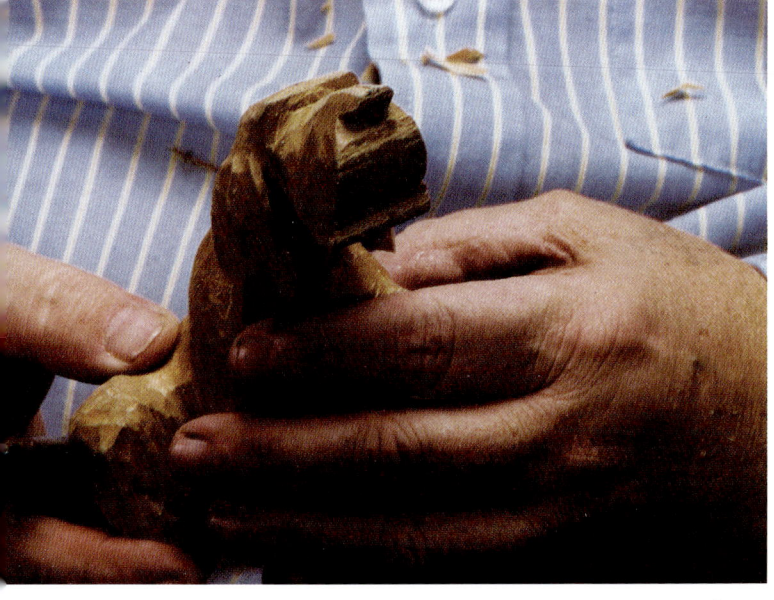

Do the same to the other side to get to this point.

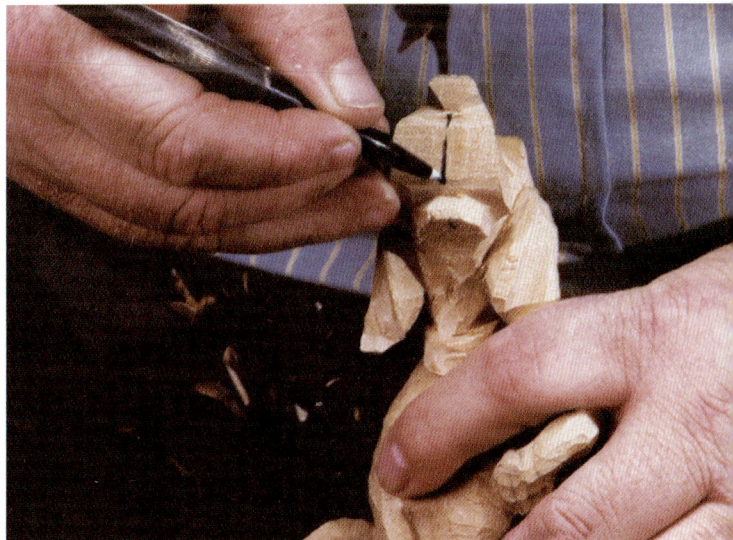

Trim around the lower jaw and make a mark down from the nose.

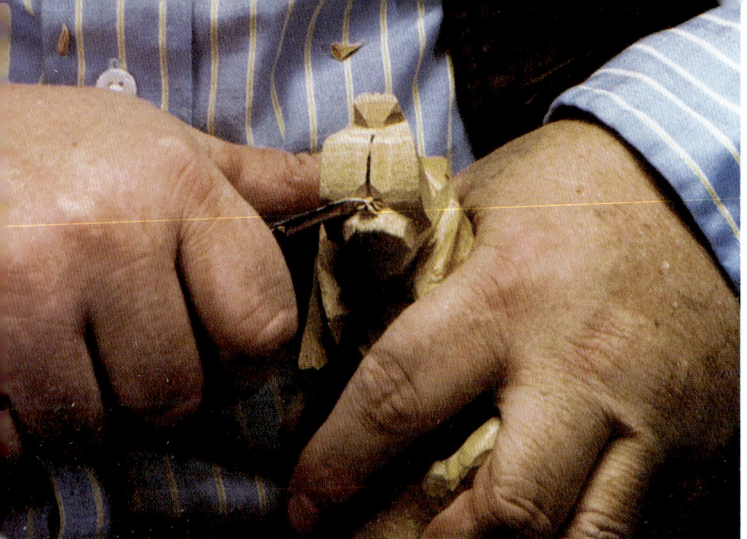

Cut a V into the upper lip at the center line...

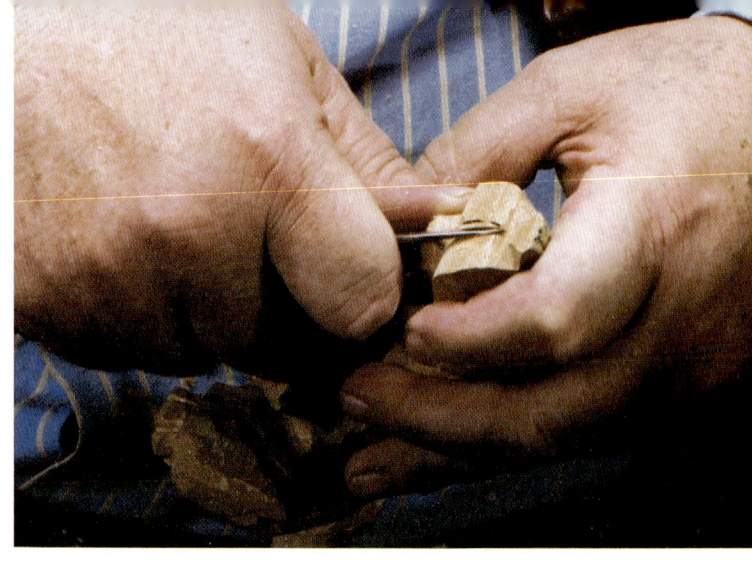

then the other.

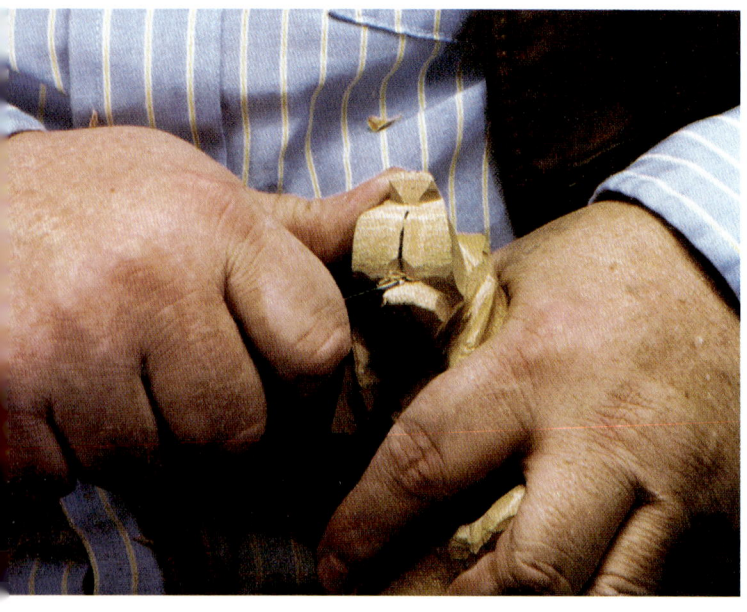

and pop it out.

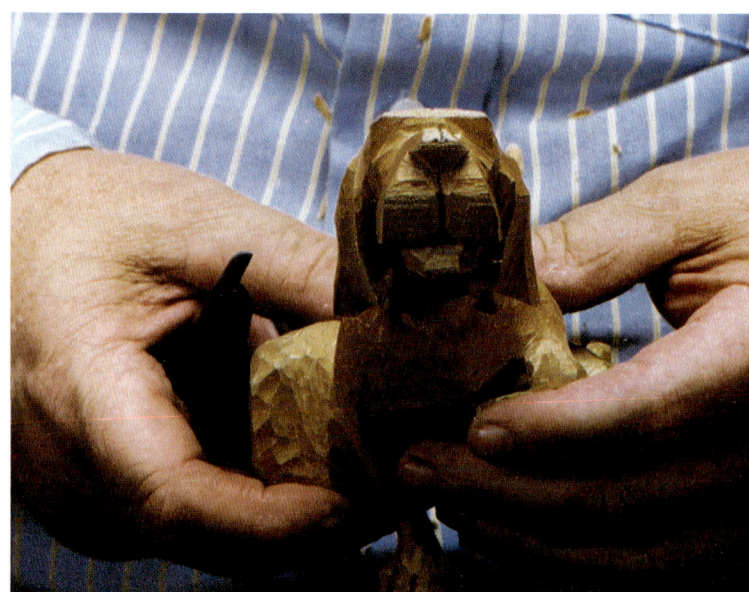

This results in a nicely defined mouth.

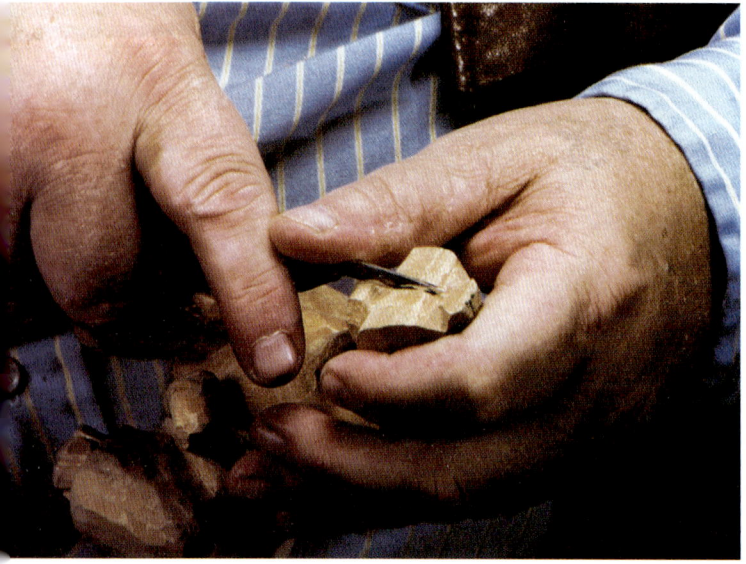

Make an angled cut into the center line from one side...

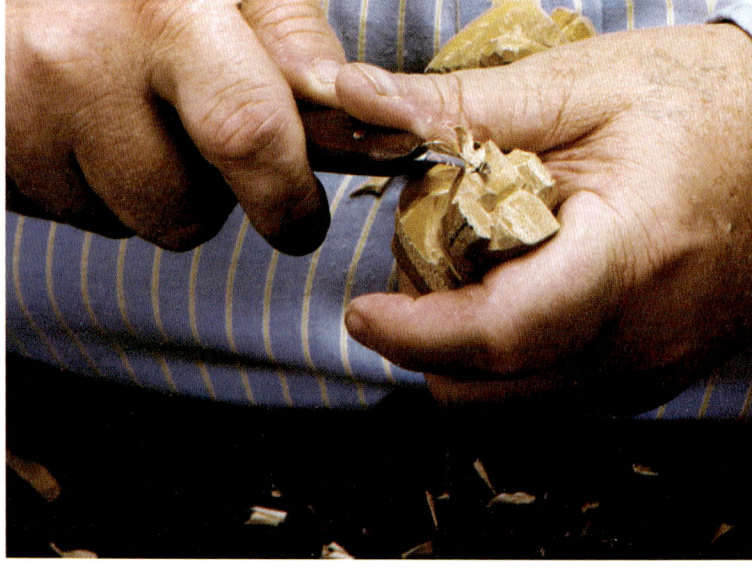

Use the knife to round up the face.

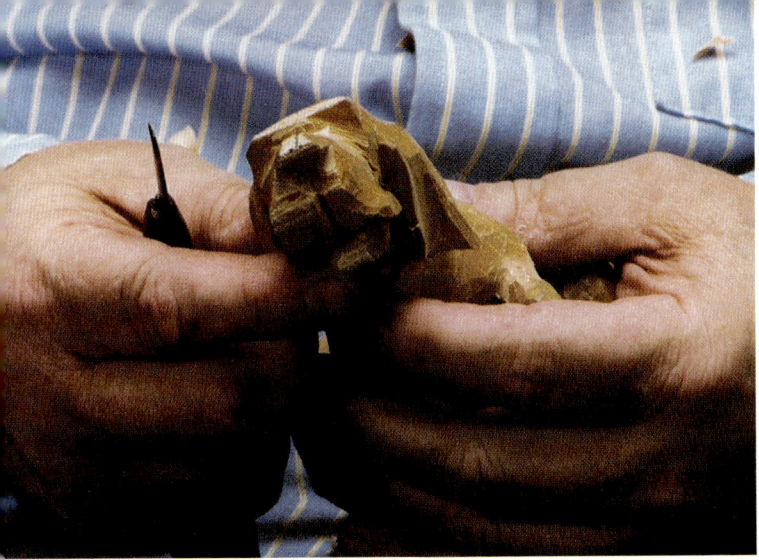

I usually leave the upper lip a little full for comic effect. Continue the shaping on the other side.

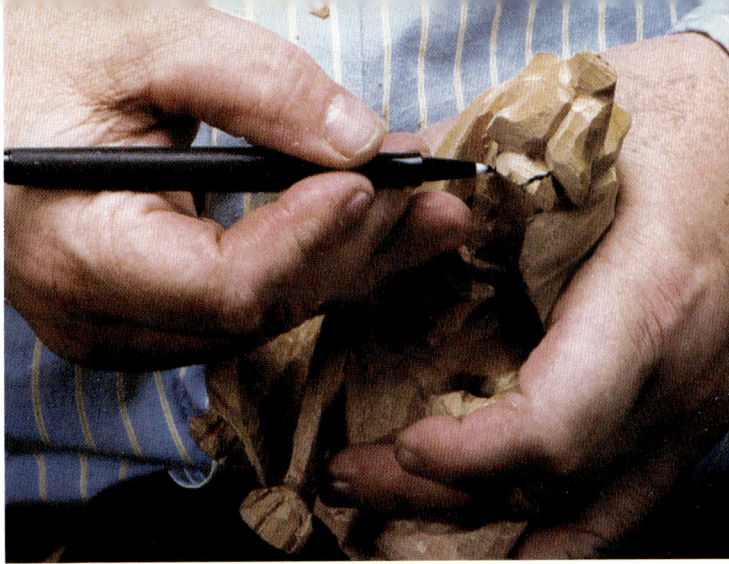

I want his tongue to be hanging out, and for balance I've decided to have it on the opposite side from the raised paw.

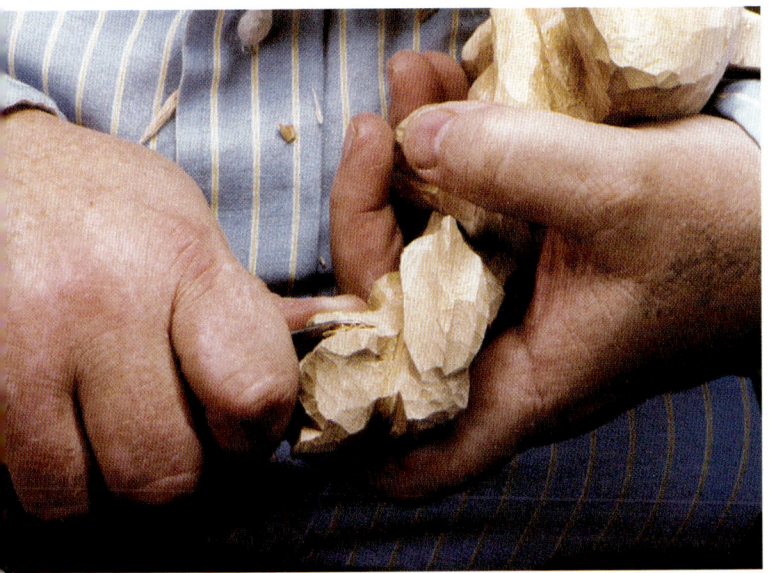

Define the mouth line by cutting a stop and trimming back to it.

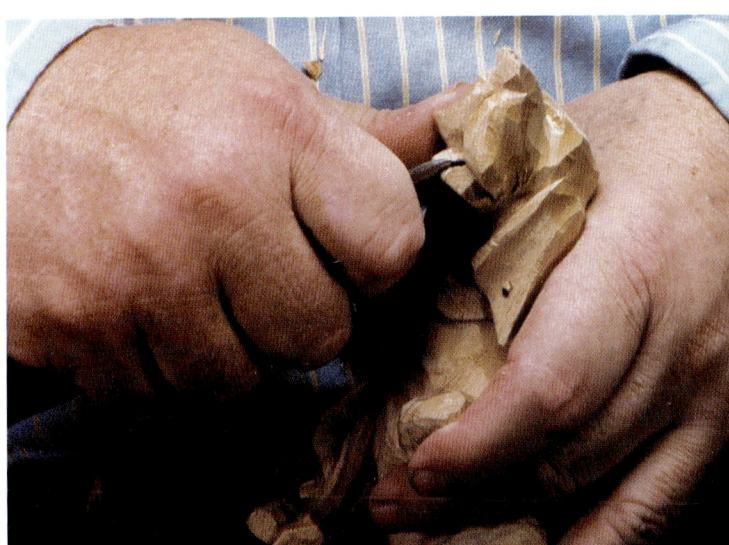

Cut stops around the tongue. This area is likely to chip so don't bear down on the knife. Just gently rock it back and forth.

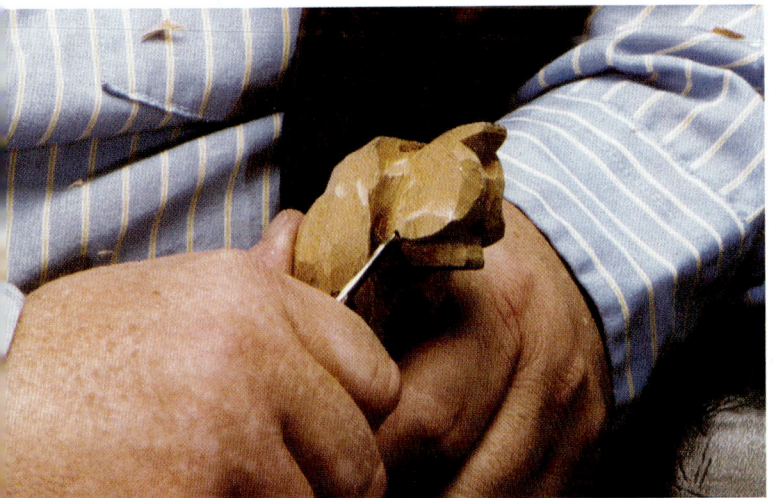

Carry the mouthline back behind the jowl with a little upturn at the end. This gives the hound a slight smile that seems right for him.

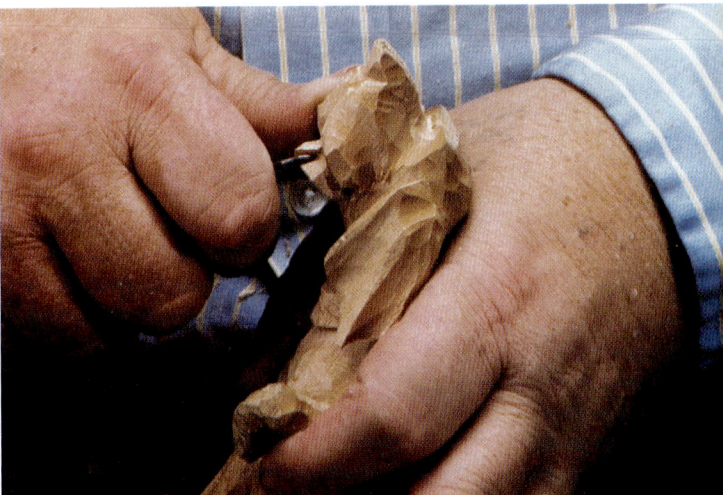

Cut back along the lip to the stop on either side of the tongue.

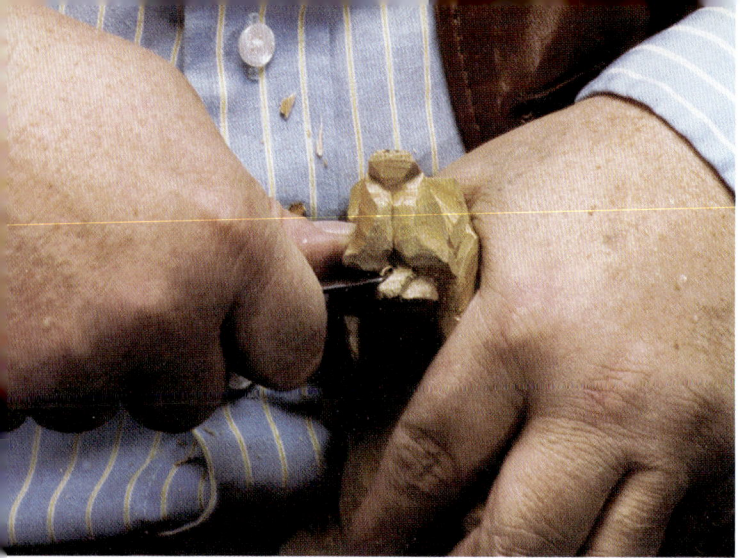

Make a crease in the tongue by cutting a shallow nitch.

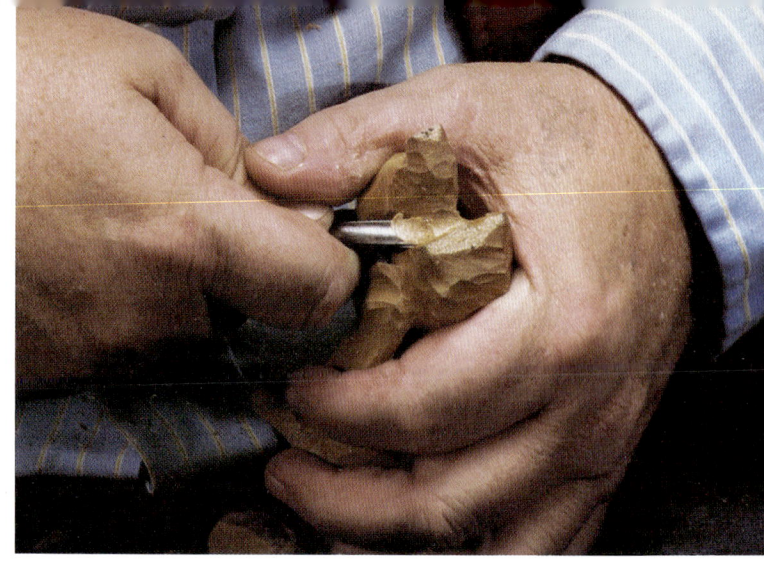

Cut in from the outside and toward the bridge of the nose. These gouged sockets help get that sad look that a hound dog should have.

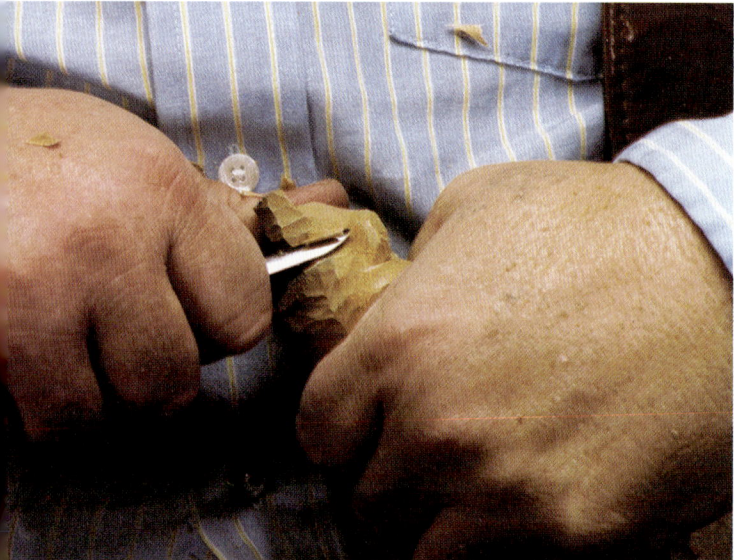

Go over the face, dressing it up and removing any unseemly marks.

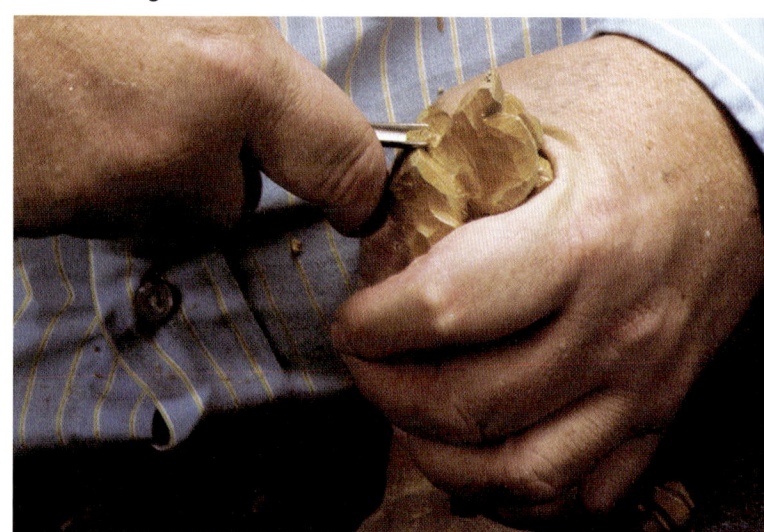

Gouge a space in the brow right over the nose.

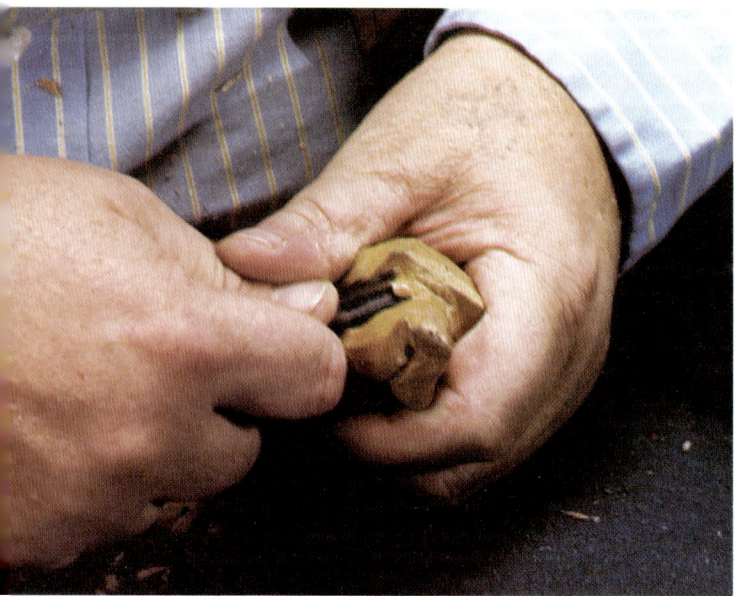

Use a gouge to create the sockets for the eyes.

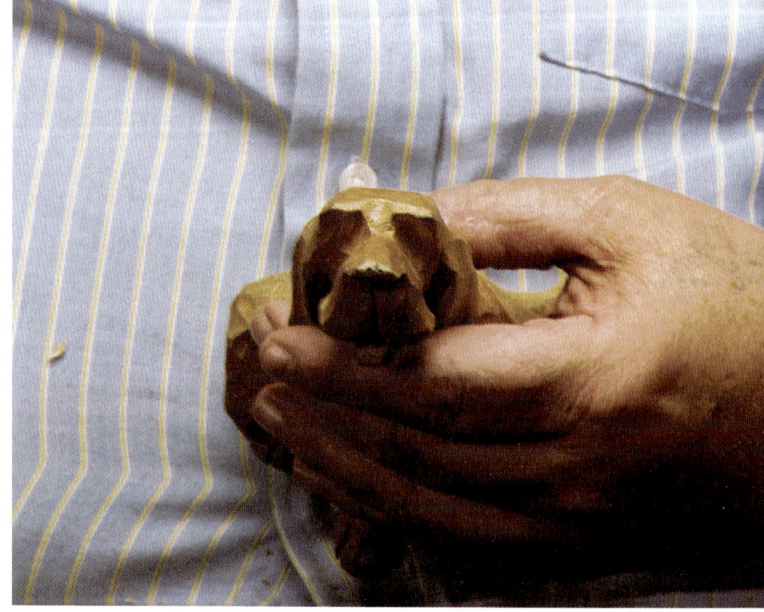

The face should look like this now.

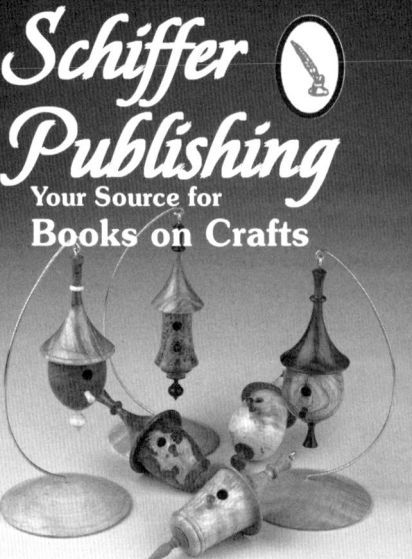

Schiffer Publishing
Your Source for Books on Crafts

Shorebird Carving–Rosalyn Daisey
8 1/2" x 11", 207 color, 611 b/w photos, 256 pp.
ISBN: 0-88740-219-4, hard cover, $49.95

Favorite Santas for Carvers–Ron Ransom
Size: 8 1/2" x 11", 225 color photos, 64 pp.
ISBN: 0-7643-2362-8, soft cover, $12.95

Carving Caricature Heads–W. "Pete" LeClair
8 1/2" x 11", 33 caricature carvings, 64 pp.
ISBN: 0-88740-784-6, soft cover, $12.95

Dick Sing Turns Miniature Birdhouses
8 1/2" x 11", 395 color photos, 80 pp.
ISBN: 0-7643-2080-7, soft cover, $14.95

Pens From the Wood Lathe–Dick Sing
8 1/2" x 11", 273 photos, 64 pp.
ISBN: 0-88740-939-3, soft cover, $12.95

Constructing a Fireplace Mantel–Steve
Penberthy
8 1/2" x 11", 330 color photos, 64 pp.
ISBN: 0-7643-2457-8, soft cover, $14.95

Making Mobiles–Bruce Cana Fox
8 1/2" x 11", 199 color photos, 80 pp.
ISBN: 0-7643-2474-8, soft cover, $14.95

For our complete catalog of books visit
www.schifferbooks.com

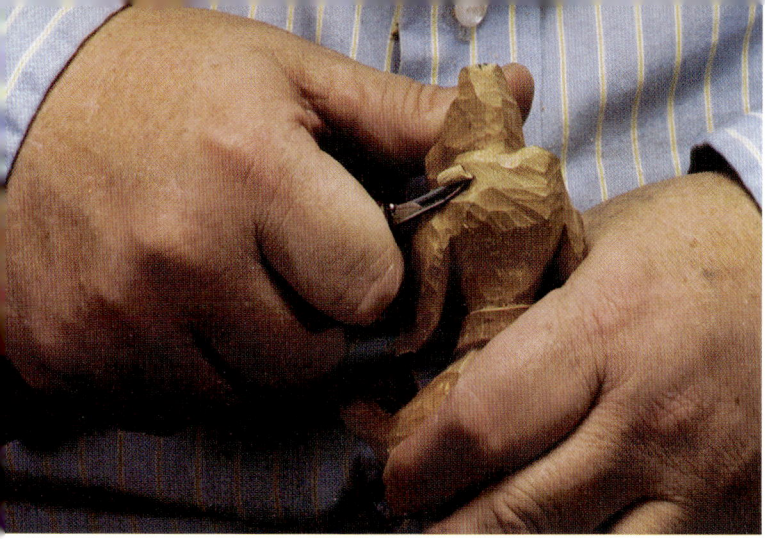

Cut a groove behind the eyebrow, making it appear to rise even more.

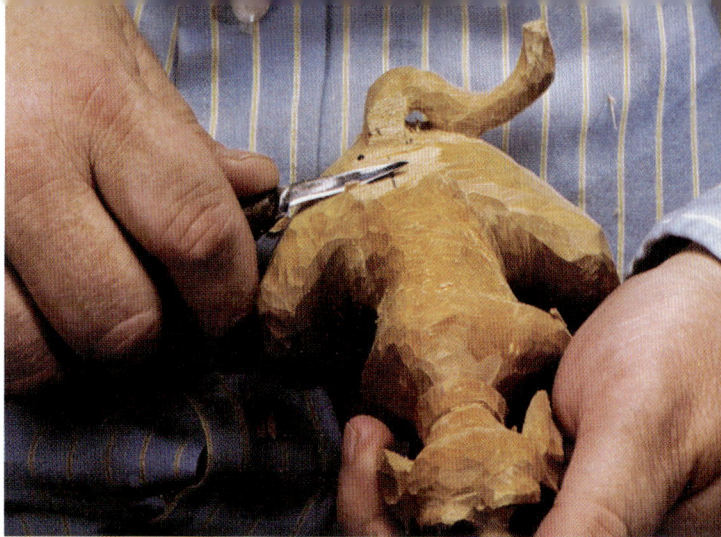

Remove remaining marks. They will sometimes throw you off and should be removed as soon as you can live without them.

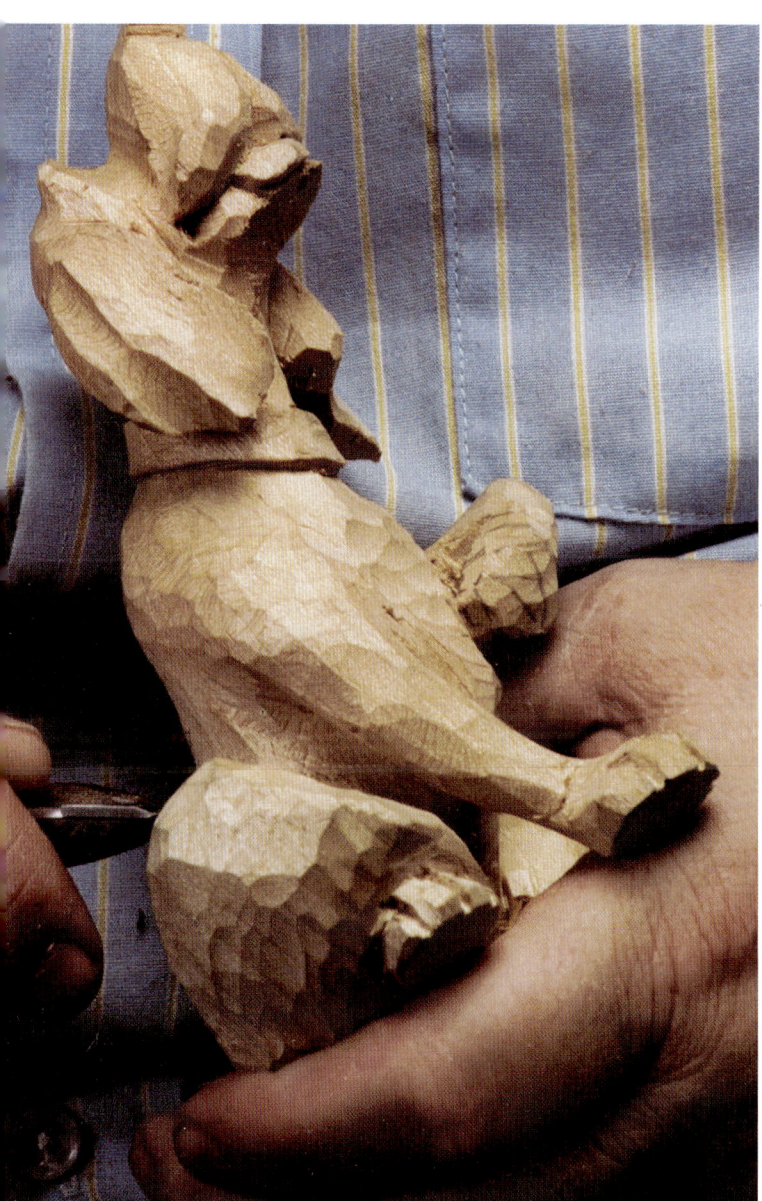

Go over the dog again. This time I catch the fact that the legs are too thick. They need thinning on both sides.

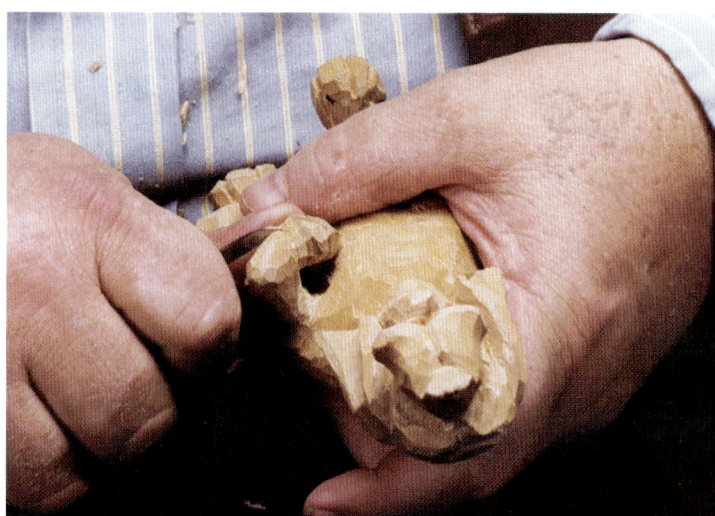

Make shallow stop cuts along the lines you have drawn for the bandage...

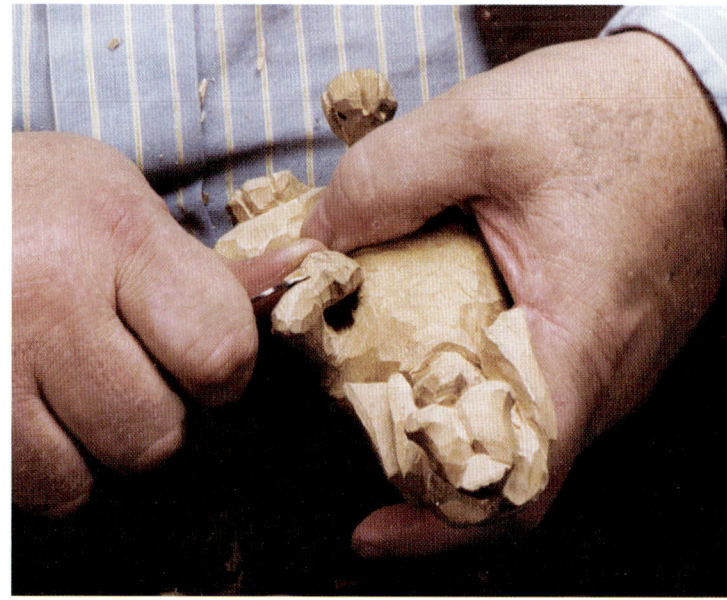

and cut small nitches back into them.

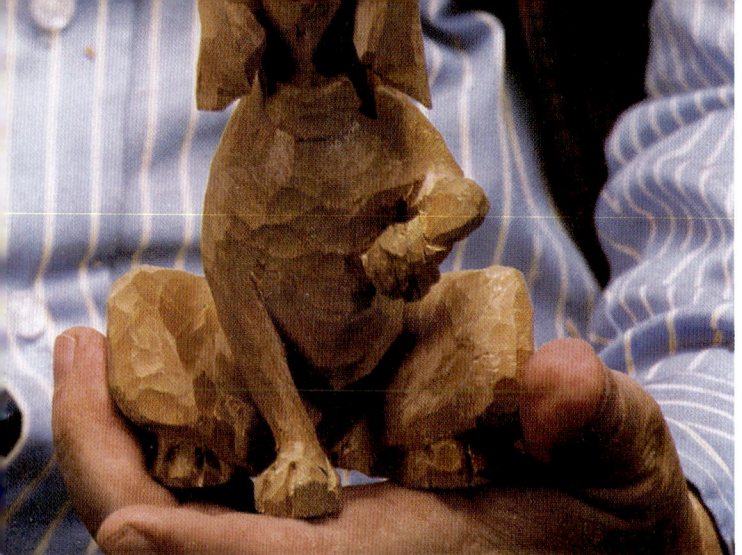

The bandaged paw.

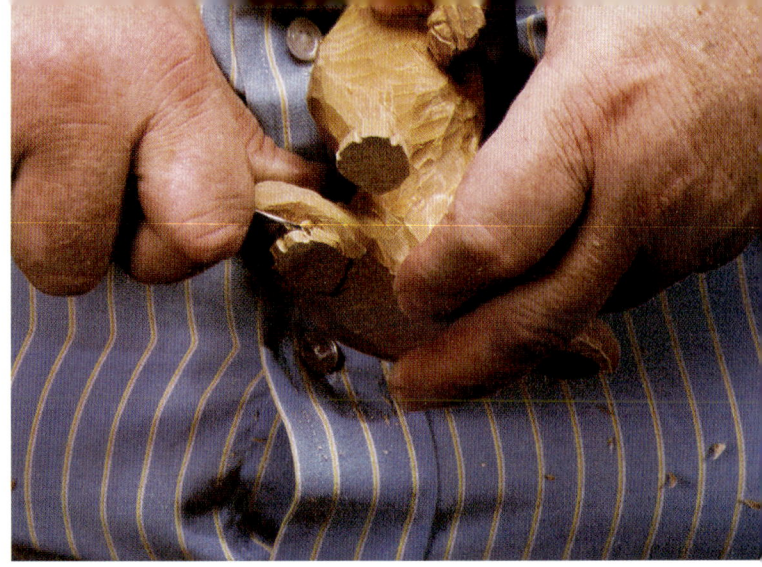

Clean up around the toes.

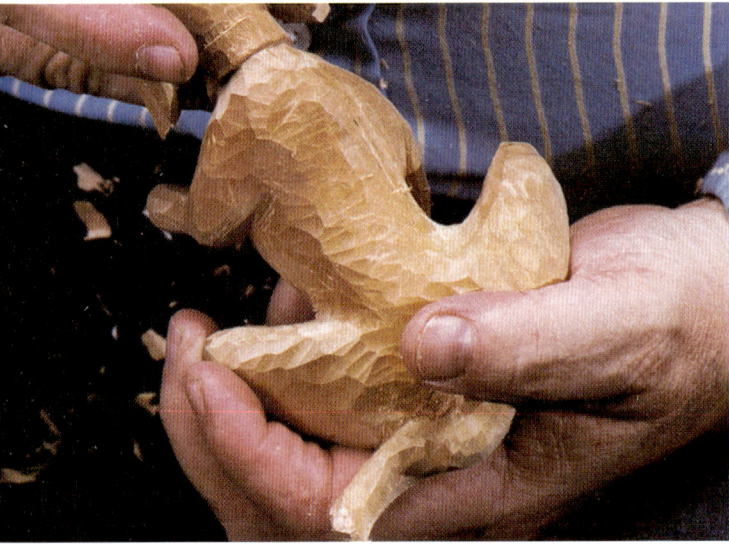

In some tight places the grain is raised when cutting up or down.

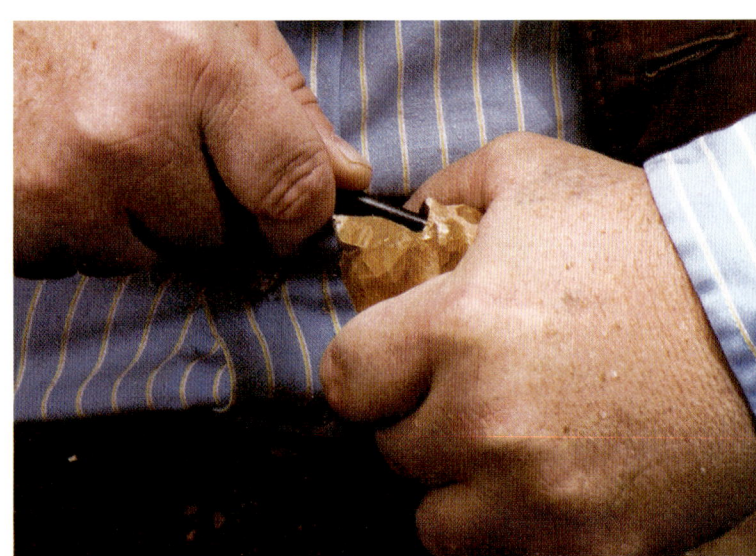

Using a large eyepunch, push and twist it into the left eye first. This gives you the best perspective on the right eye (provided you are right handed), and makes it easier to keep the eyes even.

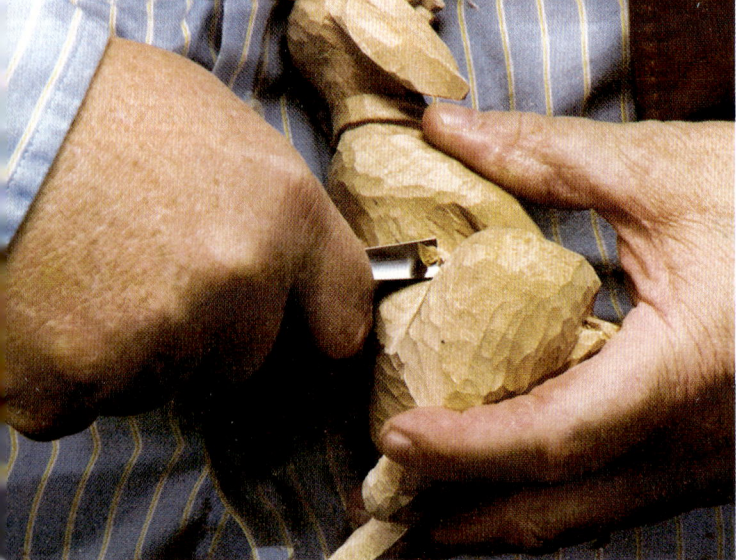

To remove it, use a sharp flat chisel and go across the grain.

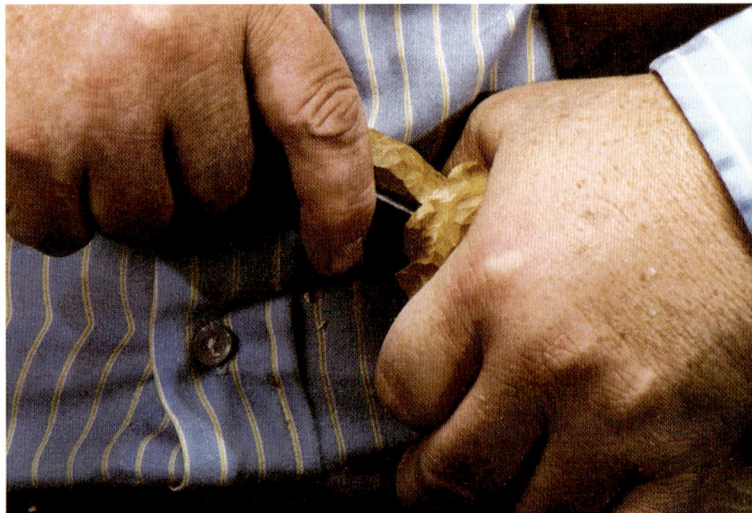

Do the right eye second.

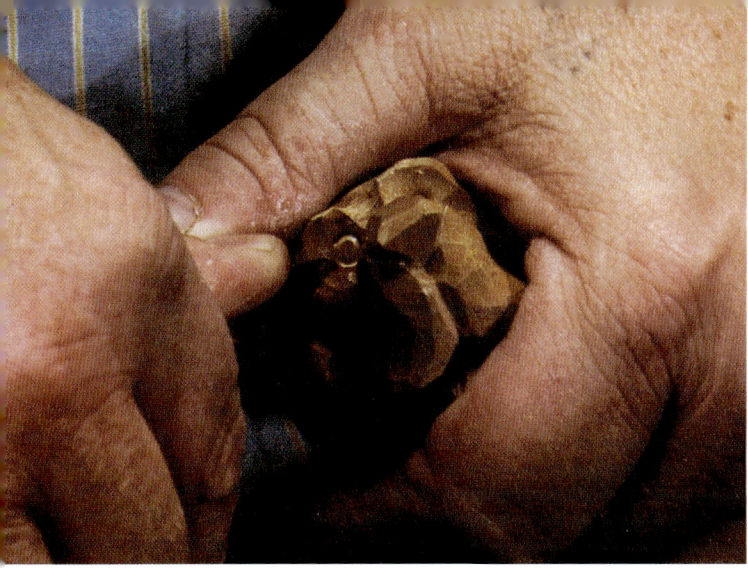

Cut a small triangle at the outside corner of the eye.

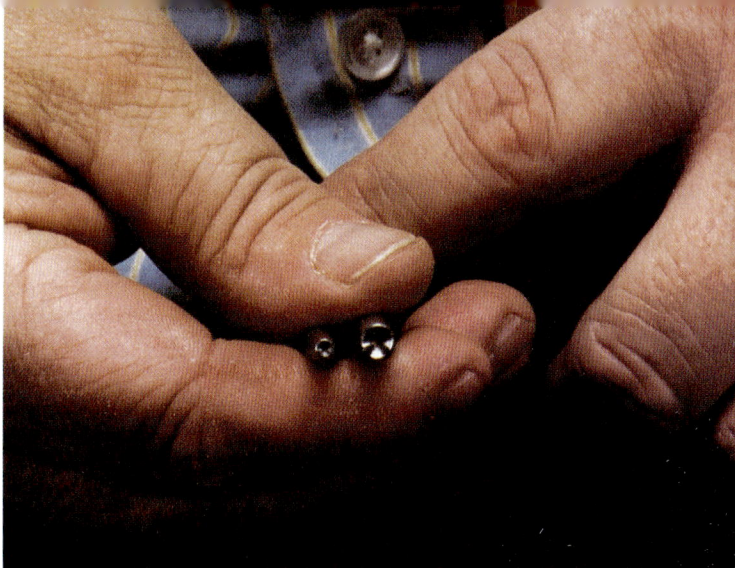

Use a smaller eyepunch in the same way...

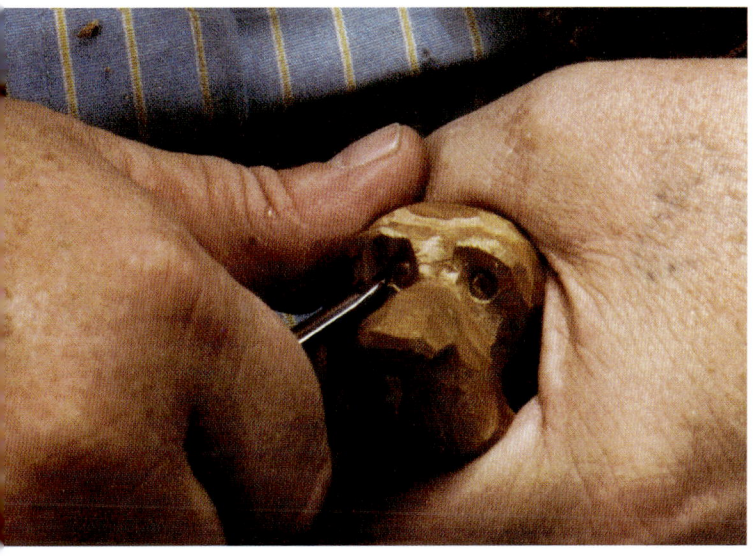

Pop the triangle out, defining the shape of the eye.

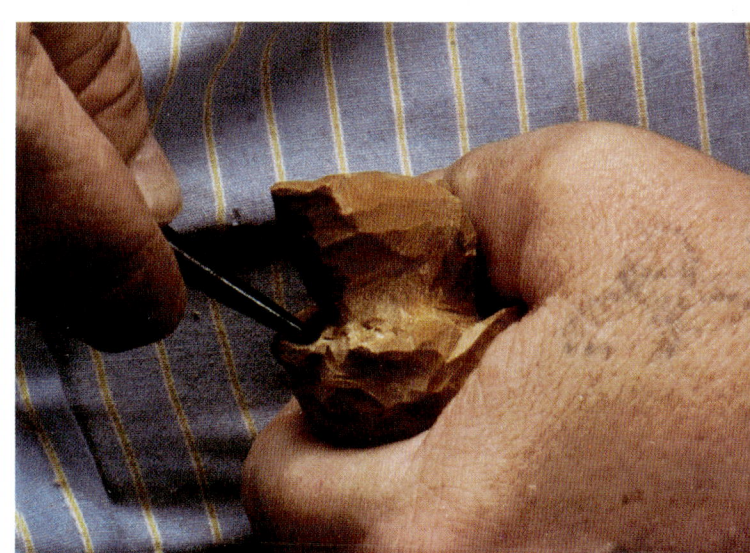

pushing and twisting...

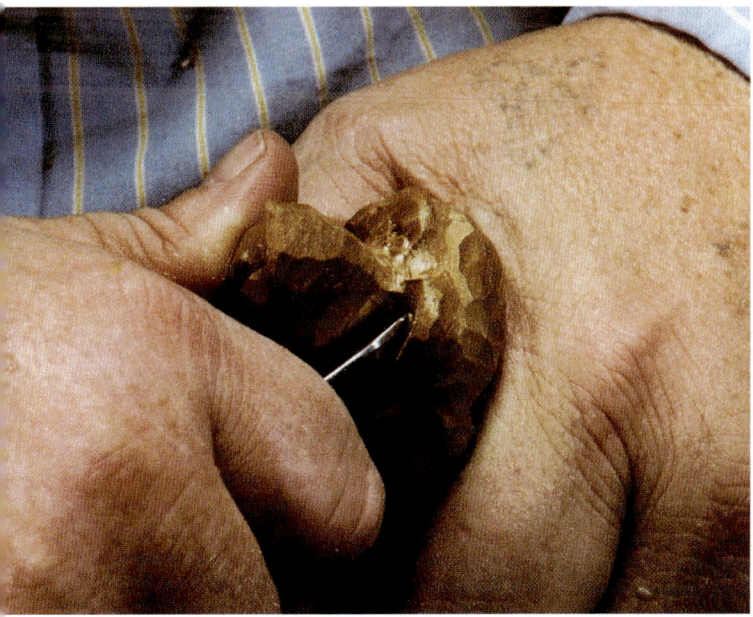

On the inside corner of the eye, place just a tiny triangle.

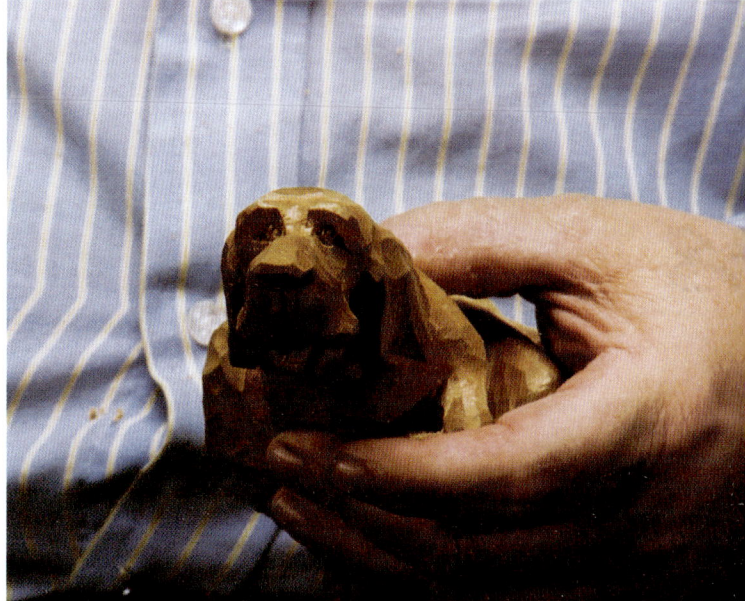

to make the pupil.

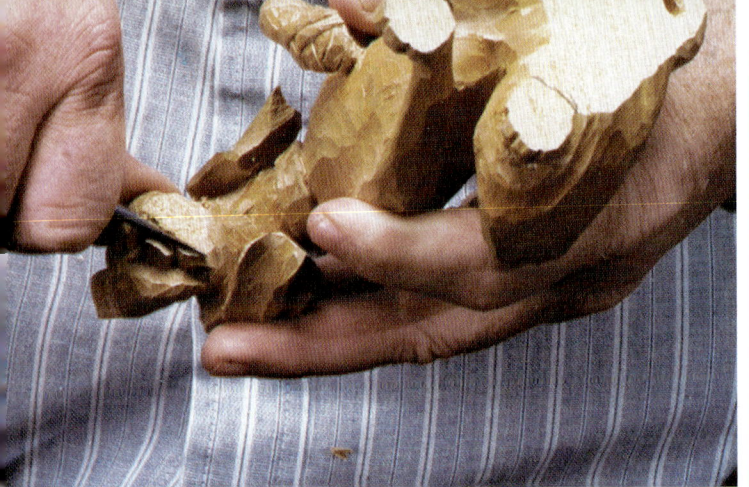

Go over the piece and smooth it out. Pay particular attention to saw marks as you go.

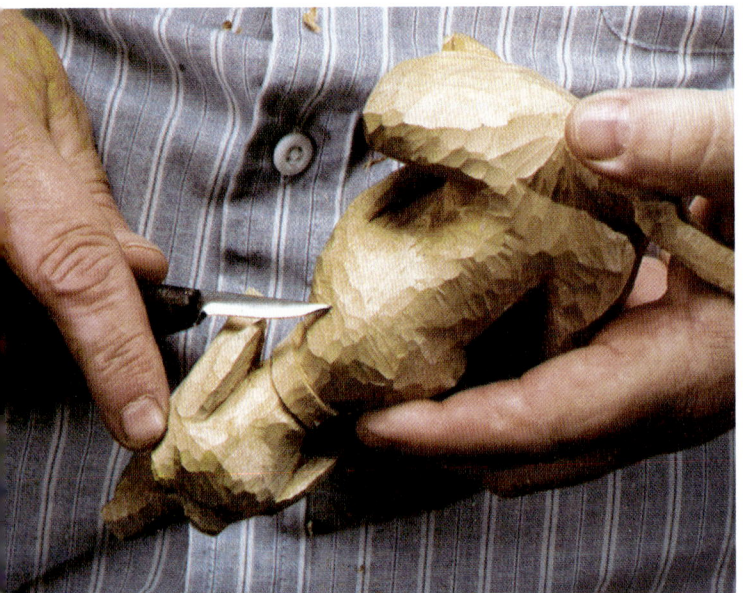

Keep an eye out for chip marks that form lines, like they do here.

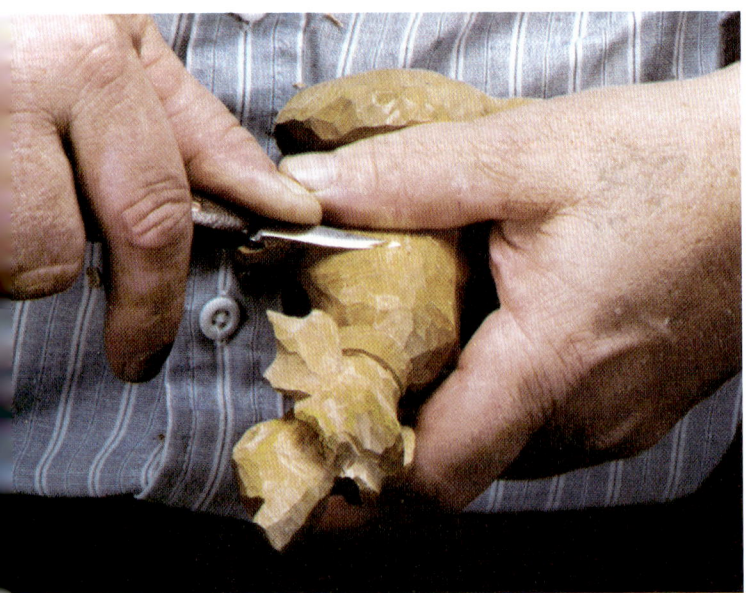

Smooth them out.

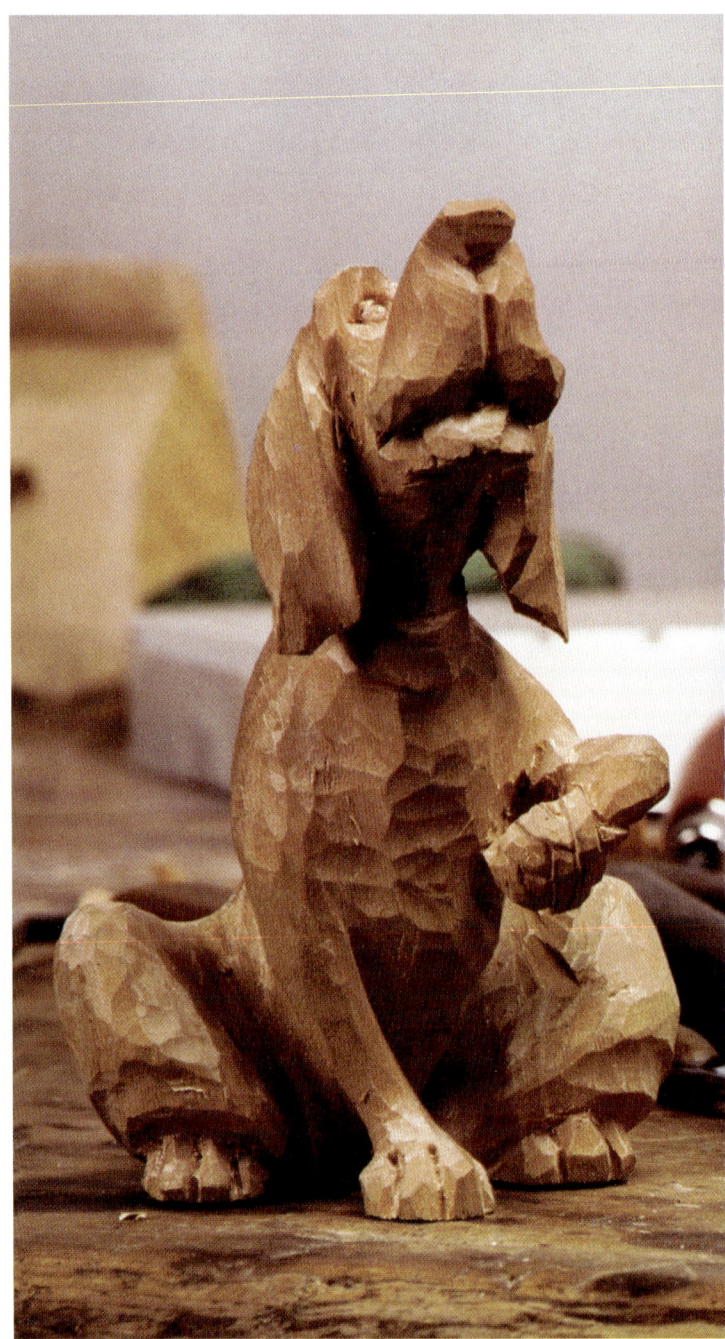

The hound dog is ready to be painted.

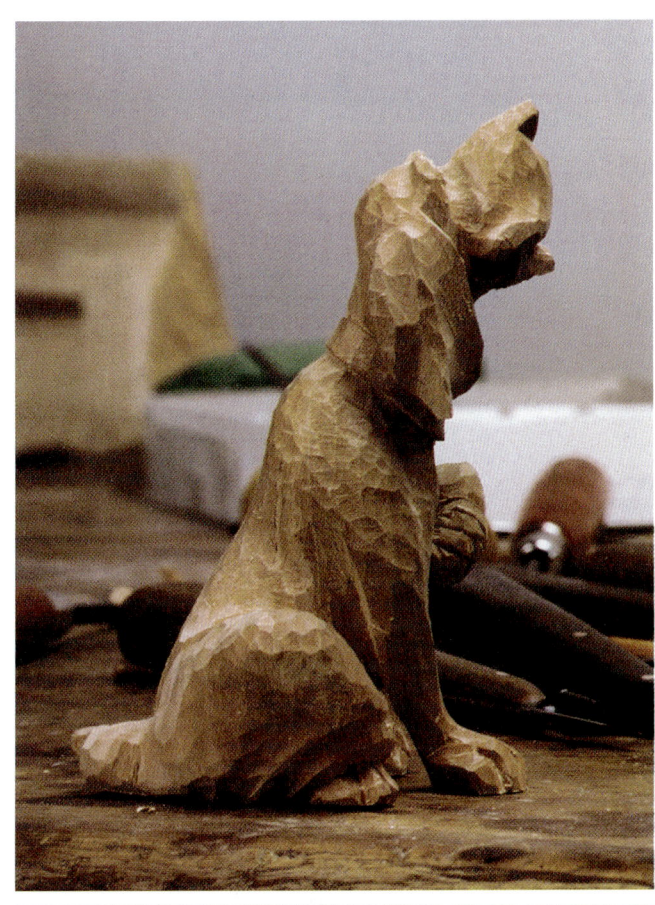

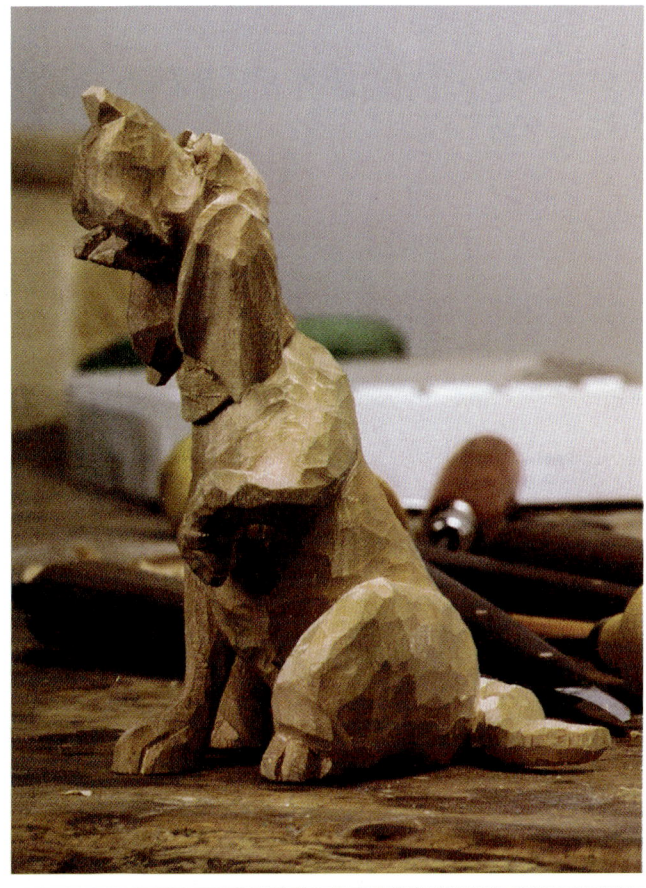

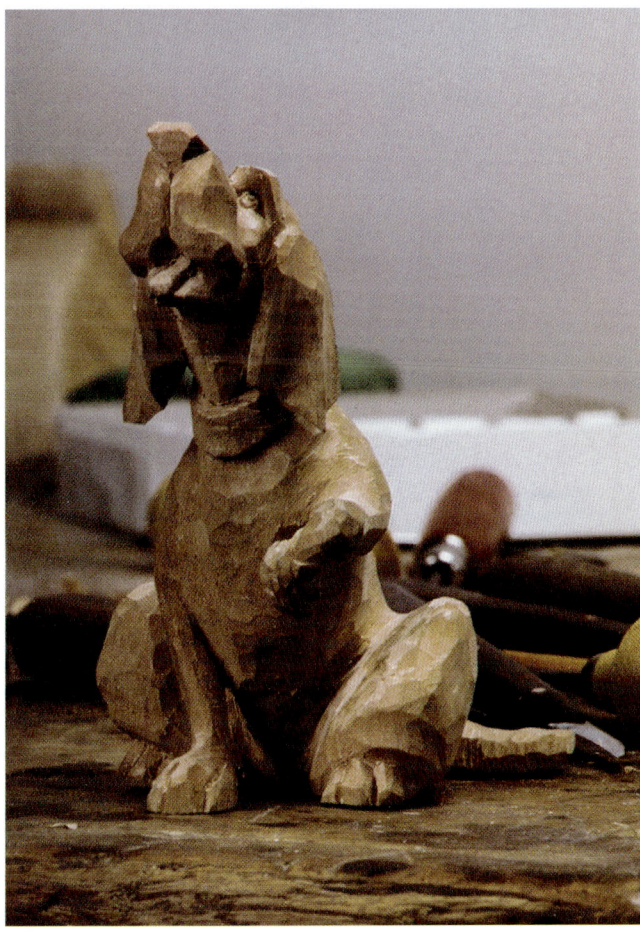

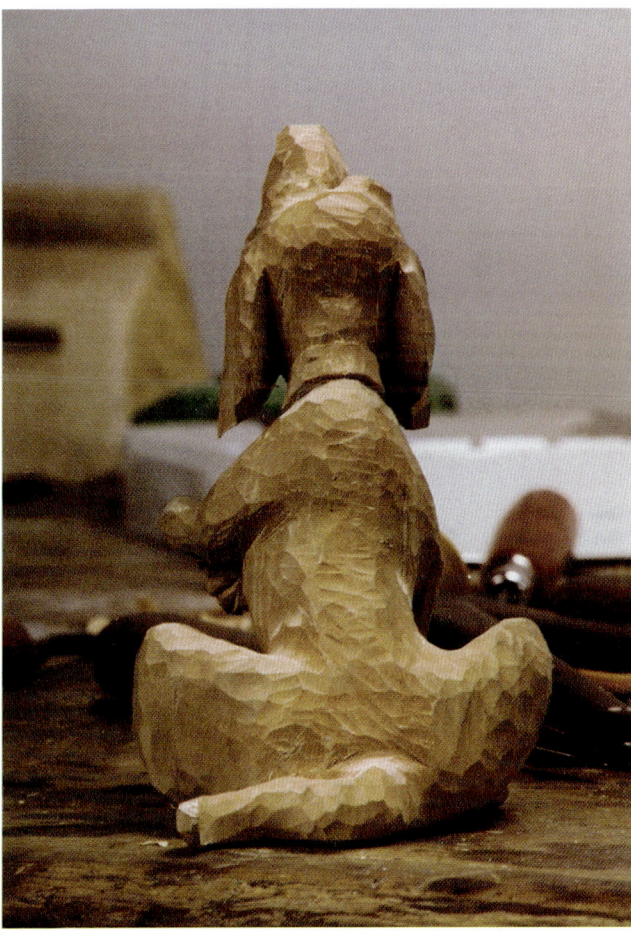

Painting the Dog

For wood carving I use Winsor and Newton Alkyd tube paints. These are thinned with turpentine to a consistancy that works with the carving. I mix my paints in glass juice bottles, putting a bit of paint and adding turpentine. I don't use exact measurements. Instead I use trial and error, adding a bit of paint or a bit of turpentine until I get the thickness I want.

What I look for is a watery mixture, almost like a wash. In this way the turpentine will carry the pigment into the wood, giving the stained look I like. It has always been my theory that if you are going to cover the wood, why use wood in the first place.

The juice bottles are handy for holding your paints. They are reclosable, easy to shake, and have the added advantage of leaving a concentrated amount of color on the inside of the lid and the sides of the bottle which can be used when more intense color is needed.

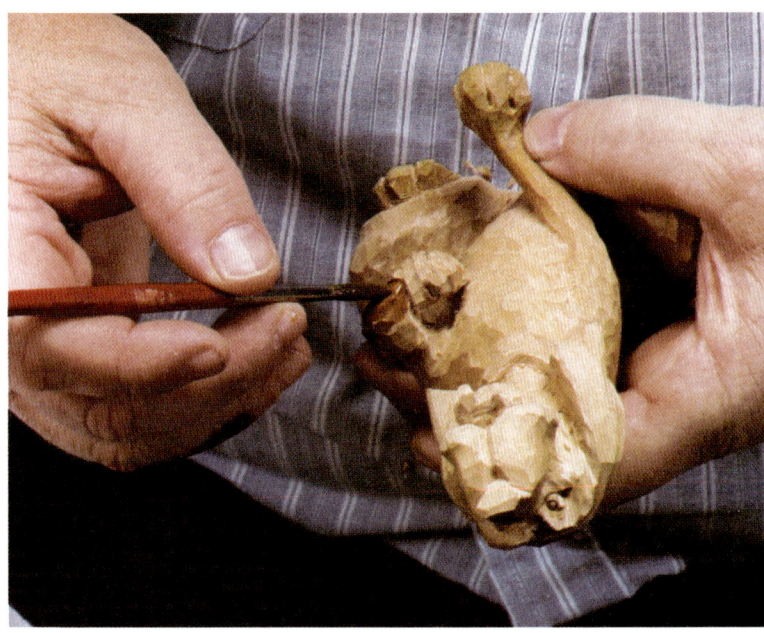

Start around the bandage on the hurt paw.

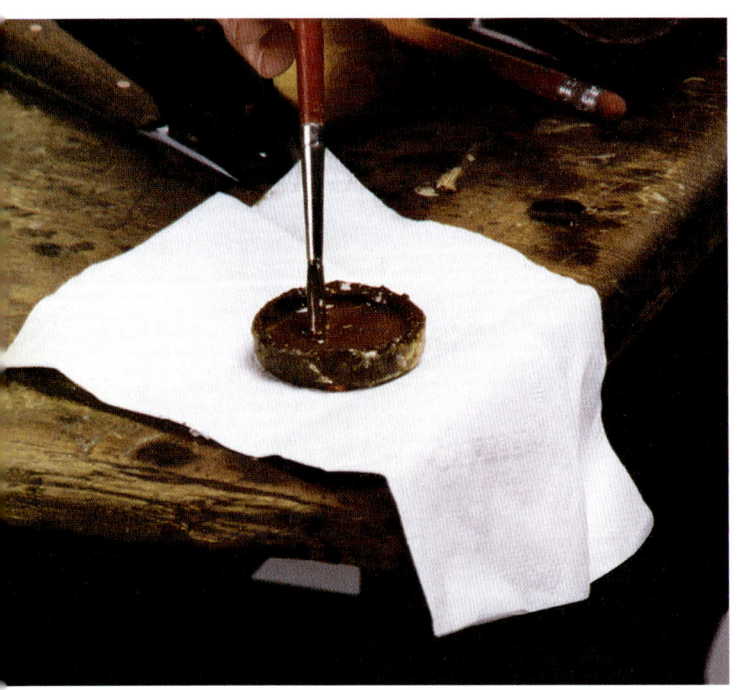

We're going to make this a red bone hound. Pour a bit of raw sienna in the cap and mix it with the brush.

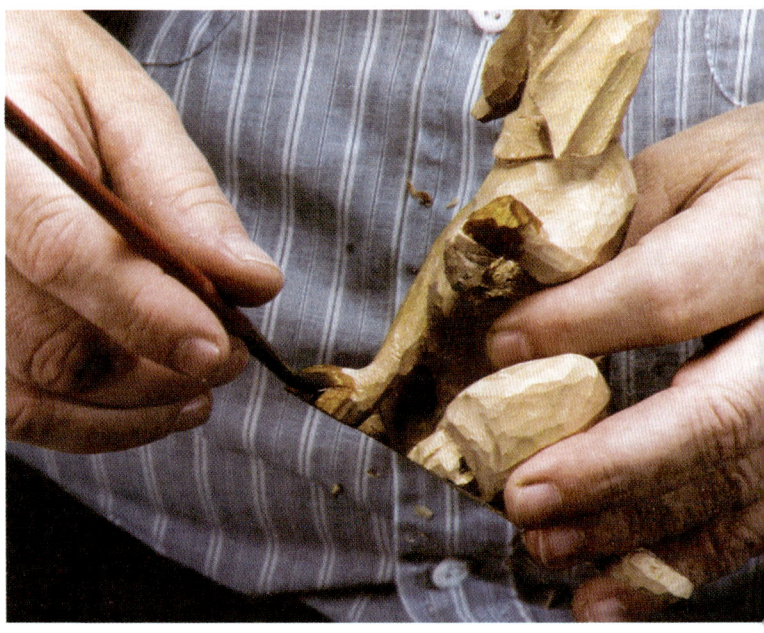

Then go around all the paws and a little bit up the leg.

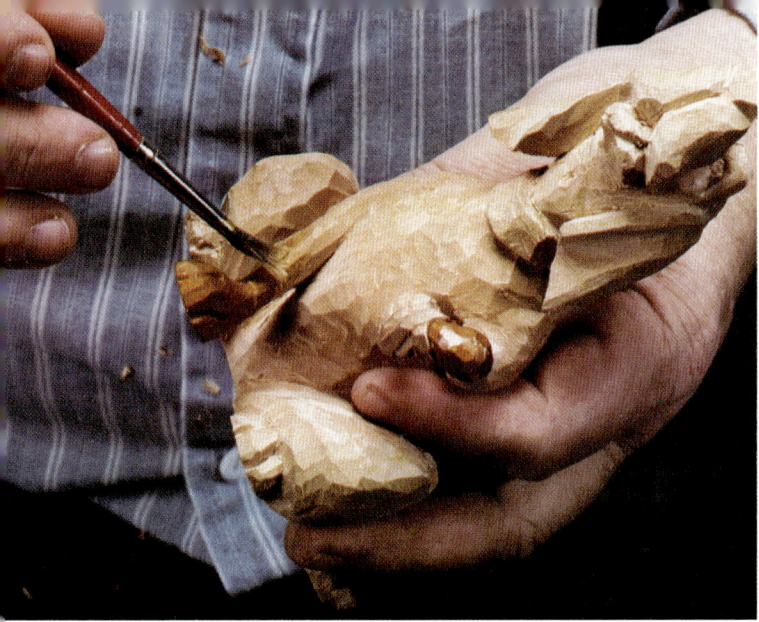

Keep brushing up the leg until your brush gets dry and the color fades. In these dogs the delineation of color is not critical because the colors overlap and, besides, no two dogs are colored alike.

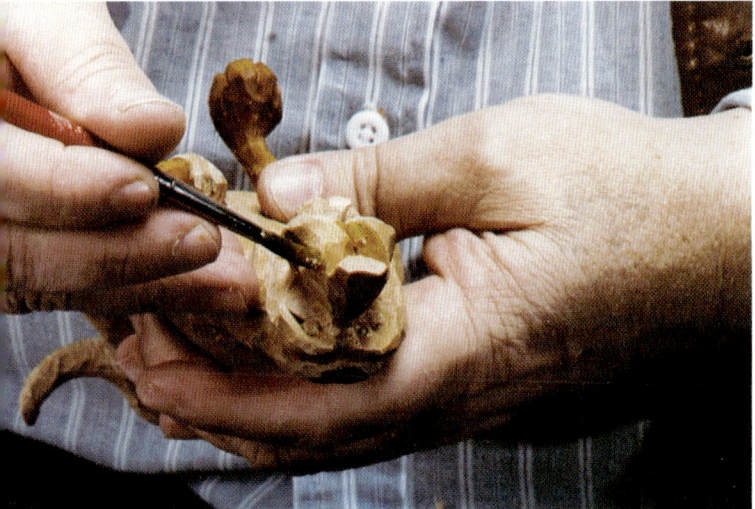

Paint the raw sienna under the nose

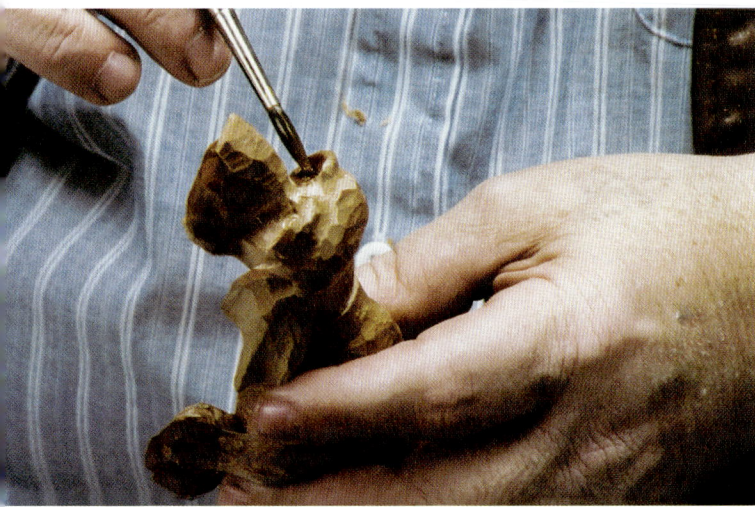

Cover the whole face, eyes and all.

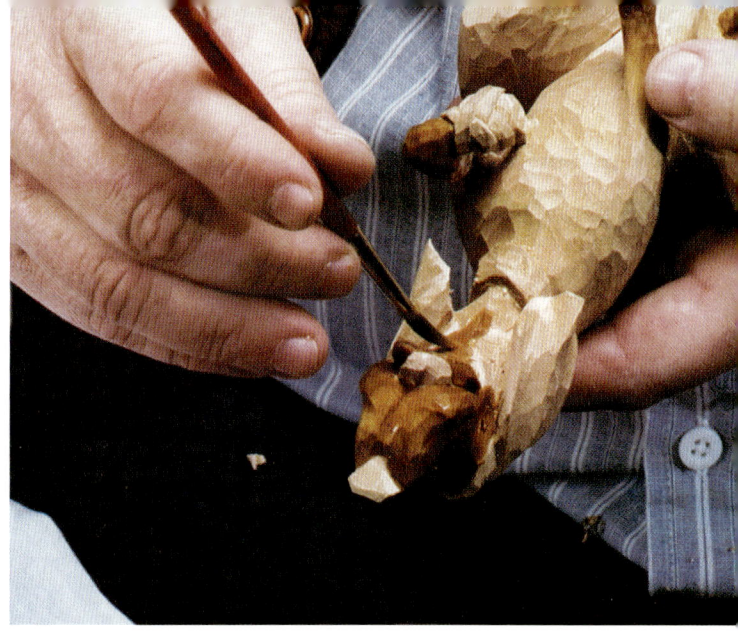

Underneath the chin bring the paint down a little bit, and then drybrush it out until your brush is dry.

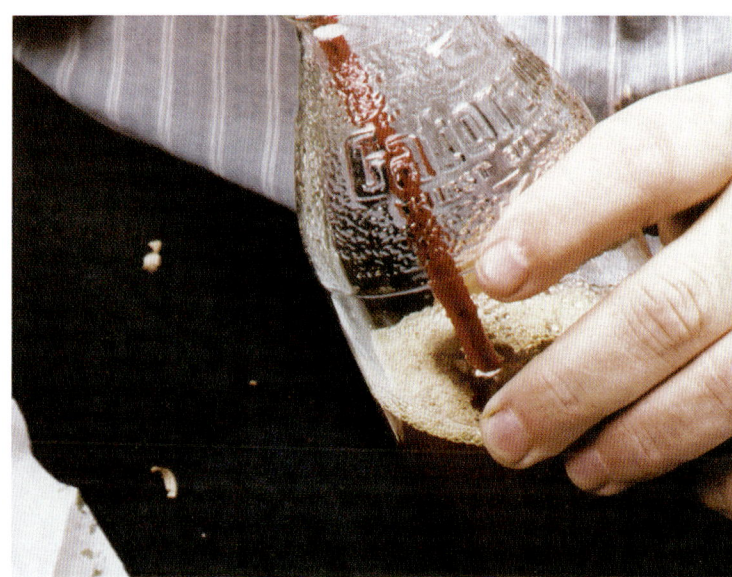

Keep a wash bottle of turpentine and use it to keep your brushes clean.

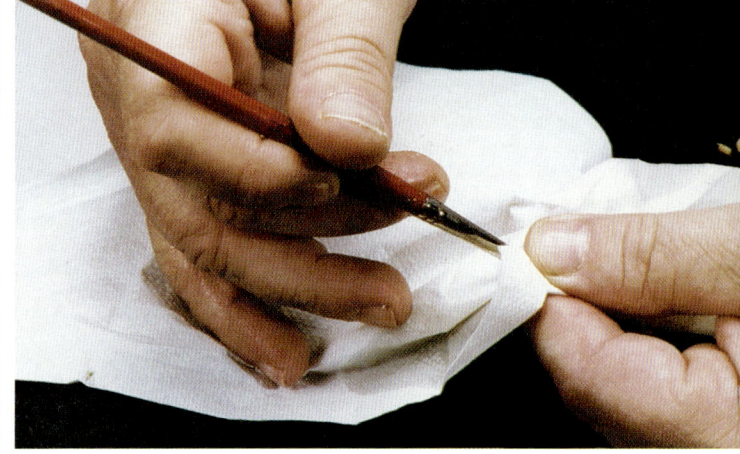

After washing your brush, be sure to get the excess turpentine out of it, or it will affect your next color.

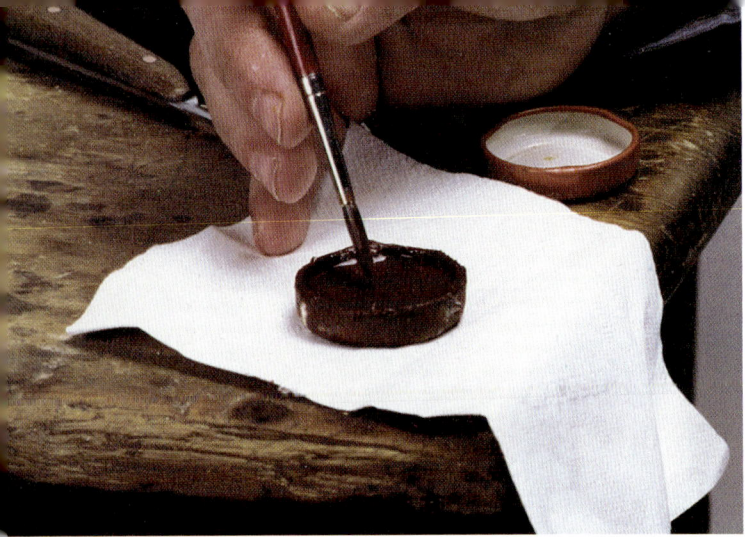

The reddish color of burnt sienna is going to be the dominant color of the redbone.

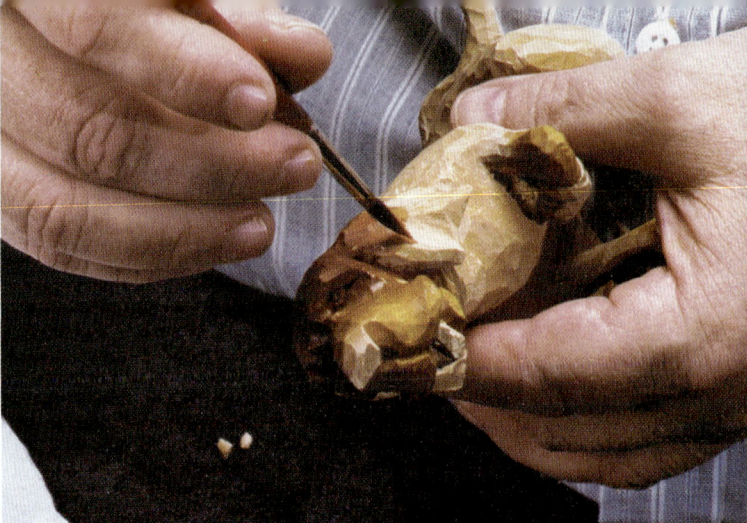

Come down the ear and feather the color out as you did with the legs, using a dry brush.

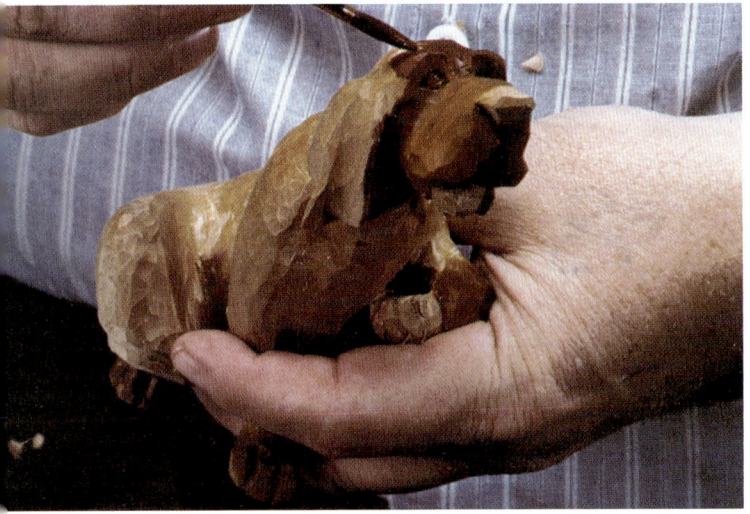

Start with the brow and head and work your way down the body.

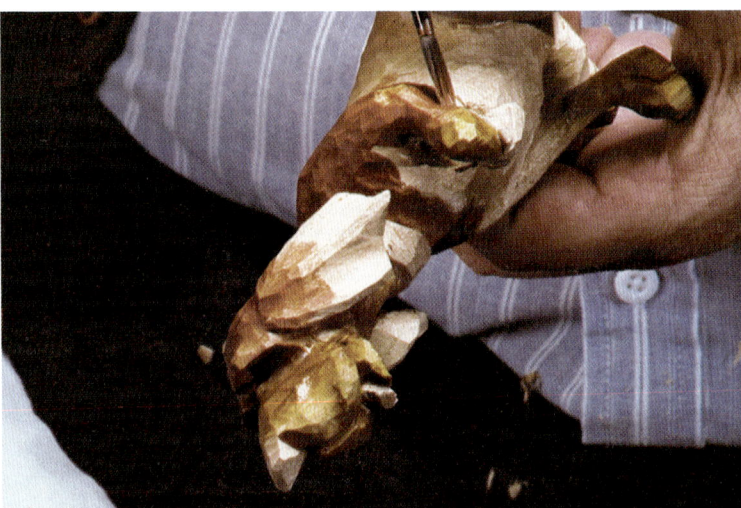

When you come to the places where you earlier applied raw sienna, be sure your brush is fairly dry. Overlap and blend the two colors.

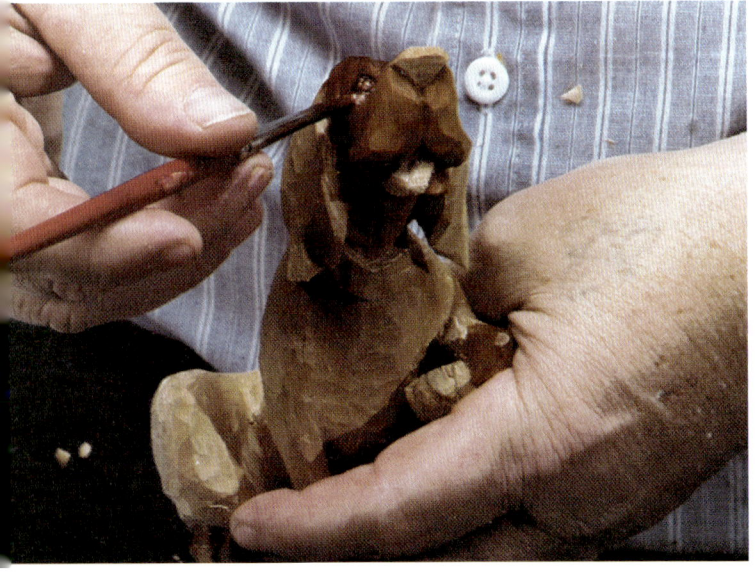

The eye and some other places will have several colors overlapping. Go over the raw sienna with the burnt sienna.

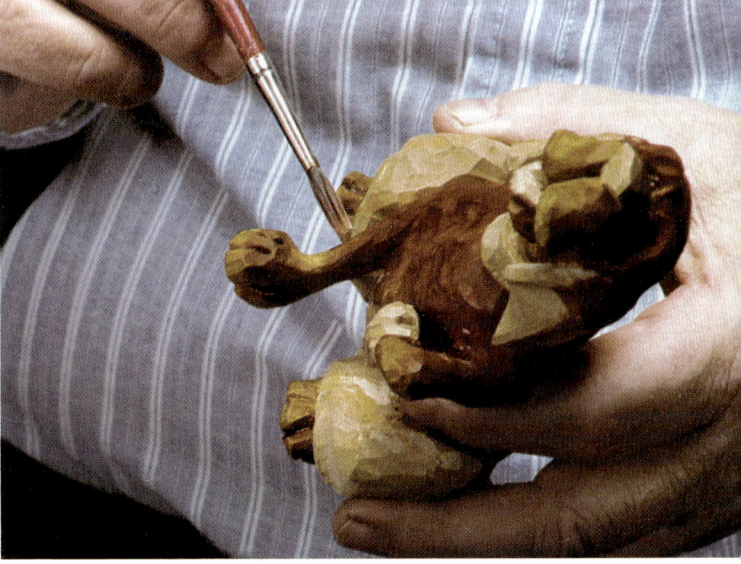

You want hardly to be able to tell where one shade ends and the other begins, having them fade one into the other.

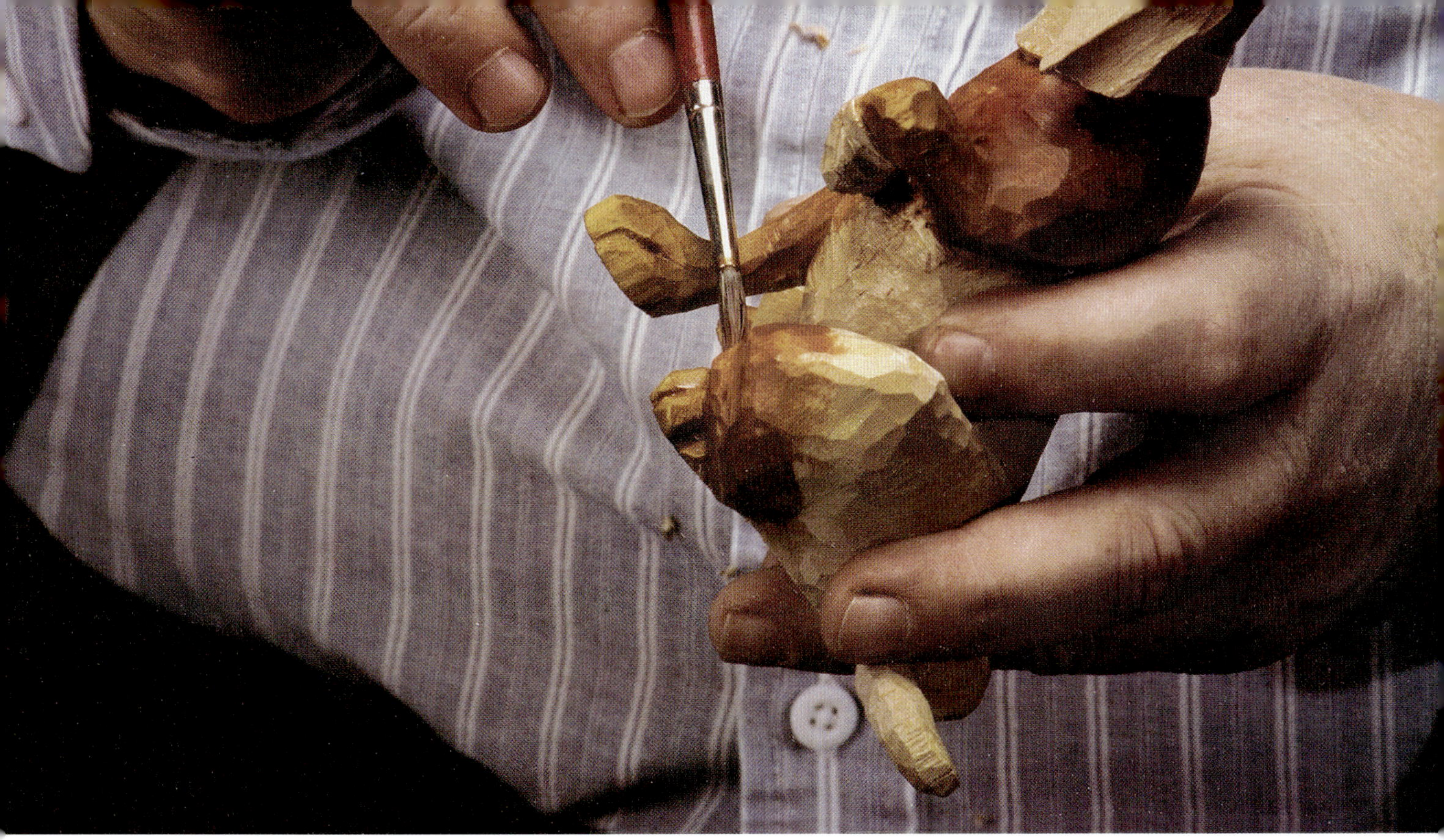

The back legs are a little different. There should be a
clear contrast between the raw sienna foot sticking out
from the burnt sienna haunch.

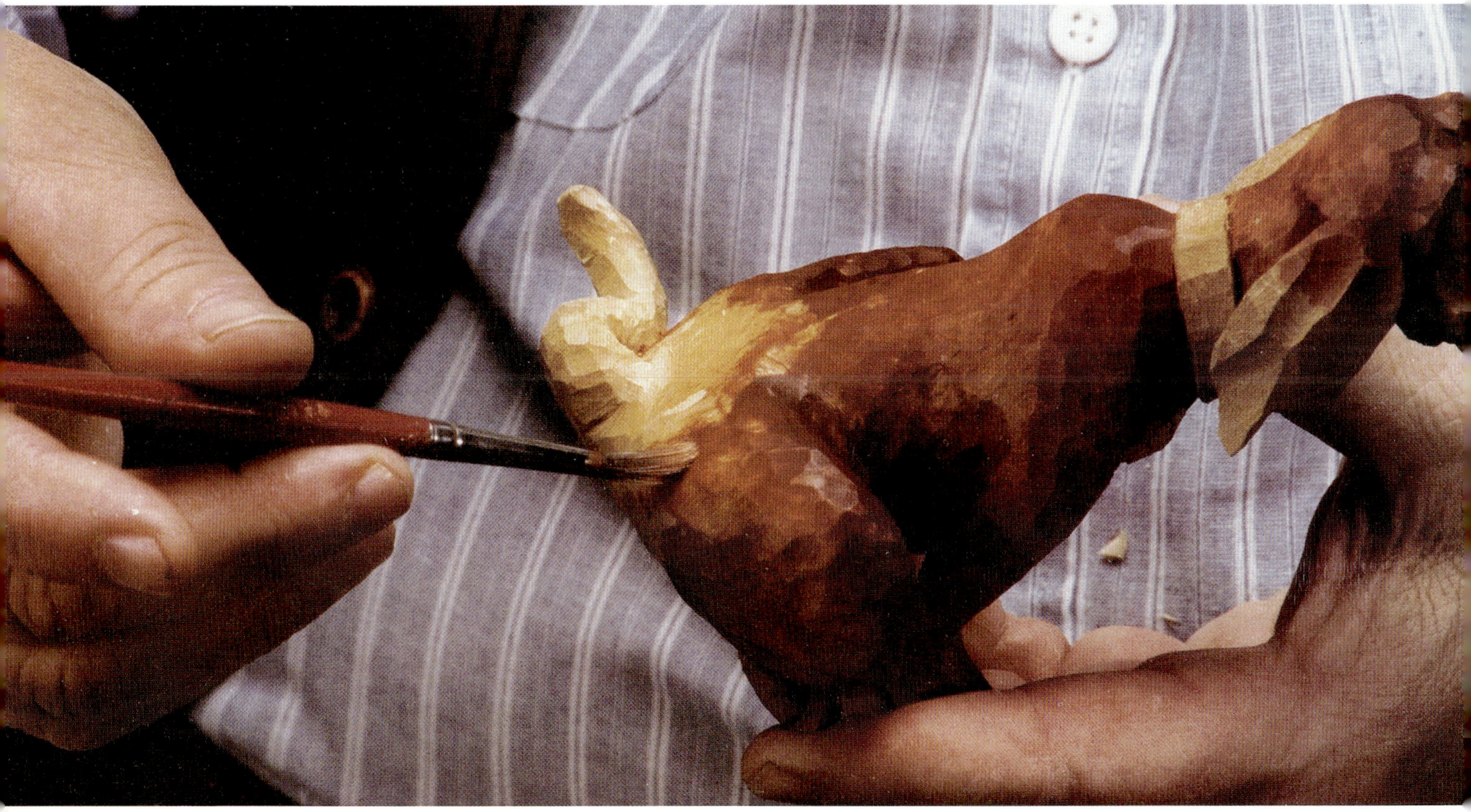

I want to leave a saddle around the tail for darker colors,
so I feather the burnt sienna into the area and leave it
unpainted.

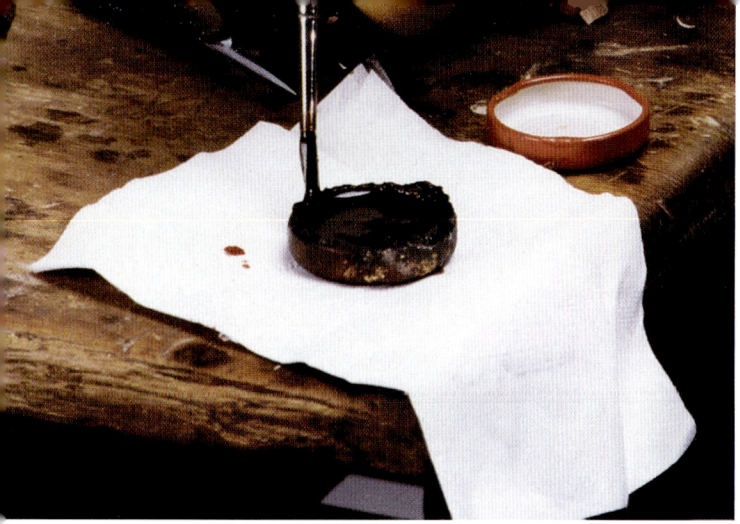

The next color is burnt umber.

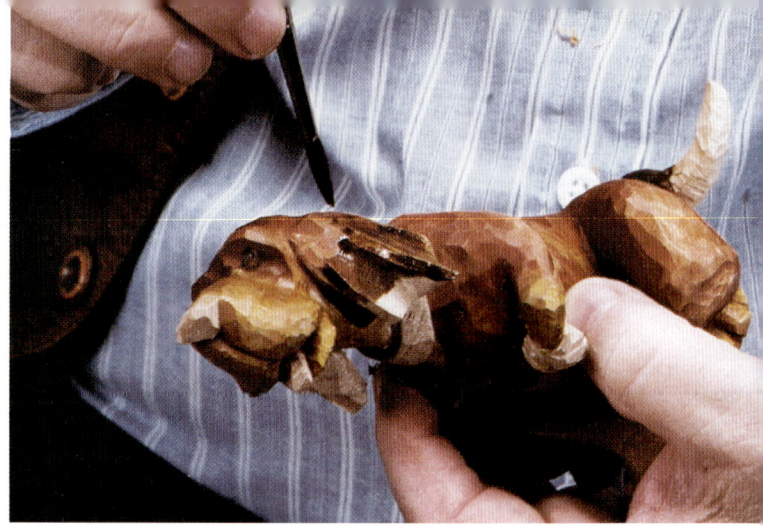

On the ears, again, feather the burnt umber into the burnt sienna and paint the tips.

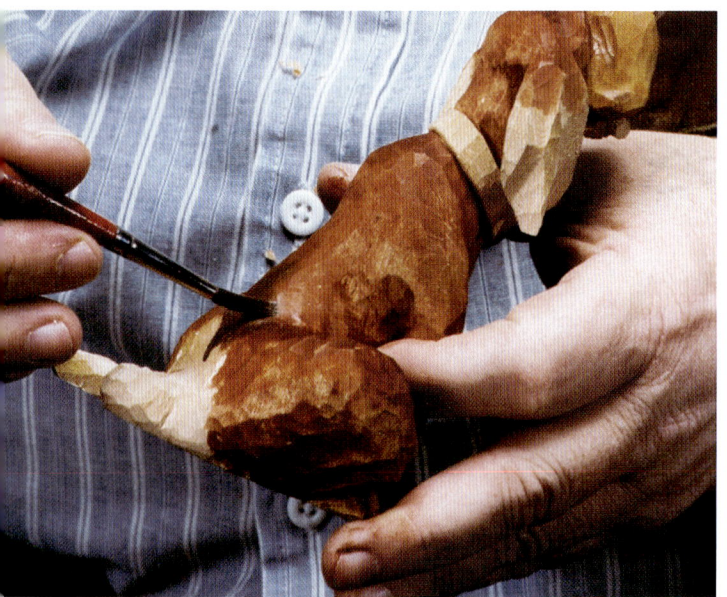

Around the edges of the saddle, feather the burnt umber into the burnt sienna.

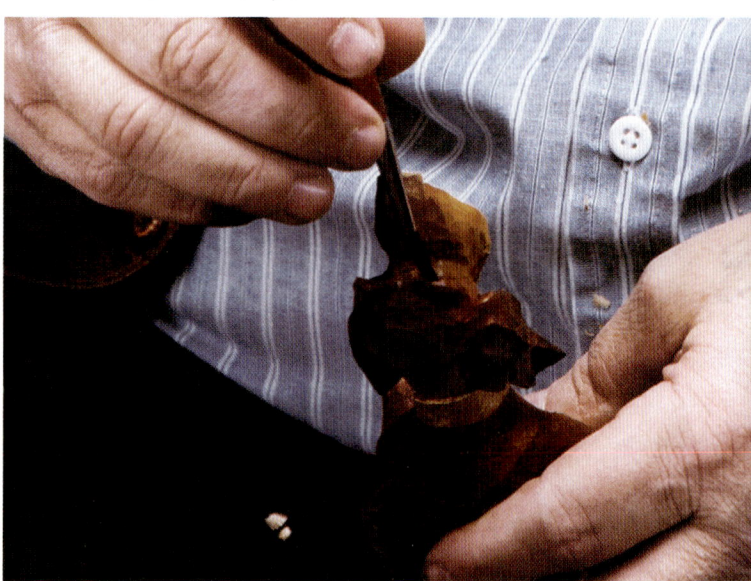

Wash the eye, just slightly, with the burnt umber.

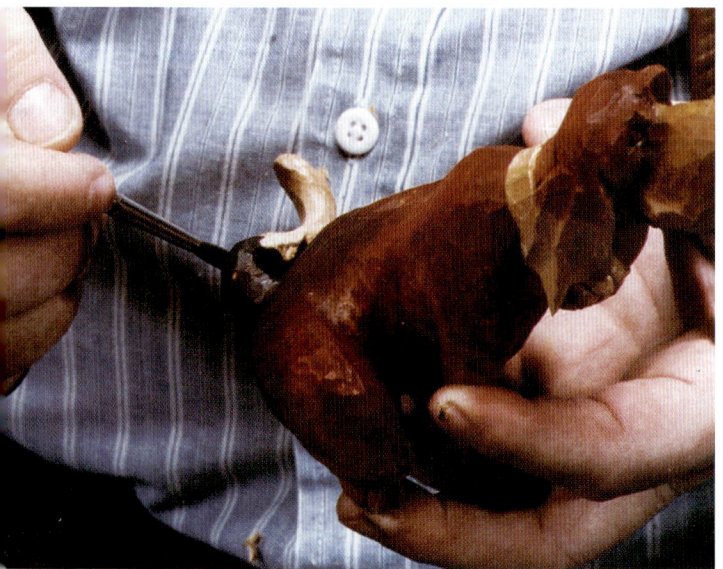

Continue with the burnt umber about halfway down the tail.

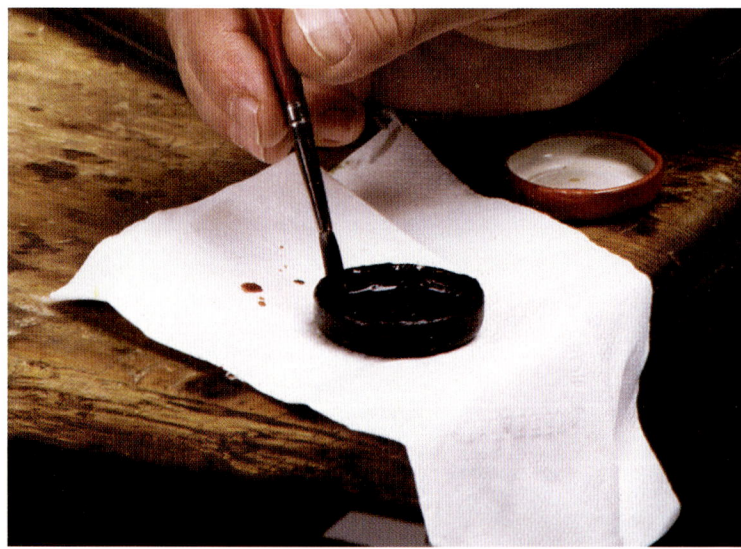

Next comes black. It is important to start with the lighter shades because the darker shades (and white) are dominant and are difficult to cover. Be sure to clean your hands between colors.

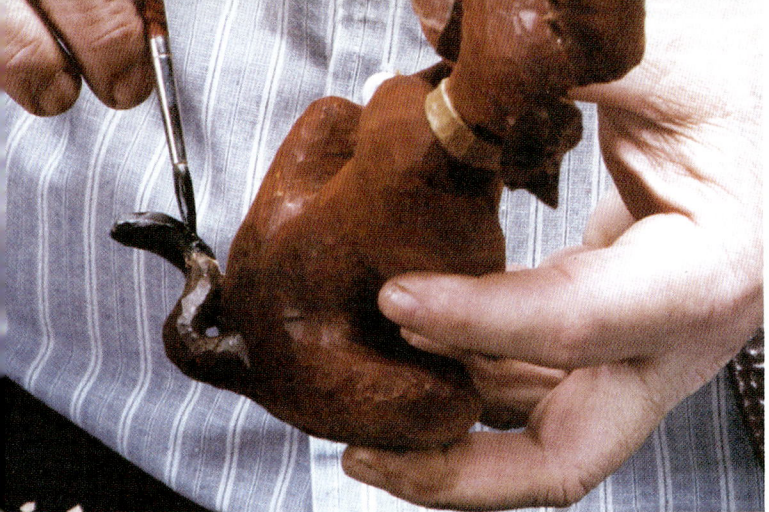

Begin with the tip of the tail...

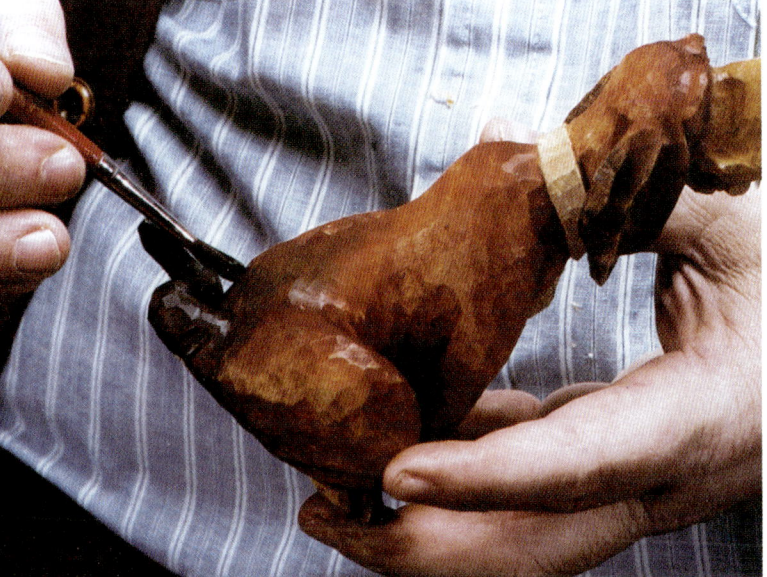

and feather the black over the burnt umber on the upper tail and the saddle.

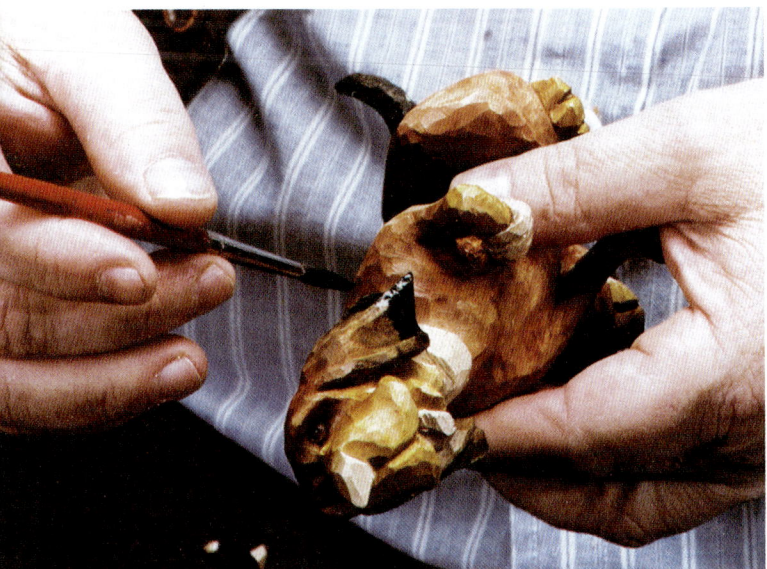

Apply black to the tips of the ears and feather it up the ear. If you get too much paint, as I did here...

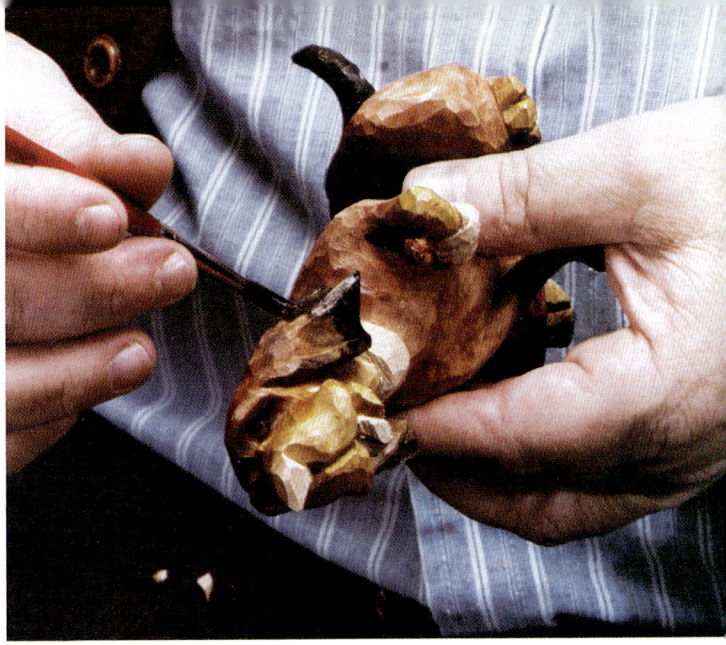

simply dry your brush and continue.

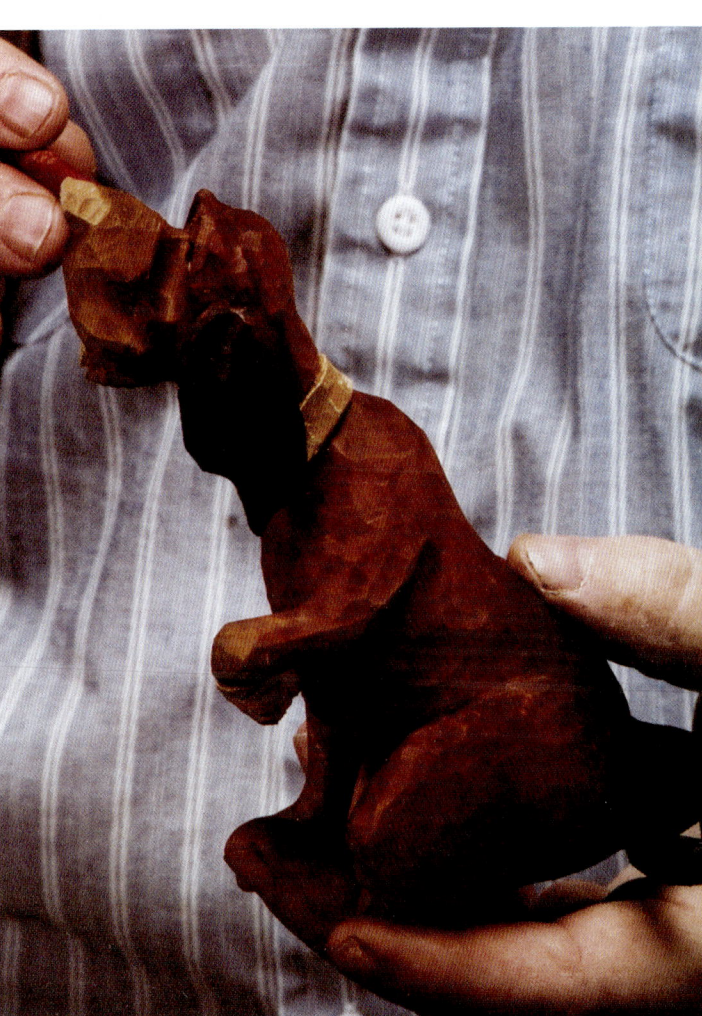

You can see the blending of the colors on the finished ear.

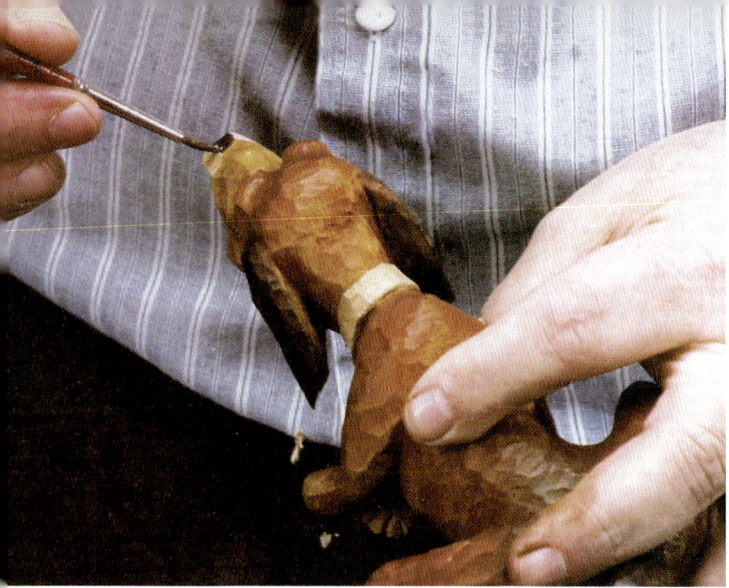

Switch to a little smaller brush and apply pure black to the nose.

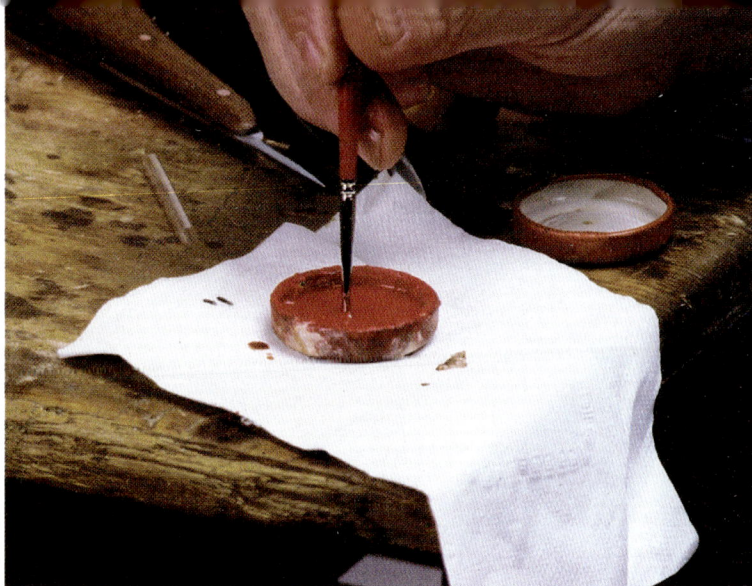

I have chosen red for the collar, though any color may be chosen.

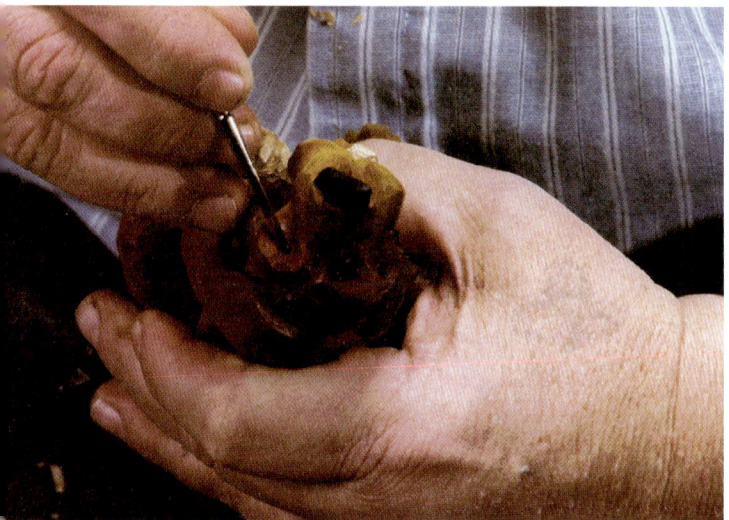

Use a fine pointed brush to paint the pupil of the eye.

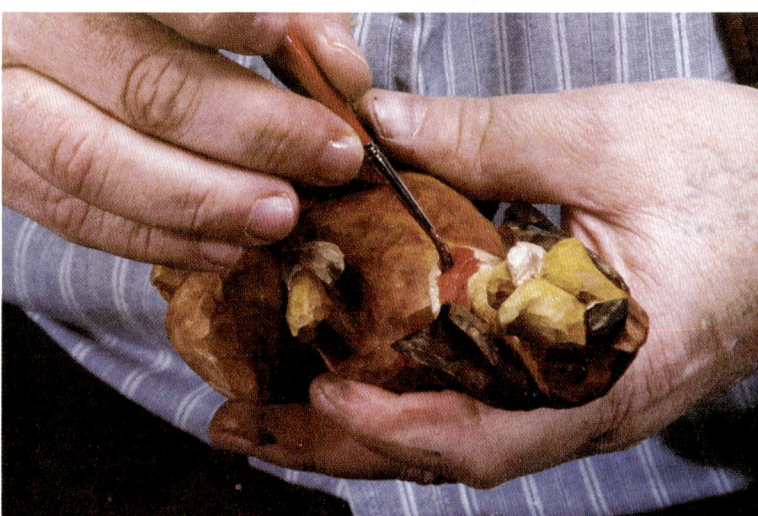

Apply it carefully. If you slip and paint over previously painted areas, you should be able to wipe it off. If not, remember that when you're working with wood, the knife is your eraser.

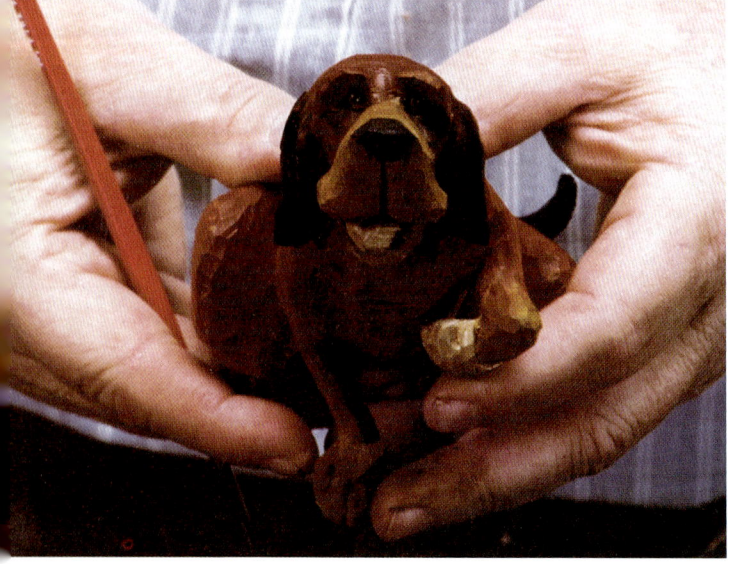

The finished eyes. In the eye area you don't want a cold black, but degrees of brown.

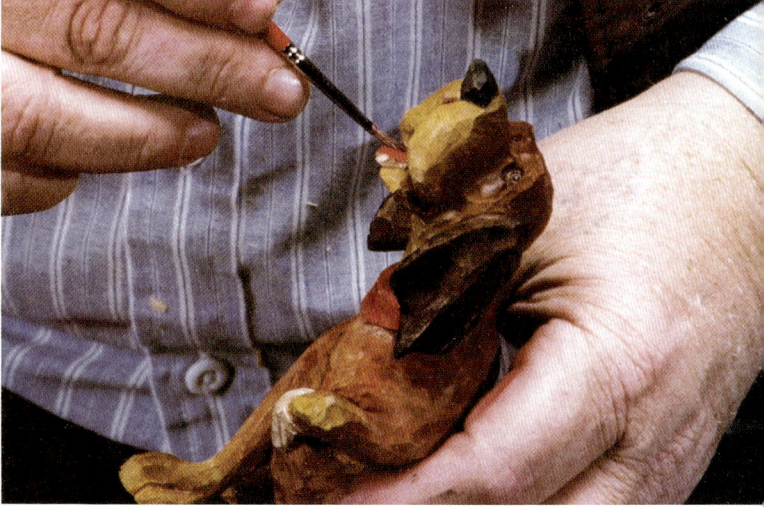

Apply the red paint to the tongue.

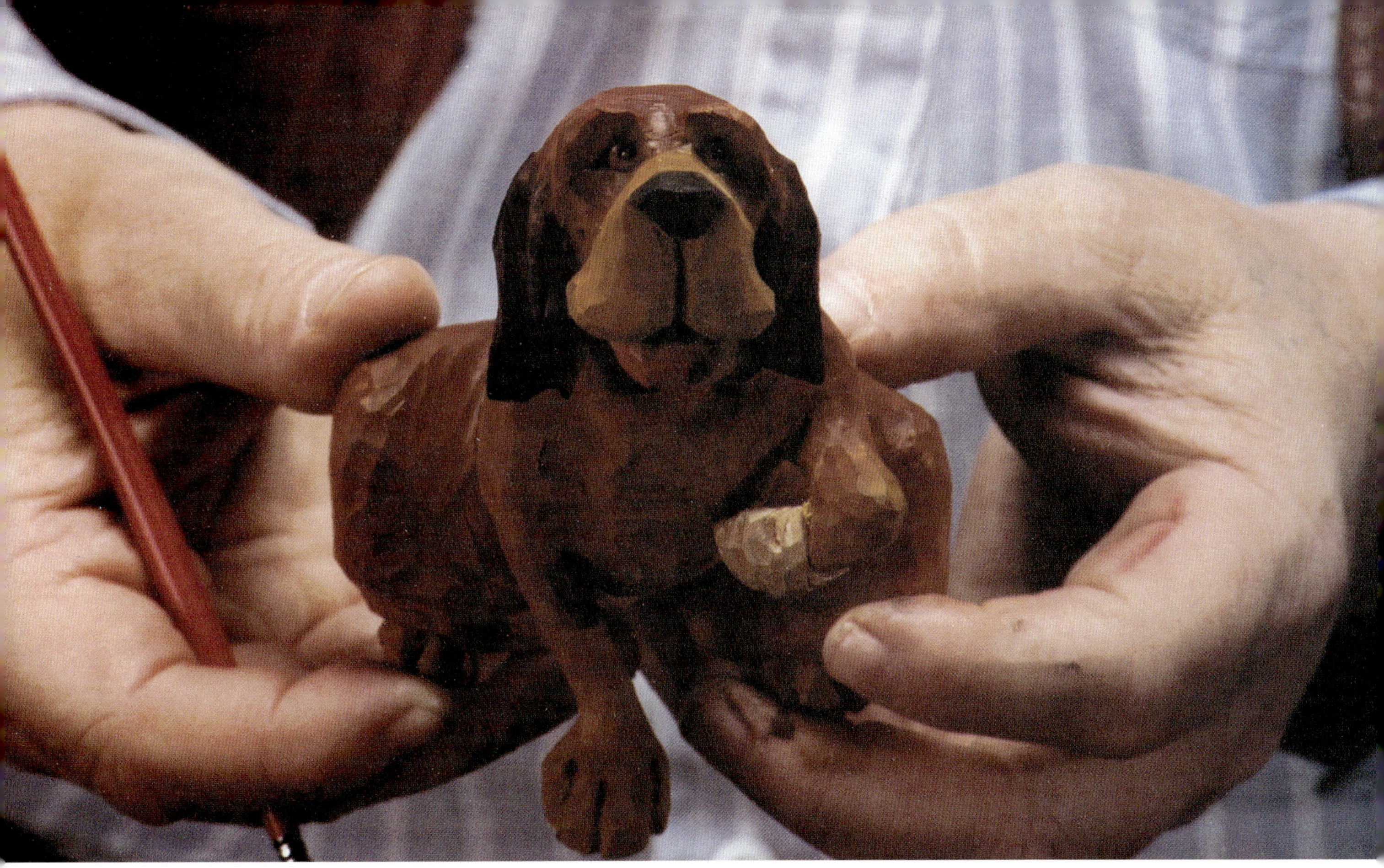

The painted face.

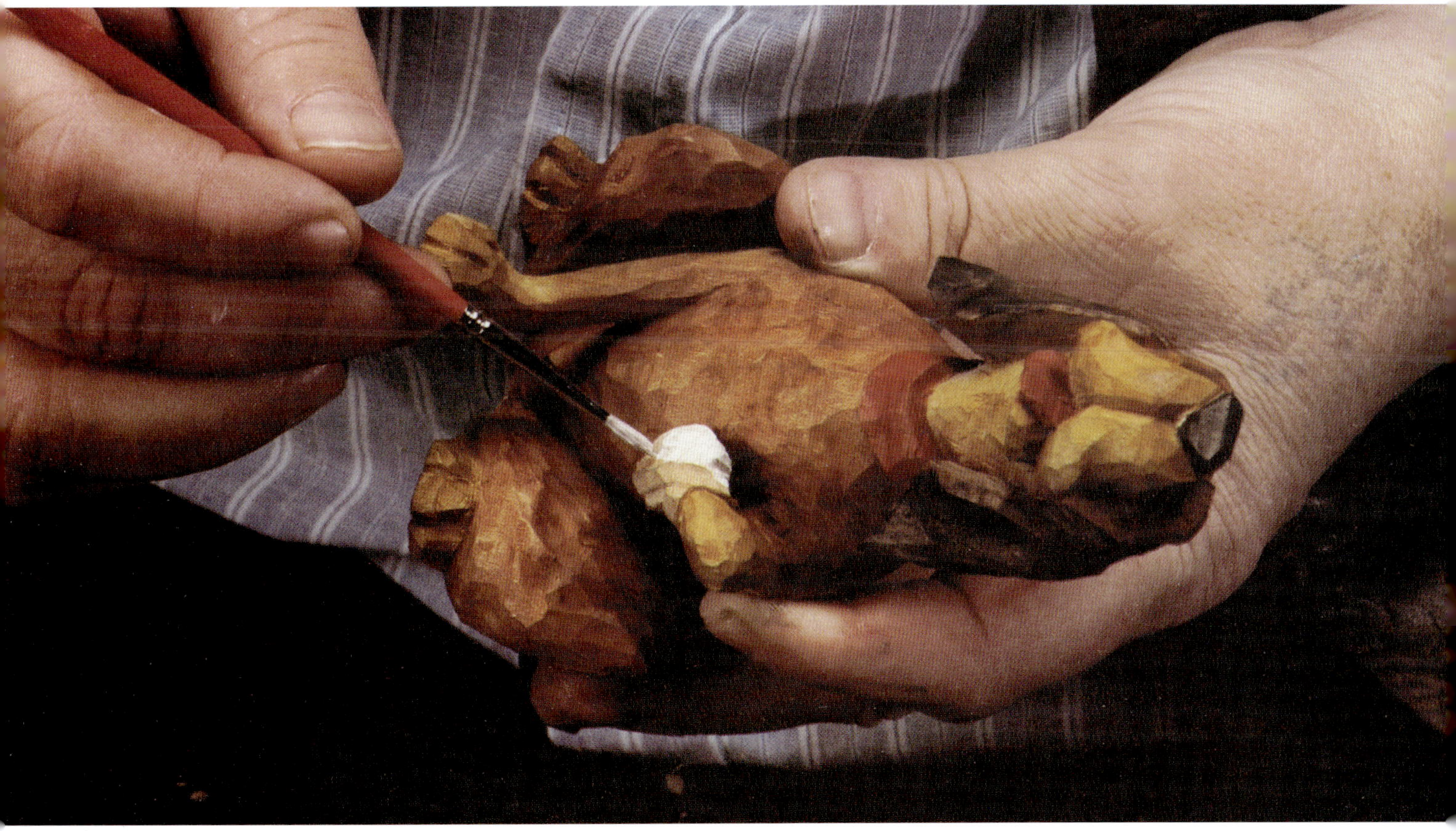

Apply white paint to the bandaged paw.

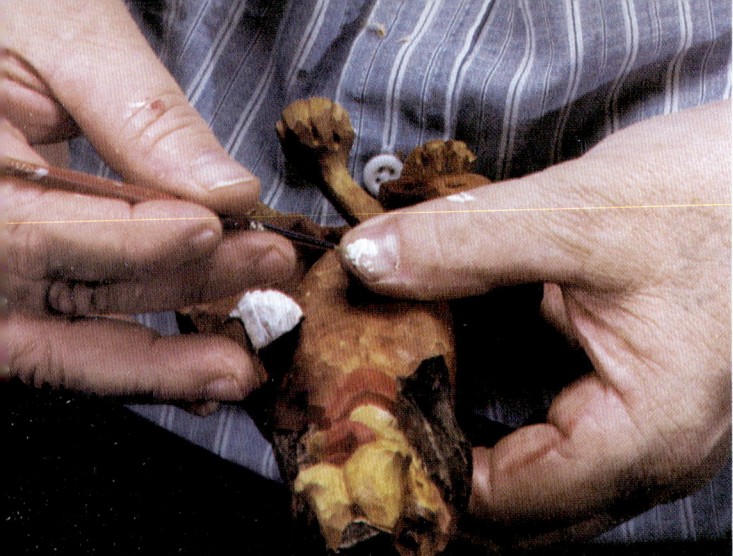

While I don't usually do this with dogs, I think I will add a slight white glint to the eyes. I use my thumbnail as a palette, and use a fine brush with just enough paint to make the spot I want.

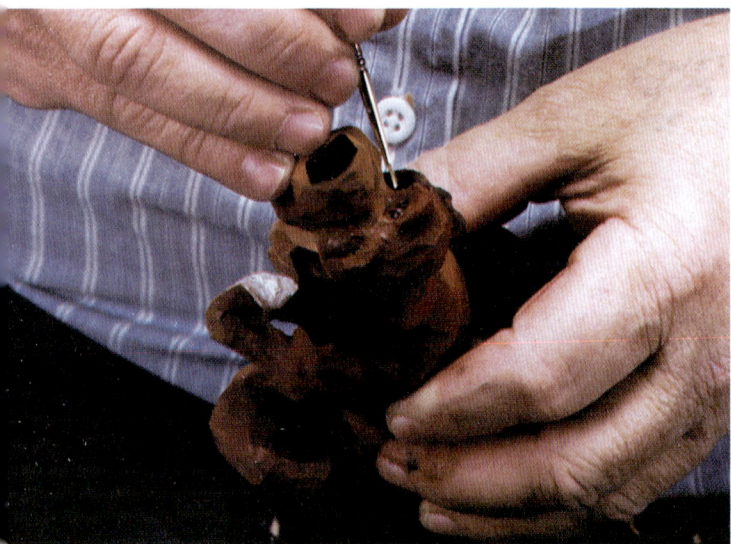

Apply a spot to the same side of each iris.

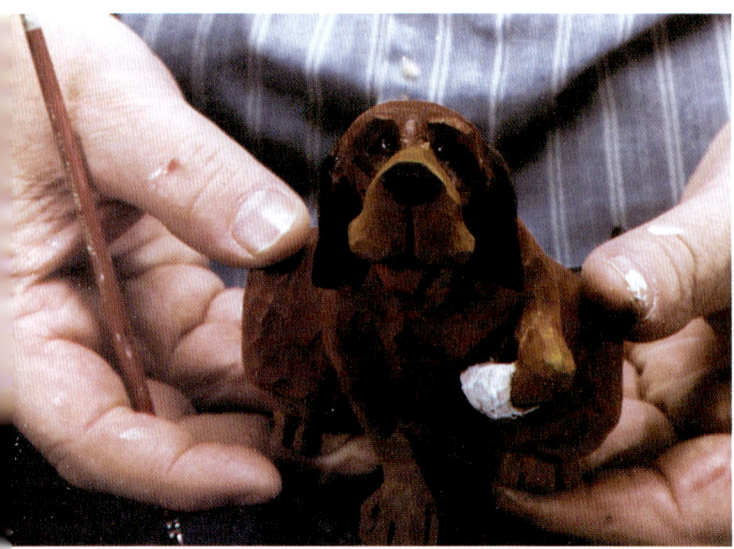

The eyes come to life with just this little hint of white.

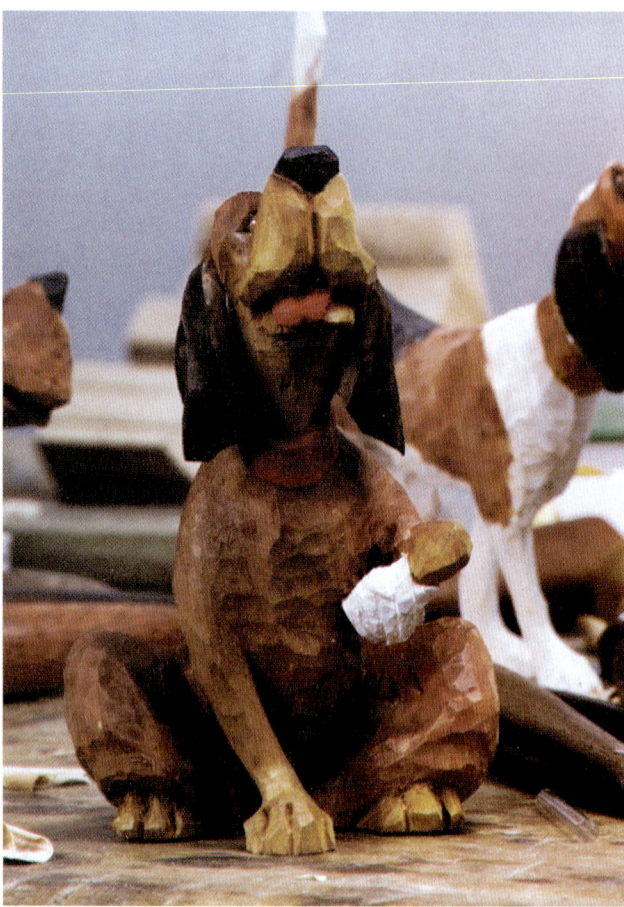

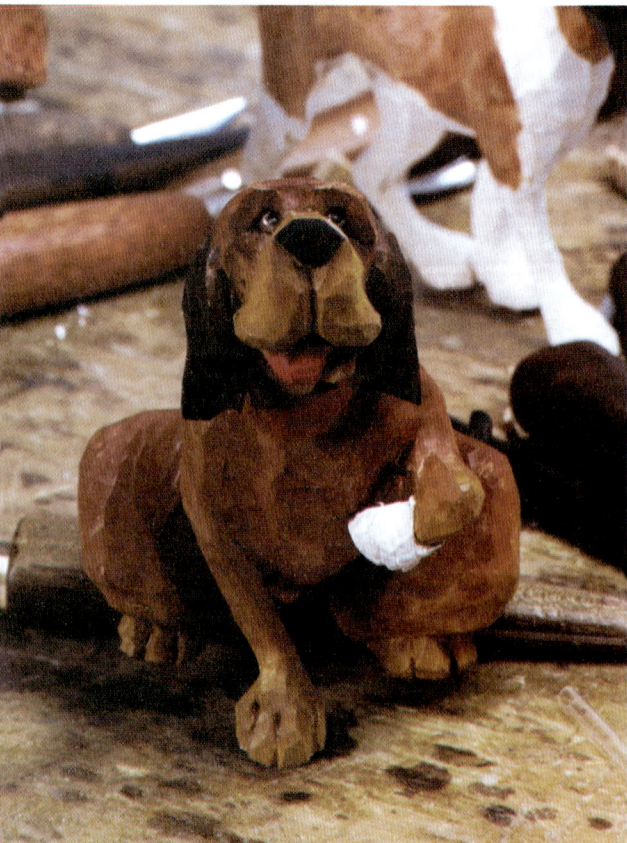

The finished dog.

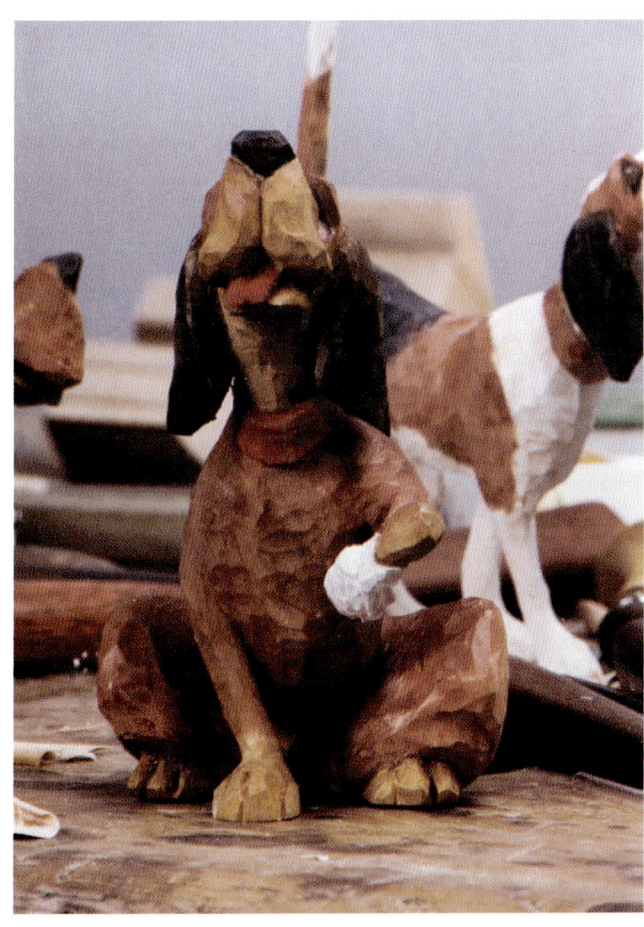
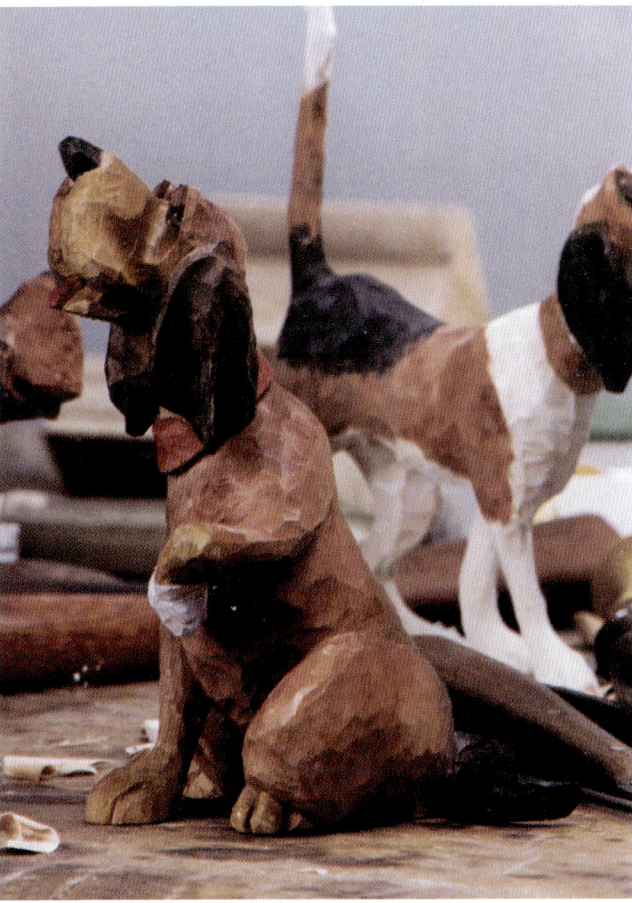
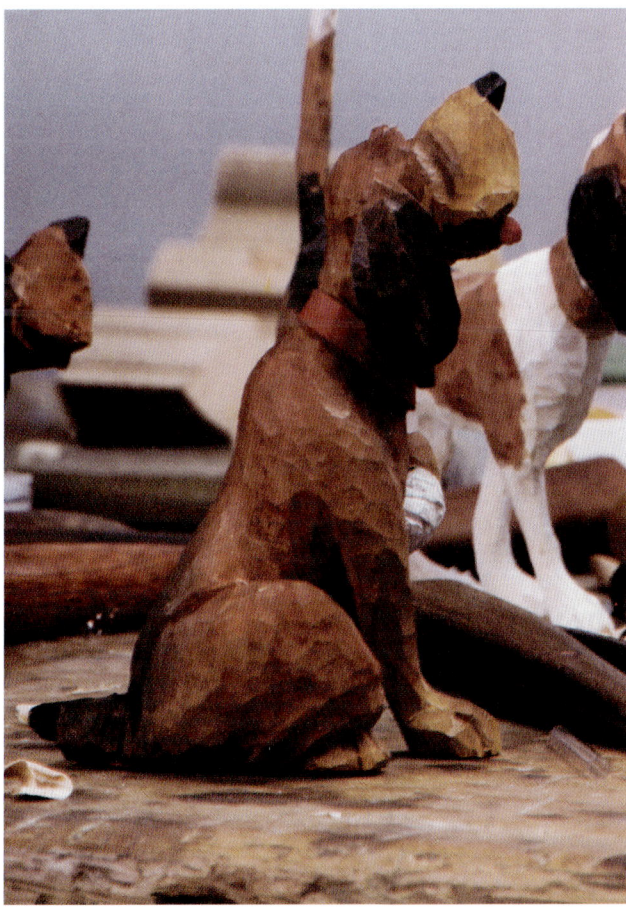
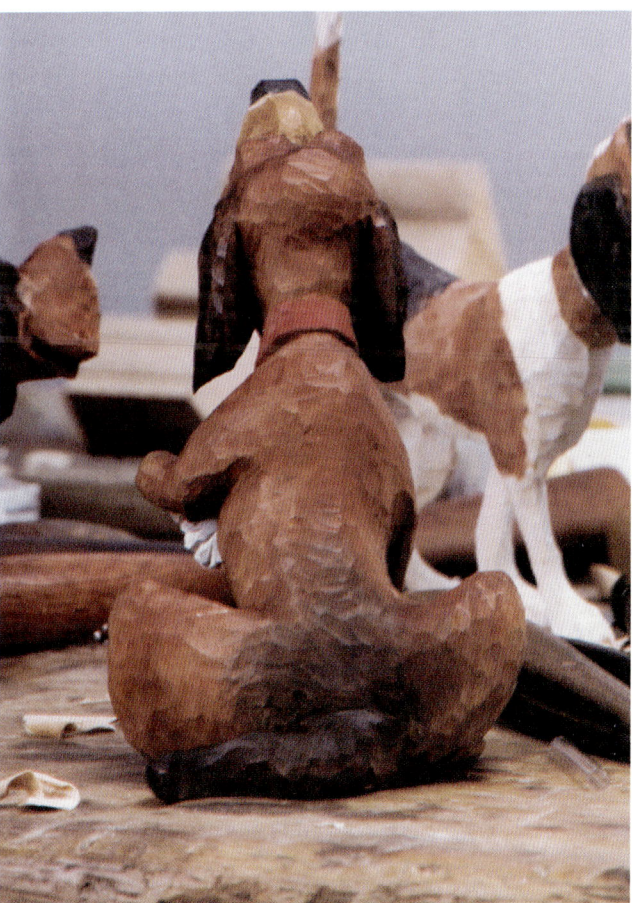

Gallery of Carved Dogs

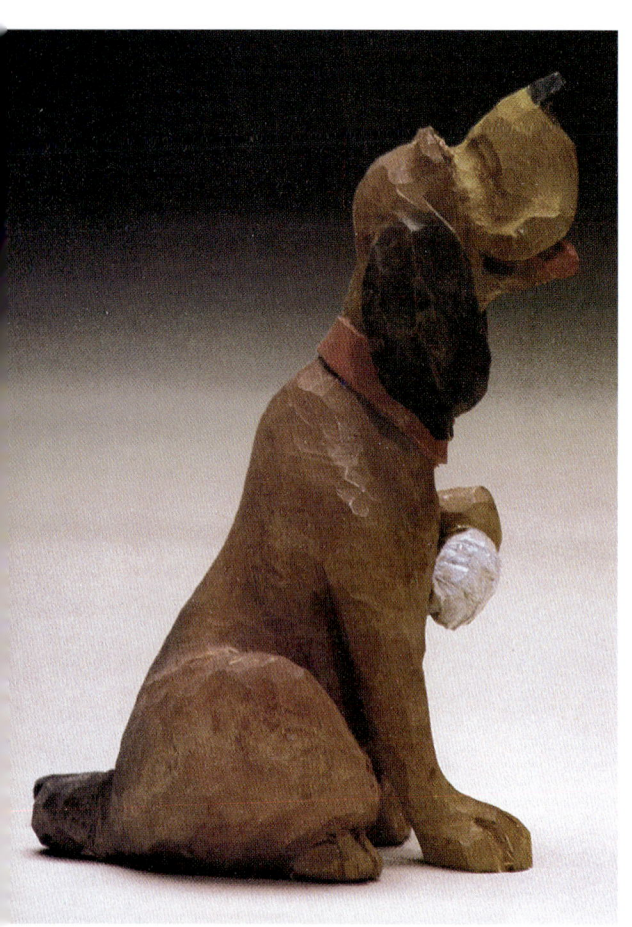
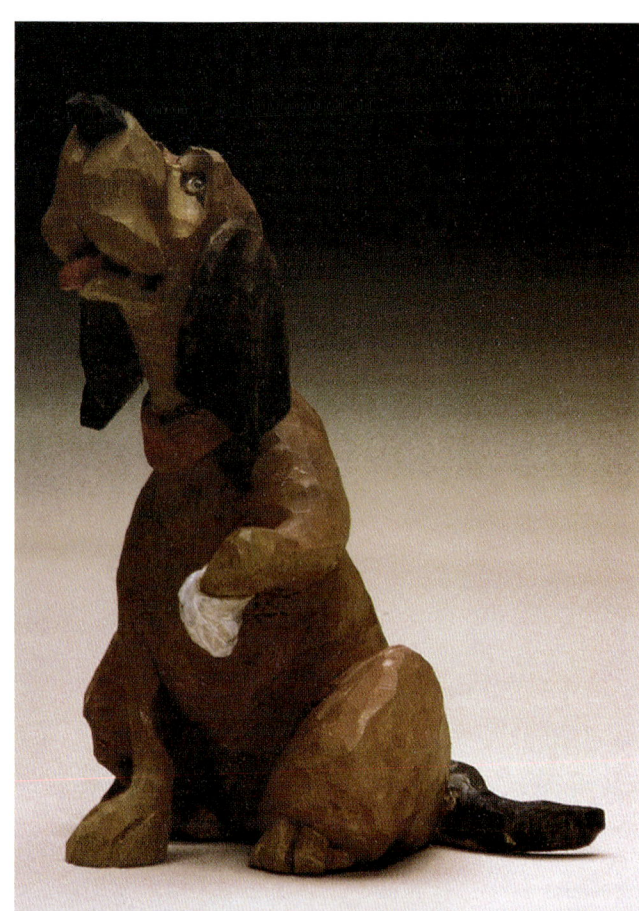
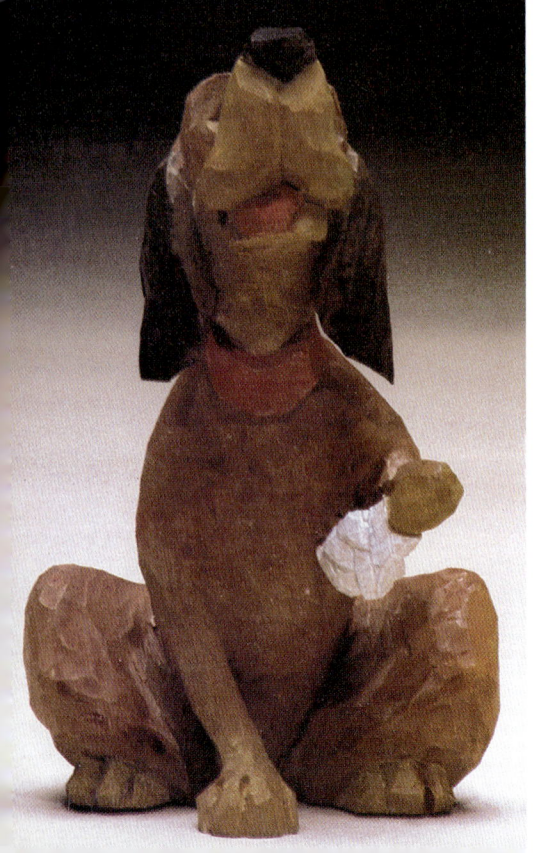
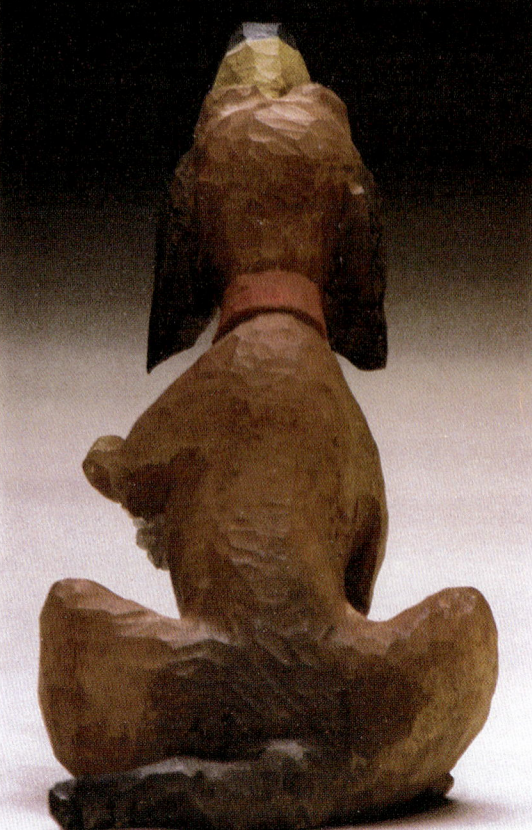
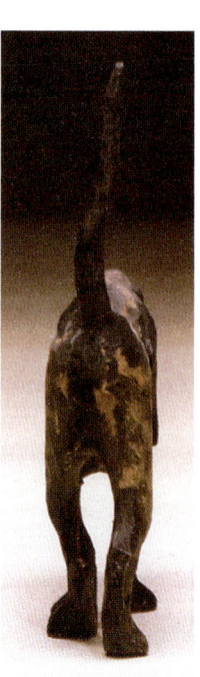
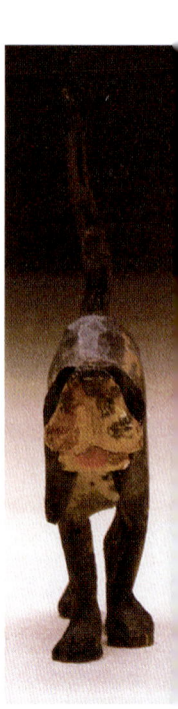

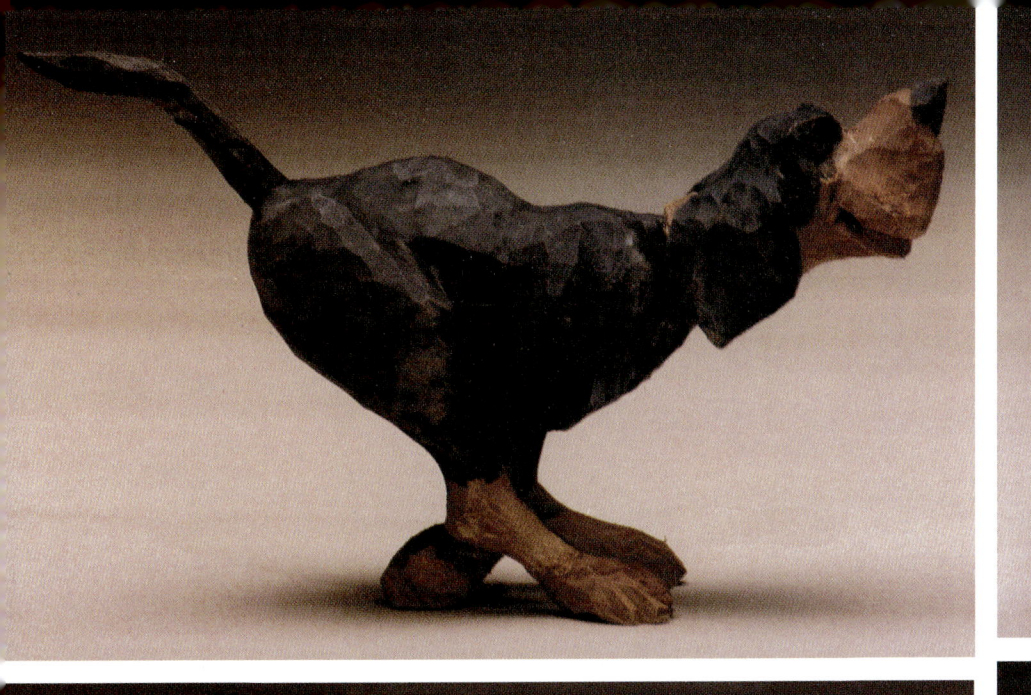
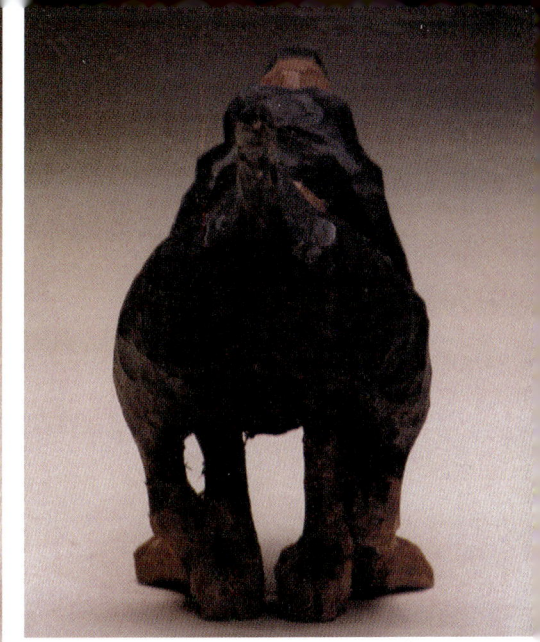
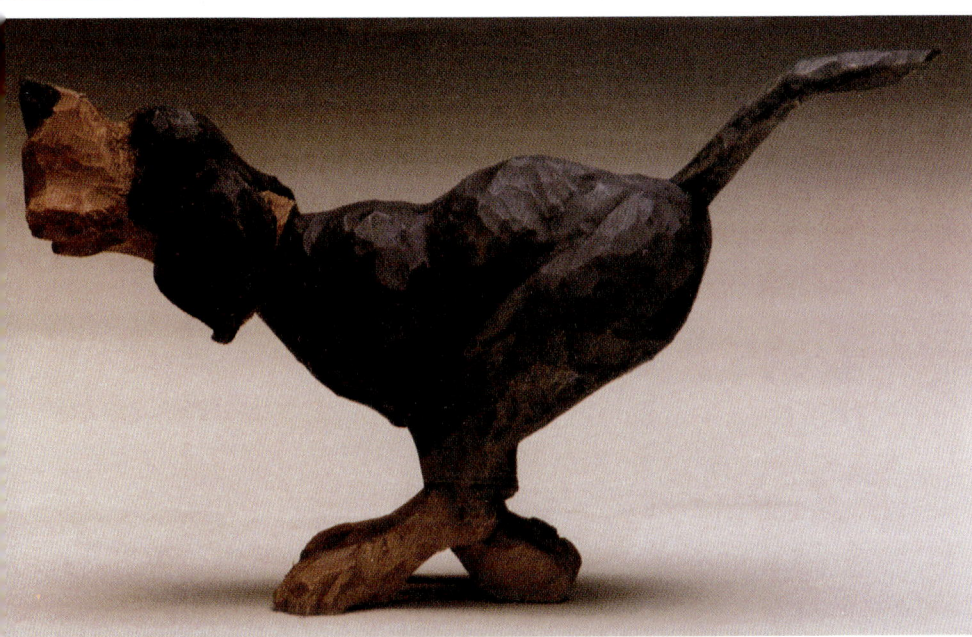
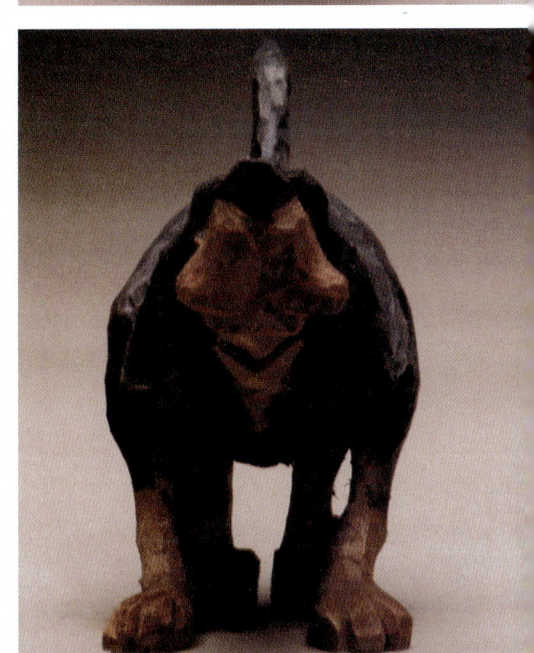
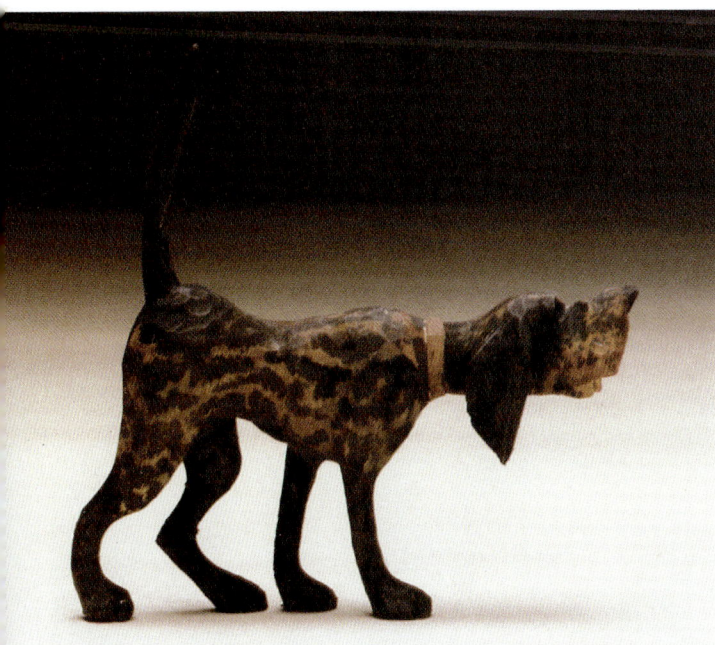
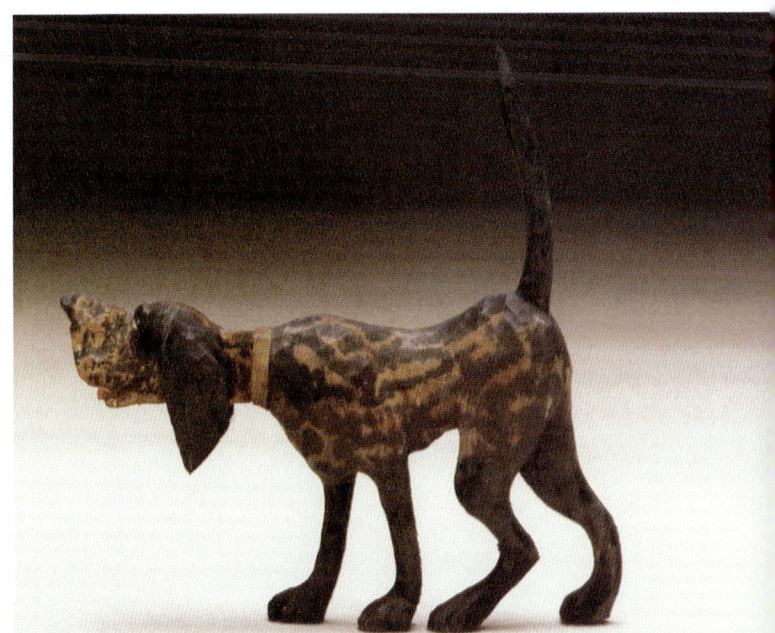

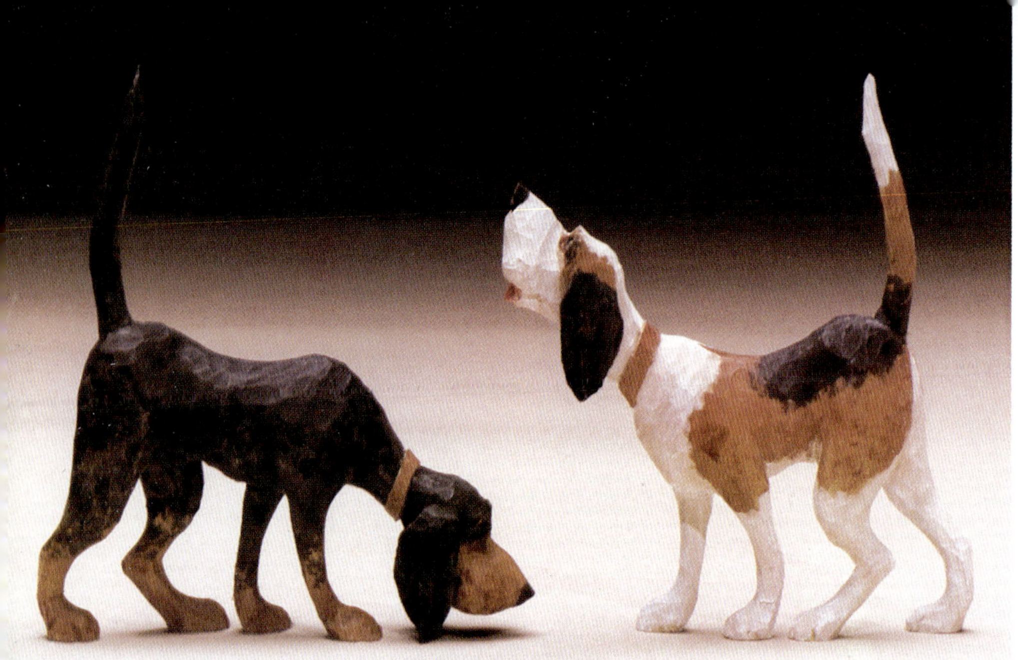

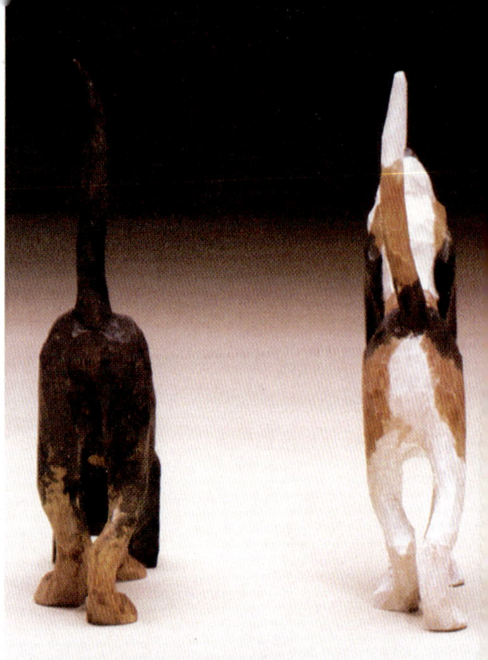

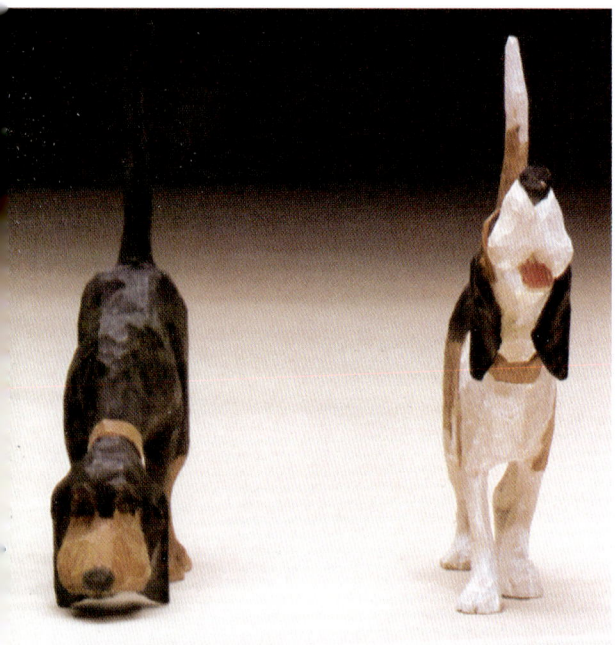

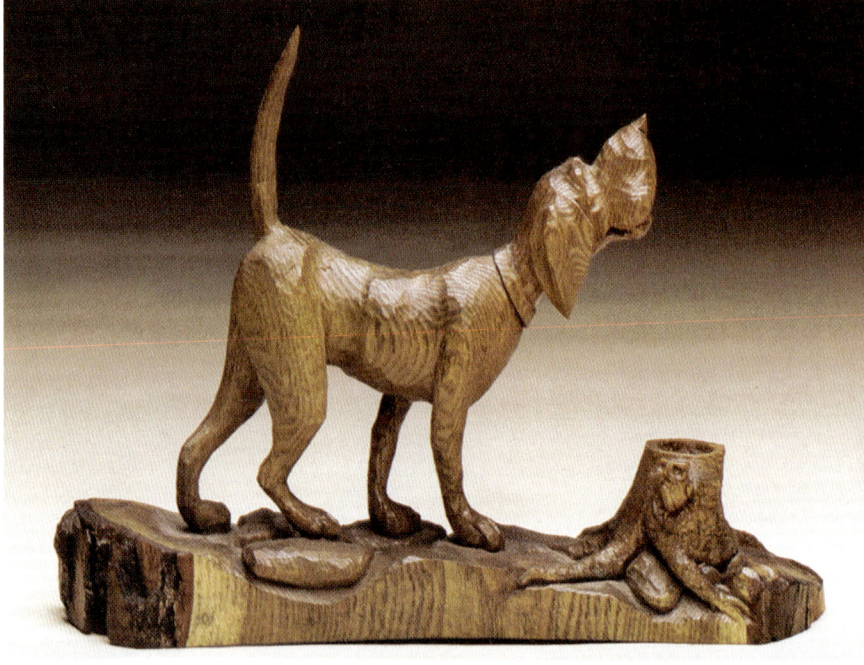

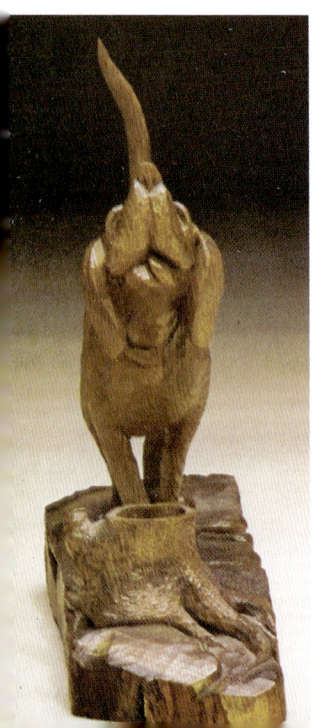

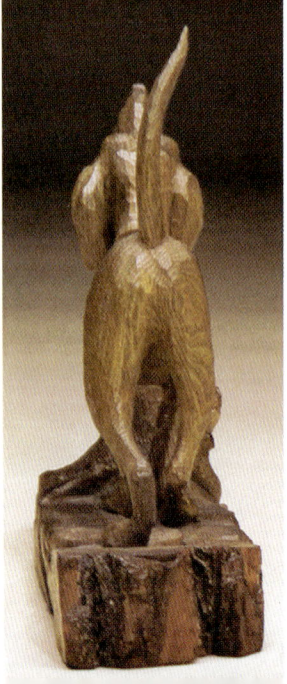

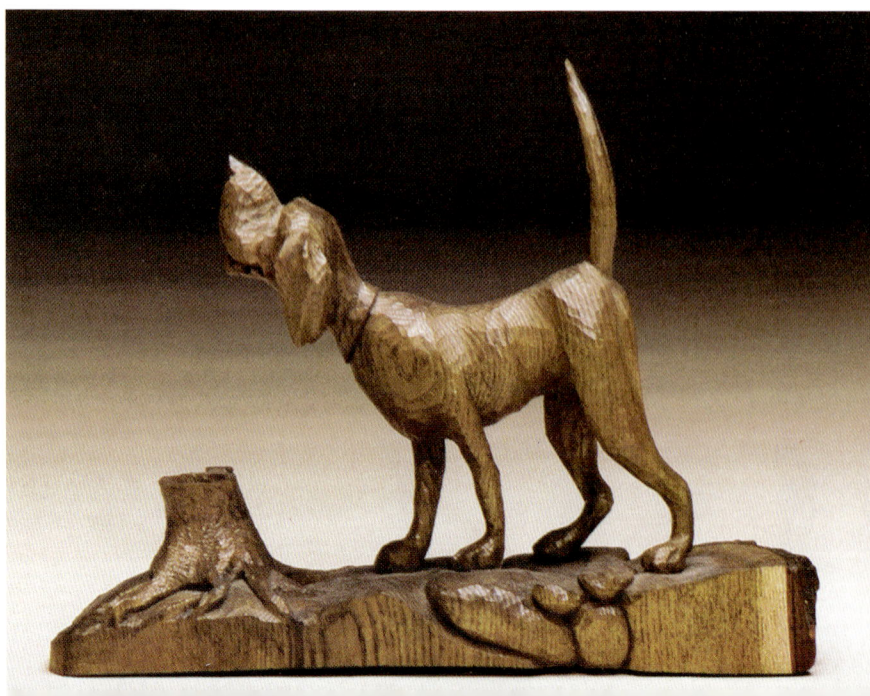

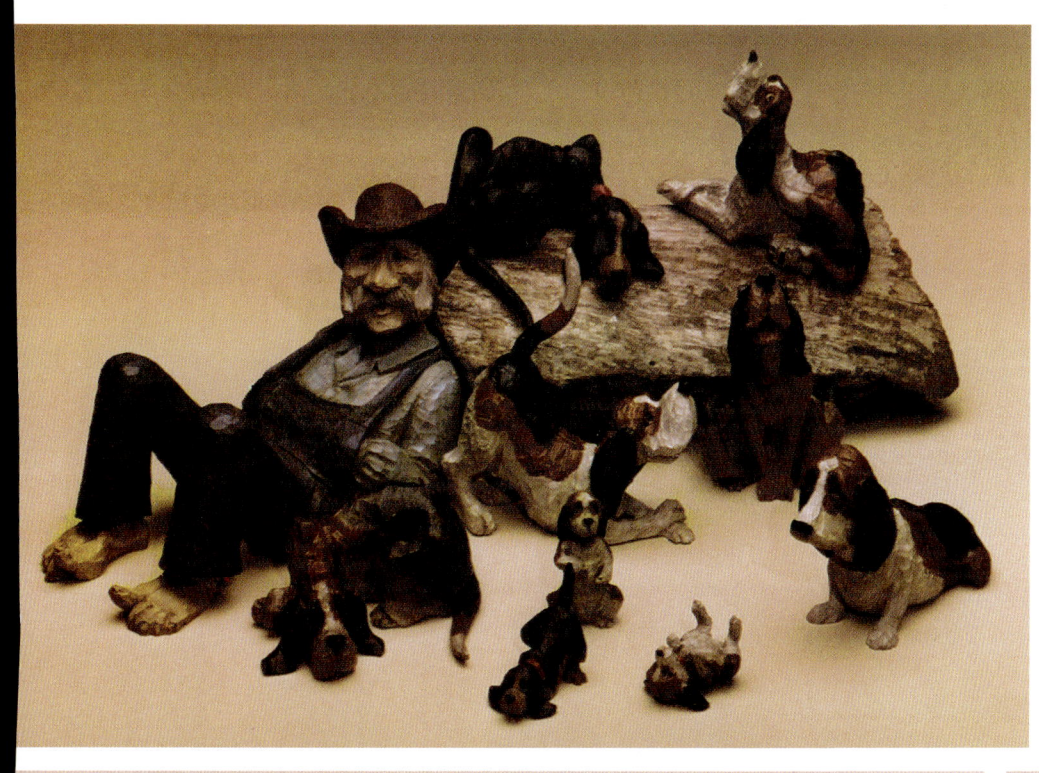

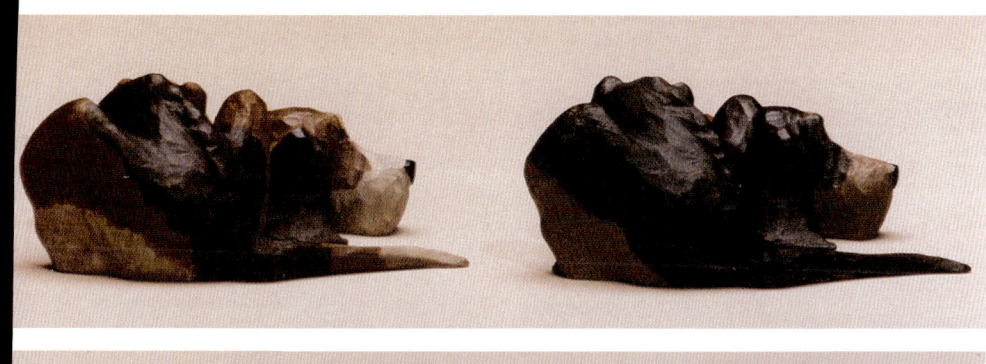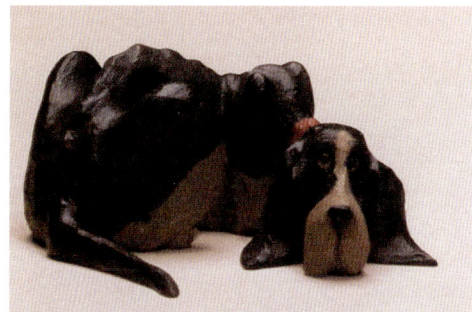

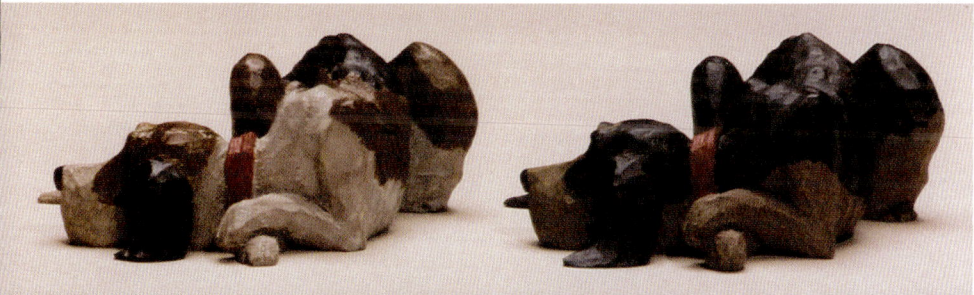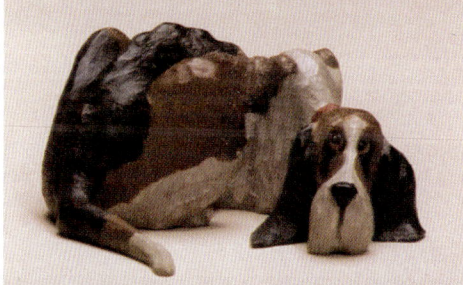

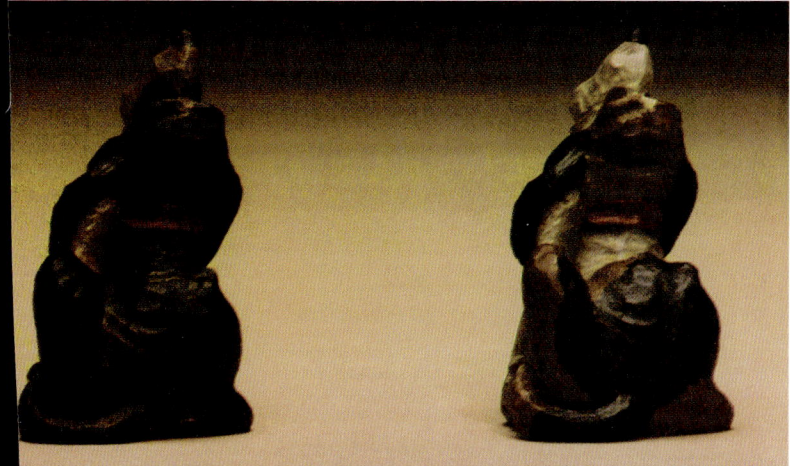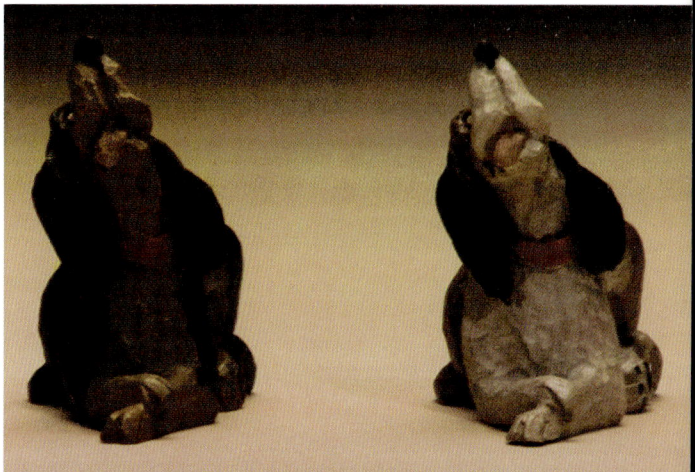

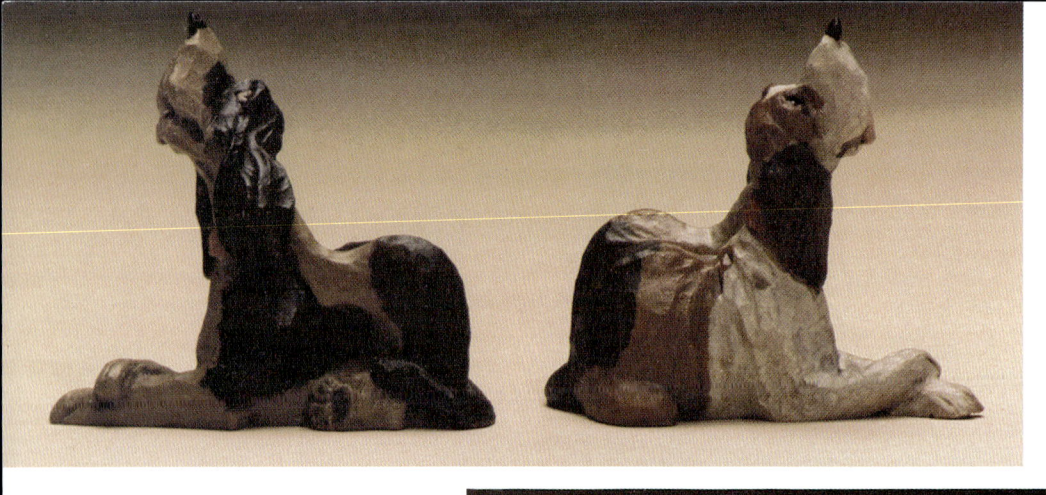

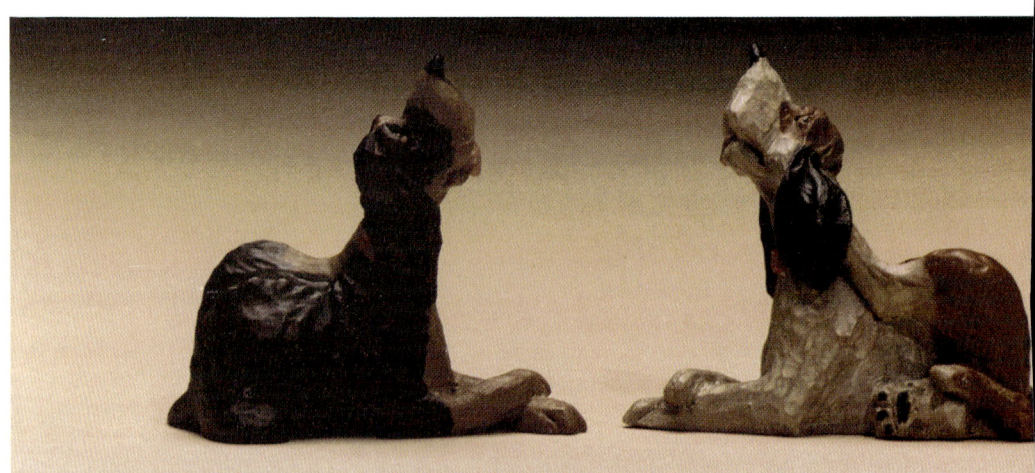

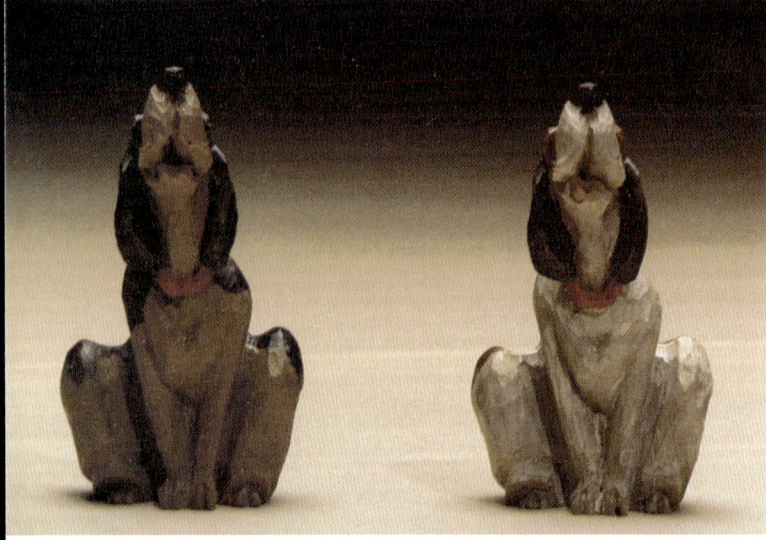

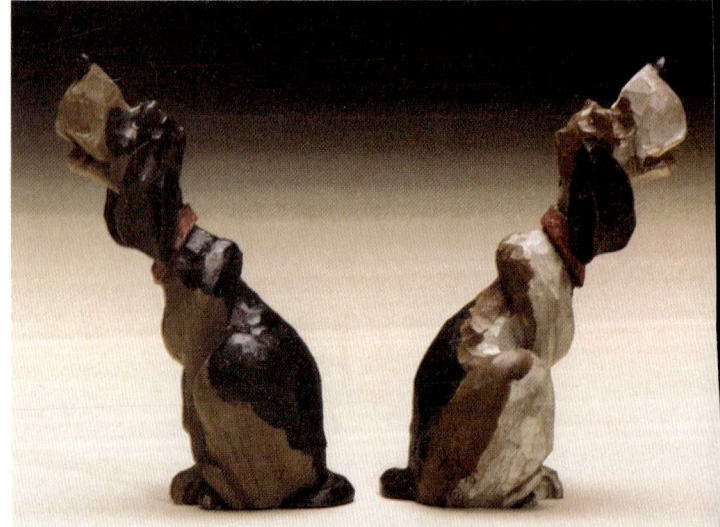

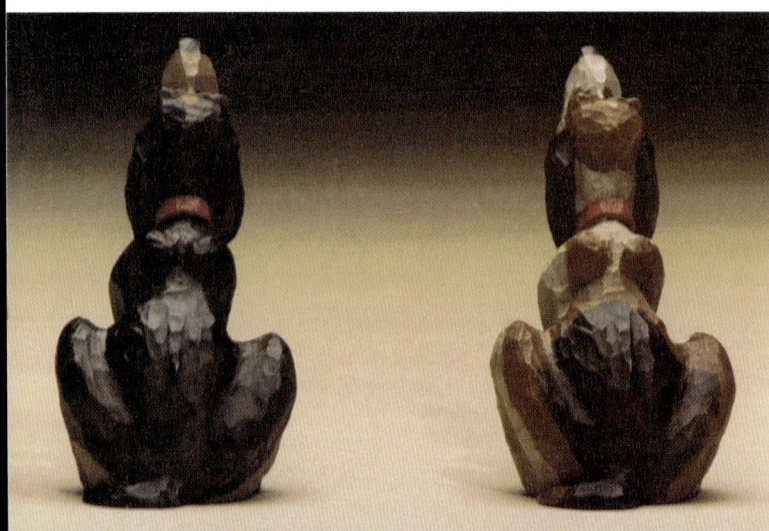

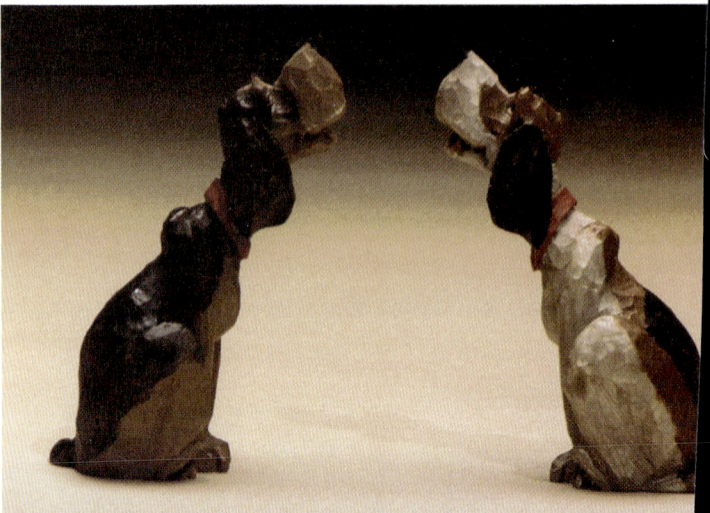